Field Work

Elihu Vedder, *The Questioner of the Sphinx*, 1863
Bequest of Mrs. Martin Brimmer
Courtesy Museum of Fine Arts, Boston

Field Work

Sites in Literary and Cultural Studies

Edited by
Marjorie Garber,
Paul B. Franklin,
and
Rebecca L. Walkowitz

Routledge » New York & London

CULTUREWORK

A book series from the
Center for Literary and Cultural Studies
at Harvard

Marjorie Garber, Editor
Rebecca L. Walkowitz, Associate Editor

Media Spectacles
Marjorie Garber, Jann Matlock, and Rebecca L. Walkowitz, Editors

Secret Agents:
The Rosenberg Case, McCarthyism, and Fifties America
Marjorie Garber and Rebecca L. Walkowitz, Editors

The Seductions of Biography
Mary Rhiel and David Suchoff, Editors

Published in 1996 by
Routledge
29 West 35th Street
New York, NY 10001

Published in Great Britain by
Routledge
11 New Fetter Lane
London EC4P 4EE

Application has been made to the Library of Congress for cataloging-in-
publication data.

Contents

Acknowledgments

The editors are delighted to acknowledge the many friends and associates who helped bring this volume about. We are especially grateful to Barbara Akiba, Jim Dawes, Ted Gideonse, Toby Kasper, Jeffrey Reiser, Herrick Wales, and Steve Wolf for their energy and talents. William Germano and Eric Zinner encouraged us to collect these essays as a volume. Mark Tansey most generously permitted us to reproduce *Secret of the Sphinx (Homage to Elihu Vedder)*. Phillip Brian Harper and Joseph Koerner contributed wise and stimulating thoughts about substantive matters.

Time Warner's continuing support of the intellectual initiatives of the Center for Literary and Cultural Studies at Harvard has been crucial to our work. It is a pleasure to offer special thanks to Peter Wolff for his interest in our programs. We would also like to express our gratitude to Neil and Angela Rudenstine, and to Jeremy Knowles, for their kind words on the occasion of the Center's tenth anniversary, and for their commitment to scholarship in literary and cultural studies.

Introduction

Field Work

The key to a riddle is another riddle.

—Emerson[1]

In Mark Tansey's 1984 painting, *Secret of the Sphinx (Homage to Elihu Vedder)*, a white, male figure in a modern business suit crouches before the massive stone head of a Sphinx, holding out a microphone to catch its every utterance. At his feet a reel-to-reel tape recorder turns; both sartorial and technological style mark this as a mid-century event, an anthropologist's—or journalist's—scoop for posterity along the lines of Walter Cronkite's early television show "You Are There," which placed the reporter on the scene at key moments in past history. ("Columbus discovers America—and YOU ARE THERE.")

Who is the inquirer in Tansey's painting, and what does he seek to know? Is he a professor, an antiquarian, or a newsman? Is the "secret" to be used as the basis of an academic article, a news-magazine report, a scientific or cultural breakthrough for the benefit of all humanity? Tansey's ironic eye notes the earphones, the intensity, the meticulous mechanical preparedness of the seeker. Will he, like some characters in T. S. Eliot's poetry, have had the experience and missed the meaning?

Tansey has been described as both a "literary" and an "archaelogical" painter. His canvases are intellectual as well as painterly; in one well-known work, the celebrated literary theorists Paul de Man and Jacques Derrida struggle at the edge of the abyss in a scene reminiscent of Sherlock Holmes's final contention with Professor Moriarity at the Reichenbach Falls. The "archaeological" elements in Tansey's work include his practice of building up layers of paint on the canvas and then wiping them down to create a sedimented effect in dense yet muted tones—as well as his more directly thematic interest in archaeological subjects, as in the droll and witty *Secret of the Sphinx*. Like Sigmund Freud, who drew an analogy in *Civilization and Its Discontents* between archaeological remains and "preservation in the sphere of the mind,"[2] Tansey sees the quest for a full and objective knowledge of the past as what Freud called a "fantasy." Interpretation will always alter what it seeks to remember and preserve; the investigator, as is now commonly acknowledged, inevitably becomes part of the investigation. Yet both enterprises—the excavation of the traces of human memory and "wisdom" and of the traces of material history and culture—remain in a sense idealized, even as they are quietly ironized, by their interlocutors. And both find a perfect metaphor in the figure of the Sphinx.

Tansey's own fieldwork for *Secret of the Sphinx* is acknowledged in his subtitle, which directs attention to Elihu Vedder's 1863 canvas, strikingly titled *The Questioner of the Sphinx* (frontispiece). In this painting by a once popular, now largely neglected American Romantic painter and illustrator, another male figure kneels intently by the head of a Sphinx, ear close to its mouth. But this inquirer is dark skinned, and wears the robes of the desert. His walking staff lies at his feet, a provocative reminder of the third "age" of the traditional Theban Sphinx's riddle ("What goes on four legs in the morning, on two at noon, and on three in the evening?"—a riddle to which Oedipus famously declared the answer to be "Man").

The desert landscape of Vedder's painting is strewn with fragments of statuary and of human bodies; a skull lies beside a broken pillar. The spirit is more that of Shelley's "Ozymandias" than of Western technology, a report from the field as relayed to the poet-speaker of this sonnet by a "traveler from an antique land": "on the sand, / Half sunk, a shattered visage lies, whose frown / And wrinkled lip, and sneer of cold command, / Tell that its sculptor well those passions read / Which yet survive, stamped on these lifeless things /....Nothing beside remains." But where Shelley's tyrant mocked—and was mocked by—history ("'Look on my works, ye Mighty, and despair!'"), Vedder's Sphinx, the archetypal questioner, is itself put to the question. For if the answer to the riddle was "Man" (or even, in Muriel Rukeyser's feminist rewriting of the scene, "Man" and "Woman"[3]), has that answer not immediately and always disclosed itself as another question?

"This sphinx," wrote Nietzsche, "teaches us too to ask questions." "*Who* really is it that here questions us? *What* really is it in us that wants 'the truth'?... Which of us is Oedipus here? Which of us Sphinx? It is, it seems, a rendezvous of questions and question marks."[4] As Shoshana Felman observes, "What Freud discovered in the Oedipus myth is not an answer but *the structure of a question*, not any given knowledge but a structuring positioning of the analyst's own ignorance of his patient's unconscious."[5] Not only in philosophy and psychoanalysis but within the entire field of what the French nicely call "the human sciences," from literature to sociology and anthropology, it is not so much that questions beget other questions, but rather that attention to the structure of a question disciplines knowledge, frames discussion, and directs the investigator toward one answer rather than another. The necessary dialectic of question and answer is the enabling structure of education and inquiry, even if all "answers" are provisional. (After all, so, if it comes to that, are all questions.)

The listener in Vedder's painting may *be* Oedipus, or one of his successors and emulators. Vedder's interest in exoticism, a hallmark of Romanticism in both painting and poetry, figures the human investigator as "native" rather than "foreign," and as individual or personal rather than professional and collective: the quest is presumptively—though only presumptively—for wisdom for oneself, not for a colossal sound bite for the evening news. Yet as James Clifford has pointed out, the tension between "native" and "traveler" is being rethought by modern anthropology in the light of recent work on hybrid, cosmopolitan experiences. "The goal is not to *replace* the cultural figure 'native' with the intercultural figure 'traveler.' Rather the task is to focus on concrete mediations of the two, in specific cases of historical tension and relationship," since "both are constitutive of what will count as cultural experience." As Clifford notes, with some satisfaction, "anthropological 'culture' is not what it used to be."[6]

If "culture" is changing, so also is the notion of the "field." Here are some of Clifford's observations—and worries—about that contested and contestatory term, many of which are illuminating when juxtaposed not only to the disciplinary expectations of professional anthropology, but also to a reconceptualizing of other intellectual and research "fields" from foreign language to the history of art:

> The field is...a set of discursive practices. Dwelling implies a kind of communicative competence. One no longer relies on translators, but speaks and listens for oneself...*the* language, singular, as if there were only one? What does it mean to learn or use a language?... What about stranger talk, the specific

kind of discourse used with outsiders?… It's worth pointing out…the fallacy, culture (singular) equals language (singular). This equation, implicit in nationalist culture ideas, has been thoroughly unraveled by Bakhtin for whom a language is a diverging, contesting, dialoguing set of discourses that no "native"—let alone visitor—can ever learn.

Among the other perceived "dangers of construing ethnography as '*fieldwork*'" (Clifford's emphasis) are the elision of "the global world of intercultural import-export in which the ethnographic encounter is always already enmeshed" and the degree to which culture is written by so-called informants as well as by anthropologists or other professional investigators. The old formula "the native speaks, the anthropologist writes"[7]—so aptly challenged in visual terms by the pendant paintings of Vedder and Tansey—is exposed as a simplifying and distorting fiction. New inquiries into ethnicity, urban popular culture, "identity politics," diaspora (the Holocaust; the Atlantic slave trade), cosmopolitanism, border-crossing, transnationalism in economics and the entertainment industry, sexuality studies—all suggest in different ways a repositioning of the roles of questioner and knower.

What if Tansey's Sphinx were to interview the interviewer, to ask him to account for his costume, his apparatus, his audience, the very form of his inquiry? If the quest is for a secure ground (or "field") on which to "ground" one's assumptions, whether about culture, "human nature," philosophy, aesthetics, or values, intellectual inquiries into how we know what we know give rise to a discomforting sense that what we see as figure may be ground, and what we take as ground may—to alter the metaphor slightly—be imperceptibly shifting beneath our feet. Earthquake or evolution? As vertiginous as these shifts in authority and point of view may seem, they are part of the continuum of humanistic study.

> For out of old feldes, as men seyeth,
> Cometh al this newe corn fro yer to yere;
> And out of olde bokes, in good feyth,
> Cometh al this newe science that men lere.
>
> —Geoffrey Chaucer, *The Romaunt of the Rose*

Chaucer's translation of a passage from Guillaume de Lorris equating old fields with old books as the source of new corn and new science stood at the head of John Bartlett's preface to the 1891 edition of *Familiar Quotations*. The "field" was the seedbed of knowledge, the ground of inquiry. By the mid- to late nineteenth century (a time that saw the evolution of modern university "departments" like English literature and the classics, as well as of modern social sciences like anthropology and psychology), the word "field" had come to mean "a department or subject of activity or speculation," and also, in a related sense, a description of work "carried out in the natural environment of a given material, language, animal, etc., and not in the laboratory, study, or office"[8]—a fair approximation of modern-day "fieldwork." What is the relation between an academic "field" and the concept of "fieldwork"?

A modern archaelogical text defines fieldwork as "the examination and recording of the surviving remains of past human activity without excavation,"[9] describing it as "the discovery, planning, description and analysis of archaeological sites" and as "essential if our knowledge of the past is to be advanced."[10] For sociologists and anthropologists, "field research consists of the simultaneous tasks of data collection, coding, and analysis," closely related to three key issues affecting the researcher: "validity and reliability, questions of ethics, and study of the unfamiliar."[11] It thus falls on the "qualitative" rather than the "quantitative" side of the putative divide, and is, potentially, highly influenced—and rendered subjective—by the experiences and responses of the investigator. Was Margaret Mead conned by canny Samoans? Did Bronislaw Malinowski skew his conclusions about Melanesian society to accord with his prior assumptions? "Fieldwork," say the editors of one anthology on fieldwork experience, "must certainly rank with the more disagreeable activities that humanity has fashioned for itself. It is usually inconvenient..., sometimes physically uncomfortable, frequently embarrassing, and, to a degree, always tense."[12] But, notes another expert, "Fieldwork *is* the central activity of anthropology," distinguishing it—in this view—from psychology, sociology, political science, and economics. "It is fieldwork, more than the distinctive content of the material, that produces the uniqueness of anthropology."[13]

Thus defined, "fieldwork" seems to typify certain investigative processes of the humanistic social sciences. "Disagreeable," "inconvenient," "physically uncomfortable," conducted away from the safer and more familiar sites of office, laboratory, and library—how can this fieldwork be related to the presumptively agreeable, convenient, comfortable investigations of humanists and students of literature?

The title of this volume interposes a space between "Field" and "Work," inverting the model of the series title, "CultureWork," which makes one word of two. Both moves are intended to defamiliarize, and to emphasize, dislocations and juxtapositions, even superpositions, between kinds and loci of inquiry. What does it mean these days to work "in" an academic field, especially when interdisciplinarity and cross-cultural investigation are enlivening the humanities as never before, when art history and social history are important parts of many literary projects, when Freud is taught in English departments (and *not* in many psychology departments) and literary and philosophical writers such as Bakhtin and Foucault are studied by anthropologists, when political scientists discuss not only Habermas but also Derrida?

Here are some of the questions these scholar-critics seek to engage in the pages that follow:

- What does the word "culture" mean today, in its various manifestations, from "cultural anthropology" to "cultural studies" to "high" and "mass" and "popular" culture to the so-called culture wars? Is a phrase like "literary and cultural studies" an oxymoron or a redundancy? How is "culture" (and how are "cultures") related to the questions of politics, ethnicity, pedagogy, "values," and "multiculturalism" that enliven and fragment current-day discussions of education and the university?
- Are scholars working on U.S.-related literary and historical topics today "post-American studies"? What does that mean, and what are its intellectual and pedagogical consequences? What about the increasing "globalization of culture"? Is *any* culture local culture today?
- What is, and might be, the role of national literatures, and national literature departments, in a global world?
- In how many ways can a poem be read? Have some critical preconceptions about intra- and extratextual issues rigidified what was never, for either critics or poets, an either-or matter of text and context?
- How does textual editing construct, and reconstruct, the objects and subjects of knowledge?
- How is visual culture produced by and interpreted from visual images? What are the languages of the eye?
- In what ways do the disciplines and practices of law and literature offer ways of reading and understanding one another?
- What is the reason for, and the effect of, the increasing use of the personal voice in literary and cultural criticism?

The contributors to this volume look back at the questions that have engaged scholars in the humanities and related social sciences over the last ten years; they look forward toward new questions and old questions posed in new ways. The questions are always as interesting and engaging as the answers—but both "questions" and "answers" have a way of coming back, in familiar and unfamiliar guises, just when one thinks they have been resolved or rendered moot. The author; the reader; the text; the context. Values, absolute and relative; forms and structures, canons and institutions; the "self"; the "other." The "others." History and histories; theory and practice; even— of course—truth and beauty.

NOTES

1. Ralph Waldo Emerson, "Illusions," *The Conduct of Life*, in *The Complete Works of Ralph Waldo Emerson* (Boston: Houghton Mifflin Company, 1904), 6: 313.

2. Sigmund Freud, *Civilization and Its Discontents*, trans. Joan Riviere. In *The Standard Edition of the Complete Psychological Works of Sigmund Freud*, ed. James Strachey (London: The Hogarth Press and the Institute of Psycho-Analysis, 1961), 21: 69.

3. Muriel Rukeyser, "Myth." Reprinted in *The Norton Anthology of Literature by Women*, ed. Sandra M. Gilbert and Susan Gubar (New York: Norton), pp. 1787–88.

4. Friedrich Nietzsche, *Beyond Good and Evil: Prelude to a Philosophy of the Future*, trans. R. J. Hollingdale (Harmondsworth, UK: Penguin Books, 1976), p. 15. Emphasis in original.

5. Shoshana Felman, *Jacques Lacan and the Adventure of Insight: Pyschoanalysis in Contemporary Culture* (Cambridge: Harvard University Press, 1987), p. 103. Emphasis in original.

6. James Clifford, "Traveling Cultures," in *Cultural Studies*, ed. Lawrence Grossberg, Cary Nelson, and Paula A. Treichler (New York: Routledge, 1992), p. 101.

7. Clifford, p. 100.

8. *Oxford English Dictionary*, p. 880.

9. Anthony Brown, *Fieldwork for Archaeologists and Local Historians* (London: B. T. Batsford, 1987), p. 9.

10. Brown, p. 10.

11. William B. Shaffir, Robert A. Stebbins, and Allan Turowetz, eds., *Fieldwork Experience: Qualitative Approaches to Social Research* (New York: St. Martin's Press, 1980), pp. 6, 11.

12. Shaffir, et al., p. 3.

13. Nancy Howell, *Surviving Fieldwork: A Report of the Advisory Panel on Health and Safety in Fieldwork* (Washington, D.C.: American Anthropological Association, 1990), v. 26, p. 4.

PART ONE

What Is Culture?
What Are Cultures?

1

The Intellectual Challenge of Multiculturalism and Teaching the Canon

Seyla Benhabib

A brief consideration of the history of the concept of "culture" in the last century allows us to place this term in three rather different, when not contradictory, contexts of discourse. As a term that originated in the French Enlightenment and the discourse of the German Romantics, "culture," *Kultur*, was used at the turn of the nineteenth century primarily in contrast to *Zivilisation*, "civilization." *Kultur* represents those values, shared systems of meaning, signification, and symbolization of a people, usually considered as a homogeneous unity. *Kultur* refers to forms of expression through which the "spirit" of a specific people, as distinct and distinguishable from all others, is voiced. For the individual, the acquisition of *Kultur* signifies the immersion and shaping of the soul through education in the values of a spiritual collective. This classical German understanding views culture as a process of intellectual-spiritual formation, of *Bildung*.

"Civilization," by contrast, refers to those material values and practices that are shared with other peoples, and that do not reflect, therefore, individuality. "Civilization" roughly designates the bourgeois, industrial-capitalist world. Economic and legal practices, as well as the institutions of liberal democracy, would fall under the umbrella of *Zivilisation* as opposed to *Kultur*. This contrast is also associated with others, like "exteriority" vs. "interiority," "superficiality" vs. "depth," "linear constructions in time and space" vs. "organic growth," "individualism" vs. "collectivism."

With the emergence of mass totalitarian movements in Europe in the 1920s and 1930s, the concept of culture was situated within a framework of anxiety about its very possibility. Can there be mass culture? Are the masses capable of culture? This discussion about mass culture, which had already begun in the Weimar Republic in the 1920s, was transported across the Atlantic during the post–World War II period and was applied to the experience of mass consumer democracies. The idea of mass culture carries all the marks that were once associated with the concept of *Zivilisation*: superficiality, homogeneity, lack of durability, reproducibility, lack of originality. Mass culture is not educative or transformative; it does not shape the soul, nor does it express the spirit or the collective genius of a people. Mass culture is entertainment, and, in Theodor Adorno's immemorable phrase, "entertainment is betrayal";[1] a promise of happiness to those consuming masses who displace onto the screen and onto the figures of Hollywood the *promesse du bonheur* that advanced industrial capitalism cannot deliver to them.

When one considers the discussions of culture that prevail in today's academy, one is struck by the extent to which the above meanings of the term have become obsolete. What dominates today is a meaning of the term that derives from British social anthropology, from the work of Malinowski, Evans-Pritchard, the American Margaret Mead, and the structuralist theories of Claude Levi-Strauss. Culture is understood as the totality of those systems of signification, representation, symbolization, and those social practices that have a quasi-autonomous logic and independence, separated often from the intentionality or spirituality of those who constitute them. In structuralist and poststructuralist thought in particular, the step toward eliminating the subject of culture is taken all too frequently.

The battle over culture that rages today in the academy, newspapers, media, and the entertainment industry presupposes this third meaning of culture. The first two meanings of culture, however, continue to be a source of anxiety on the part of the critics of cultural studies and multiculturalism. In fact, much of the so-called debate about the "canon" is a displaced continuation of the anxiety about mass culture onto the intellectual, political, and pedagogical challenges posed by multiculturalism. In ways that would have appeared unimaginable until very recently, we are all caught in the throes of what I would call "cultural civil wars."

Some important questions to consider in this context are: How do matters of cultural representation reshape our academic and pedagogical responsibilities? Do the realities of cultural diversity expose the limits of the liberal and democratic principles at the center of the university? I would like to propose an answer to these questions by recounting some of the transformations that my own work on the history of political thought is undergoing as a consequence of the great paradigm change in the instruction of the canon, a change we are all experiencing in varying degrees.

Several years ago, while lecturing in the now destroyed Inter-University Center of the city of Dubrovnik in the Republic of Croatia, I cited a passage from John Locke's *Second Treatise of Civil Government* in which Locke discusses the "state of nature." Locke reminds us that, although a metaphor, this figure of speech may have some factual basis as well. He writes of "the two men in the desert island, mentioned by Garcilaso de la Vega, in his history of *Peru*; or between a *Swiss* and an *Indian*, in the woods of America."[2] After the lecture I was approached by a colleague from Latin America, of Peruvian descent. He asked me for the reference to the full citation; he was astonished that John Locke knew of Garcilaso de la Vega. I was in turn astonished that this detail would interest him that much, for my lecture had been a feminist critique of the concept of individuality implicit in early liberal political theory as articulated by the metaphor of the state of nature. Who was Garcilaso de la Vega? Why should he matter to my feminist critique?

Here is what my preliminary research has produced: Garcilaso de la Vega, also known as "El Inca," is hailed by Arnold Toynbee as "an early representative of a class which has been important throughout the history of the encounters between modern Western civilization and all the other surviving civilizations and precivilizational cultures on the face of our planet, and which is supremely important today."[3] Toynbee wrote this foreword to Vega's *Royal Commentaries of the Incas* in 1966, "when the impact of the West upon the rest of the world," he claimed, was becoming "a dominant motif in the present phase of world history."[4]

Thanks to his mixed Andea-European descent and to his initiation into both his ancestral traditions—a double education that was the privilege, or burden, of his mestizo blood—Garcilaso was able to serve, and did serve, as an interpreter or mediator between two different cultures that had suddenly been brought into contact with each other.[5] Born in the ancient Inca capital of Cuzco in 1539, the son of a Spanish conqueror of noble lineage and an Indian princess, Garcilaso was one of the first mestizos. As a young man, after much family misfortune and the forced separation of his parents and the annulment of their mixed marriage by the Catholic Church, he left his native Peru, never to return, and it was in the seclusion of a small Andalusian town that he wrote his great work, *Royal Commentaries of the Incas and*

General History of Peru. It is divided into two parts published separately, one in Lisbon in 1609, and the other in Cordova posthumously in 1616–17.

In 1690, when John Locke published anonymously his *Two Treatises of Civil Government,* had he actually read Garcilaso? Was his construction of the "state of nature" based on Garcilaso's *Royal Commentaries of the Incas* or upon another work called *Florida,*[6] in which Garcilaso tells the tale of an expedition to explore and occupy territories inhabited by half-savage Indians, many of them cannibals? What is surprising in this story is how my interests as a feminist led me to focus on some of the marginalia in the text of the *Second Treatise,* and how the interests of another scholar showed me the way to the encounter with another culture implicit in the subtext of John Locke's famous work. Depending indeed upon how Locke read or misread, presented or misrepresented Garcilaso, we will gain a fascinating insight into the process of the construction of the "others" in the texts of Western political thought.

What conclusions can we draw from this example? I certainly am not ready to stop teaching John Locke's *Second Treatise of Civil Government* in my courses on the history of political thought. For what gives John Locke canonical status in the history of modern political thought is his elaboration of the philosophical foundations of modern liberalism through the argument that the voluntarily given consent of the people is the only basis of legitimate government.[7] But increasingly, it is inadequate and disingenuous to keep teaching the canon as if these texts were not also cultural sedimentations of struggles among genders, races, cultures, and social classes. This much I will grant my deconstructionist friends, and this much I have learned from Jacques Derrida.[8]

However, for many colleagues who are practitioners of cultural studies, what seems to follow from this new hermeneutics of textuality is a radical contextualism. By this I mean the assumption that any claim to universality and generalizability, any claim gesturing toward a shared humanity also contained in these texts, must be met with skepticism, must be cut to size, must be radically deconstructed. Much deconstructionist methodology, as opposed to Derrida's own work, implies cultural relativism, when not nihilism. This, I think, is wrong.

A distinction first introduced by Max Weber may be our guide in untangling some of the complex issues involved. In a famous essay titled "The Meaning of Ethical Neutrality in Sociology and Economics," Weber distinguished between "value relevance" and "value freedom."[9] "Value relevance" refers to those sets of interests, questions, and puzzles that demarcate an area of knowledge and research as worthy of inquiry and analysis. What makes a given subject matter worthy of analysis, Weber wrote, is its perceived relevance for the value interests of the investigator situated in the present. These interests change over time and are culturally, historically, and politically motivated. "Value freedom," however, refers to the standards and criteria of scholarship, research, and theoretical presentation that a scholar has to follow and live up to once she has demarcated her subject matter and defined her techniques of investigation. Value freedom does not mean that a scholar should have no ethical or political commitments, or that she should not communicate them to others; it means that she should distinguish as carefully, as honestly, and as forcefully as she can between the demands of her subject matter and scholarship and her own stance on these issues. In disputing the opinion of one of his colleagues that an anarchist could not be a good jurist, Weber writes: "My own opinion is exactly the opposite. An anarchist can surely be a good legal scholar. And if he is such, then indeed the Archimedean point of his convictions, which is outside the conventions and presuppositions which are so self-evident to us, can equip him to perceive problems in the fundamental postulates of legal theory which escape those who take them for granted. Fundamental doubt is the father of knowledge."[10]

Nothing seems to me more important today than to disentangle the morass around this struggle over values, culture, and scholarship. We should distinguish between those cultural, political, moral, and aesthetic values and interests that guide our scholarship, research, and teaching, and those skills of the craft that make a great scholar, an ingenious researcher, and an inspiring teacher. It is in transmitting the latter that we must exercise value freedom in the Weberian sense; whereas the former will always be guided by the ethical and political relevance of values to us as individuals, scholars, and teachers.

If we can keep this distinction between value relevance and value freedom in sight, then we will be able to see that the questioning of the canon as expressed by feminists and gay scholars and people of color over the last twenty years has yielded and is yielding a new scholarship of tremendous depth and excitement. We are all discovering new methods and techniques of reading old and familiar texts; we are exercising an hermeneutic of moving from the margins to the center; footnotes and marginalia are assuming a significance that they never had before. For when we search these texts for those others whose presence is never quite erased but is continuously marginalized, we must move from the periphery to the center, from the text to the subtext.

In facing up to this challenge, we need to understand the historical process whereby Western modernity has emerged as a global reality since the sixteenth century. For the challenge to the hegemony of the canon has not come from oppositional intellectuals alone. It is the global complexity of the twenty-first century that has placed this hegemony in question. As civilizations, cultures, and peoples are drawn together by the technological, economic, and military realities of this century approaching its end, the hegemony of the Western canon from Plato and Aristotle over Aquinas, Machiavelli, Hobbes, Locke, and Rousseau to Kant, Hegel, Marx, and Freud will be challenged. The canon can survive, insofar as any tradition can endure, i.e., if we as contemporaries are still able to find viable answers in these texts to some of our perplexities concerning the deepest questions of life and death, justice and injustice, freedom and oppression, sexuality and community, creativity and anxiety.

As Homi Bhabha writes in *The Location of Culture*: "The borderline work of culture demands an encounter with 'newness' that is not part of the continuum of past and present. It creates a sense of the new as an insurgent act of cultural translation. Such art…renews the past, refiguring it as a contingent 'in-between' space, that innovates and interrupts the performance of the present. The 'past-present' becomes part of the necessity, not the nostalgia, of living."[11]

Radical contextualism or nihilism are wholly inadequate answers to the "global hybridity" or "interstitiality" that increasingly characterize and define life today. What is required is precisely a rethinking of the old Enlightenment ideal of the cosmopolis for the conditions of a humanity that is composed more and more of mestizos such as Garcilaso de la Vega, of multinational and multicultural residents, of migrants, of post- and ex-colonials. I believe that in thinking about this new cosmopolitical condition of the "in-between," in Homi Bhabha's words, the Western canon from Aristotle to Kant, from Shakespeare to Hegel, will continue to be our partner in conversation, although not our only one.

The globalization and pluralization of the canon will not destroy those values of the life of the mind that the ancient Greeks first discovered in their encounter with the power of *logos*, of reason and speech: curiosity, courage, the power to question and to resist, to challenge the given, and the urge to go "beyond the appearances," beyond the way things seem to us in our everyday lives, prior to analytical reflection, to the things themselves, to matters as they really are. Garcilaso de la Vega exercised these virtues in the sixteenth century as a mestizo; he became one of the first intellectuals of the Americas. He was apparently fond of telling how Dr. Juan de Cuellar, a canon of the cathedral who opened Latin classes in Cuzco, was so impressed by the aptitude of his mestizo scholars that he used to exclaim: "How I'd like to see a dozen of you in the University of Salamanca!"[12] The university of the twenty-first century will have to be home to the mestizos of the mind!

NOTES

1. Max Horkheimer and Theodor Adorno, *Dialektik der Aufklaerung. Philosophische Fragmente*, originally published in 1947, new and revised edition, afterword by Juergen Habermas (Frankfurt: Fischer Verlag, 1969), pp. 128ff. Although coauthored by Horkheimer and Adorno, we now know that the two authors were each mainly responsible for certain sections of the text. For the section on "Culture Industry. Enlightenment as Betrayal," see Habermas's afterword, pp. 278ff.

2. John Locke, *Second Treatise of Civil Government*, edited and with an introduction by C. B. McPherson (Indianapolis and Cambridge, Mass.: Hackett Publishing, 1980), p. 13.

3. Arnold Toynbee, "Foreword," Garcilaso de la Vega, *Royal Commentaries on the Incas and General History of Peru*, trans. Harold V. Livermore (Austin: University of Texas Press, 1966), p. xii.

4. Ibid.

5. Toynbee, "Foreword," p. xii.

6. Garcilaso de la Vega, *The Florida of the Inca*, trans. and ed. John Grier Varmer and Jeanette Johnson Varmer (Austin: University of Texas Press, 1980).

7. See John Locke, *Second Treatise*, pp. 47ff.

8. See the essay, "The Ends of Man," reprinted in *After Philosophy, End or Transformation*, ed. Kenneth Baynes, James Bohman, and Thomas McCarthy (Cambridge, Mass.: MIT Press, 1987), pp. 125-161.

9. Max Weber, "The Meaning of 'Ethical Neutrality' in Sociology and Economics," in *From Max Weber*, trans. and ed. Edward A. Shils and Henry A. Finch (New York: The Free Press, 1949), pp. 1-50, here pp. 10ff.

10. Weber, "The Meaning of 'Ethical Neutrality' in Sociology and Economics," *The Methodology of the Social Sciences*, p. 7.

11. Homi Bhabha, *The Location of Culture* (London and New York: Routledge, 1994), p. 7.

12. Garcilaso de la Vega, quoted by Toynbee in his foreword, *Royal History of the Incas*, p. xxi.

2

What Is Culture? Does It Matter?

Mary Margaret Steedly

As an anthropologist, I spend a lot of time thinking about what culture is doing to us. I mean this in two ways. First, as a teacher of anthropology, I incorporate local cultural artifacts as illustrative examples in my lectures—Madonna, Gap ads, an episode of *Star Trek: Voyager*, a poem by Elizabeth Bishop, a walk across Harvard Yard—in the hope of keeping my students attentive, or at least awake. What do these things have to say about who we are and how we experience the world? What can we make of them? What are *they* making of us? Is it possible anymore, even in the relatively homogeneous space of a Harvard classroom, to speak with any assurance of "we" and "us"?

Such reflections are a part of the anthropologist's classroom stock in trade, our way of linking cultural processes studied in places off the beaten track to the events, images, and practices that populate our students' cultural landscape. Such aspirations to relevance are a (perhaps wishful) way of defining ourselves into the mainstream of someone else's cultural reality, and I worry about both the inclusions and exclusions that are effected by my (or anyone else's) lists of relevant "cultural artifacts." But I have also been thinking about what this preoccupation with "culture" is doing to us in another way—what the concept of culture is doing to our academic ways of "staging the world." It is this concern that I will address here.

Quite simply, "culture" makes me uncomfortable. Not just in the old-fashioned universalizing sense, but even in the plural, relativistic sense that now seems firmly entrenched in academic discourse. "Culture" in this latter sense refers to the unique expressions of a particular collective lifeway, the distinctive "webs of significance" in which a human community finds itself enmeshed.[1]

What anthropologists properly do, as Clifford Geertz has recently put it, is to describe cultures.[2] And for all the nuanced elegance and insight that good cultural analysis can convey, it is this culture-as-the-object-of-anthropological-inquiry orientation that troubles me. Anthropologists explain cultures, and cultures serve to explain the actions of their individual members, and those individual acts are the clues that we use to "decode" the culture. But having explained all of this, haven't we missed something?

This is not an analytically derived or theoretically constructed position but one I came to through writing about people in an anthropological way. My first fieldwork experience was in Robeson County, North Carolina. This is one of the poorest counties in the state, with a roughly equal triracial—black, white, and Indian—population configuration. The Indian people of Robeson County (as they prefer to refer to themselves) have been variously labeled as "mulattos," Croatans, Cherokees, and Tuscaroras; in recent years they have been most commonly known as Lumbees.[3] They are the largest of the nonreservation Native American groups in the eastern United States.

As with many similar groups, cultural identity has become a problem for the Lumbee in recent years, with government benefits, social recognition, and cognitive salience being defined by a "tribal" status largely conceived in terms of the existence of a bounded and historically stable cultural identity. Culture in this (political) sense depends on such ethnic markers as physical appearance, native language, religion, costume, folklore, political organizations, distinctive social and economic arrangments, and the like. Not only were these all things that present-day Lumbees did not have, there was not even any historical record, written or oral, that suggested that they had ever had them in the past. In the ethnically blurred space of Robeson County, there was little that distinguished Lumbees from their black or white neighbors, aside from the pervasive sense that they were, indeed, "Indian people," and the equally pervasive acts of social and political discrimination aimed at them by outsiders.

My original plan had been to conduct a comparative study of folk curing practices in these three communities, but I soon reduced my ambitions to a study of only the Lumbee Indian tradition, and then specifically to the curing practice of one Lumbee man, Vernon Cooper. Mr. Cooper's curing practice idiosyncratically blended fundamentalist Christian faith healing, homeopathy (as a boy he worked for "Uncle Jesse" Hair, a white homeopathic doctor), and what I liked to think of as "traditional" Indian herbal medicine but which contained significant elements of cultural crossover from non-Native curing repertoires. My thesis, based on interviews and observation, discovered in this heterogeneous curing system a symbolic logic that seemed culturally "Indian," even if many of the materials and practices that were incorporated into this system had been taken from non-Indian sources. Taking a cue from Mary Douglas's *Purity and Danger*, I argued that Mr. Cooper's philosophy of curing was based on a concept of a spiritual "warfare" in which the individual body stood in a position analogous to the social body of the Lumbee community.[4] An individual's health depended on maintaining the integrity of the body's boundaries while strengthening an inner essence or core self. Such a philosophy seemed to resonate with the dilemmas of Lumbee ethnicity in Robeson County, in which both the boundaries and the core identity of the group were fragile, porous, and subject to considerable pressure, both internal and external. For Mr. Cooper and his patients, curing was a kind of self-fashioning project, in which the health of the individual patient provided a way of addressing the Lumbee social predicament and thus the health of the community as a whole.[5]

This seemed like a fairly compelling argument at the time—but I hated it. I hated it so much that I never gave Mr. Cooper a copy of my thesis, even though there was nothing in it that I thought (or still think) was not accurate; nor was there anything in it that was not respectful of him. He, being virtually illiterate, would in all likelihood not have read it anyway. But something about the writing of it bothered me immensely.

It seemed that turning people or events or texts or stories into illustrations, prototypes, or "sites" of something else erased the very thing that I wanted to capture in writing about them in the first place. In using ethnographic moments as "keys" to a larger cultural picture (like Geertz's famous cockfight), or "diagnostic events" that might reveal patterns of social tension or contradiction, or, as in this case, symbolic expressions of collective preoccupations, something about the moment itself vanished.[6] Lumbee "culture" did not explain Mr. Cooper's curing practice, and his curing activities were not just an illustration of some general cultural principle. Using them in this way felt rather like a betrayal.

My second period of extended fieldwork was conducted in a much more conventionally "cultural" situation—among the Karo Bataks, a clan-based agrarian society of northern Sumatra, Indonesia. The Karo are not a society living in "splendid isolation," nor, as far as I can tell, have they ever been so. The Karo highlands are today one of Indonesia's major commercial produce-growing areas, and the Karo claim to have the highest percentage of college graduates of any ethnic group in Indonesia. They are sophisticated if marginal players in the national political arena. But they also have all the cultural baggage dear to the anthropologist's heart: a complex kinship system (anthropologists call it a "Kachin-type" system) composed of patrilineal clans, linked together through marital ties ideally formed through matrilateral cross-cousin marriage, and ordered by a marked status distinction between wife-givers and wife-receivers.[7] The Karo speak a distinctive language, have a historical territory of residence (a "homeland"), build (or once built) unique and imposing traditional houses, some of which are still standing. They compose songs and poetry in a locally specific aesthetic style, and they have myths, legends, folktales, histories. They also, I should add, have their own anthropologists.

Although the majority of Karo are today Christian Protestants, local spirit-veneration cults are still in evidence; a decade ago, when I was learning about Karo spirit mediumship, these were flourishing. However much Karo may have been in intimate contact with other ethnic groups, however they may have been compelled to adapt (or constrained from adapting) to the pressures of colonial state formation and postcolonial state consolidation and to the fairly rigid directives of Calvinist Christianity, there is, in the Karo case, at least an obvious cultural "there" there. There is a style of doing things that Karo recognize as distinctively their own, which many Karo (and especially Karo Christians) have been working very hard to maintain or, as some would say, to "invent."

Yet once again in writing about the Karo I ran into the problem of culture. After three years of learning about Karo social life and particularly about the place of spirit mediums within that life, when I tried to write about Karo culture I found myself unable to produce anything at all. There was, first of all, the problem of definition. Karo Christians defined culture in one way, spirit mediums in another. Karo men had one view, women another. The conventions of highland villagers differed radically from those of urban Karo—and of lowland villagers. Which one should count? Then there was the problem of history: How does one describe the "ethnographic present" of a community continually reshaping itself? At what point in time does one set the cultural standard? Any definition, any fixing of the ethnographic object, generated its own set of claims to authority and its own exclusions. "Culture" in this sense has to be seen as a political category, and its definition a political act.

But my most significant obstacle was the problem of explanation.

Whenever I tried to set out a pattern of ritual performance or a structure of symbolic meaning, it felt intensely inauthentic to me. As with my earlier fieldwork in Robeson County, the act of cultural explanation seemed to drain not just the immediacy but the significance from those things I was trying to explain. So, as a kind of thought exercise, I declared a personal moratorium on the word "culture."

It was a liberating experience. Suddenly events seemed to be "about" themselves. They didn't cry out for cultural explanation. It wasn't a culture I was trying to describe, but rather a series of social moments in which people struggled to make sense (or to take advantage) of circumstances more or less beyond their control. In not attending so much to culture, in not making my work "about" culture, culture—or at least the things that made it up—seemed to slip back in, unnoticed and (on my part anyway) unremarked. Kinship was still there, of course—you can't make anything out of Karo experience without it—and so were art and ritual forms and ways of acting. They were all there, but they weren't being called on to explain anything else. They didn't have to hang together; they weren't being called on to make sense.[8]

In the exhilarating first flush of this liberation from culture, I had a conversation with a historian friend. Newly converted to the anticulture camp, and with all the enthusiasm of a fresh convert, I argued that history was being ruined by an uncritical application of outmoded models derived from anthropology, and particularly by the "culture" that had been inserted into "cultural history." To my surprise, my friend, who was a medieval historian, accused me of "trying to keep culture for the anthropologists." Culture was for her an enabling concept that allowed her to shape the fragments of archival material regarding nonelite populations into some coherent form. It allowed her—to borrow a phrase from John and Jean Comaroff—to "redeem the fragments" by situating them in the framework of a (hypothetical) total-izing culture.[9] She could bring disparate bits of information into relation with one another by recourse to the unifying concept of culture, and she could fill in the gaps in a radically incomplete historical record.

This is not a small contribution, especially when applied to medieval history or to other "from-the-bottom" accounts that are forced to deal with an incomplete (as they all are) historical or ethnographic record. In this sense, culture is an extremely useful term in historical or anthropological or literary analysis. But like such other "useful categories" as "gender" or "woman" or "experience," the concept of culture can be an instrument of dangerous utility.[10]

What makes culture analytically useful also makes it a dangerous tool to wield: that is, its inherent presumption of internal coherence, whether that coherence is expressed as "pattern" or "articulation," as "style" or "hegemony"; its assumption of formal or functional relations among its component parts or between part and whole. While the concept of culture may look delightfully "messy" and liberatory in comparison to more rigidly deterministic models of "hegemony" or "ideology,"[11] it always necessarily operates as an explanatory mechanism, even in the most offhand of contexts. As a mode of analysis, "culture" always posits itself as a replica of some objective reality out in the world.

To be sure, anthropological conceptualizations of culture are much more complicated these days than they once were. With postmodernism and poststructuralism, diaspora and transnationalism, and particularly with the extraordinarily important work being done in cultural studies, which has given a critical, political edge to cultural analyses, our notions of culture have gotten much more fluid, conflictual, disorderly, blurry, mobile, and generally unstable and uncertain. We now have culture *and* hegemony *and* ideology. We have "relative autonomy" of domains and resistances within as well as among cultures. We have domination and subordination, subalternity, subjugation, subjectivity, subjection. All this makes the concept of culture much less useful as a tool of explanation, and more puzzling as a thing to be explained, in particular cases.

Among anthropologists, the idea of culture has come to refer to increasingly smaller units. We can't speak comfortably of "American culture" any more than we can talk about "Culture" in universal terms. Now there is "white, middle-class suburban culture," "L.A. culture," "teen culture," "postmodern teen culture," "postmodern teen sci-fi fan culture," and so on. But shifting culture to smaller and smaller units will not hold it together, for the problem of difference—as the women's movement has dramatically demonstrated—remains, however small the unit of identification becomes. Each segmentation reproduces the problem it was intended to address. And, at the same time, it weakens the utility of the totalizing concept. As many feminists have argued, without a unifying, generic concept of "woman" as both identity and site of intervention, the women's movement risks eliminating the ground of its own existence.

The stakes perhaps are not so high in the world of academic discourses, but the point is the same. Every effort to resolve the problems of culture by complicating or fragmenting the totality reproduces the problem while it simultaneously reduces the usefulness of the tool. I am not suggesting that we anthropologists—or medieval historians or anyone else—stop using the concept of culture altogether, but rather that we use it with a great deal more caution than we have heretofore. Rather than continue to write "culture," or even to write "against culture,"[12] we may do well to start writing around it.

NOTES

1. Clifford Geertz, "Thick Description: Toward an Interpretive Theory of Culture." In C. Geertz, *The Interpretation of Cultures* (New York: Basic Books, 1973), p. 5.

2. Clifford Geertz, *After the Fact* (Cambridge: Harvard University Press, 1995), p. 62.

3. Key works on the Lumbees include Karen Blu, *The Lumbee Problem* (Cambridge: Cambridge University Press, 1980); and Gerald Sider, *Lumbee Indian Histories* (Cambridge: Cambridge University Press, 1993).

4. Mary Douglas, *Purity and Danger* (London: Routledge, 1966).

5. Mary Steedly, "'The Evidence of Things Not Seen': Faith and Tradition in a Lumbee Healing Practice" (M.A. thesis, University of North Carolina, Chapel Hill, 1979). The term "self-fashioning" is borrowed from Steven Greenblatt, *Renaissance Self-Fashioning* (Chicago: University of Chicago Press, 1980). For a similar examination of the politics of identity among eastern U.S. Indian groups, see James Clifford, "Identity in Mashpee," in J. Clifford, *The Predicament of Culture* (Cambridge: Harvard University Press, 1988), pp. 227–246.

6. For the term "key symbols," see Sherry Ortner, "On Key Symbols," *American Anthropologist* 75 (1973), pp. 1338–1346; the Balinese cockfight is discussed in Clifford Geertz, "Deep Play: Notes on the Balinese Cockfight," in C. Geertz, *The Interpretation of Cultures* (New York: Basic Books, 1973), pp. 412–453; for the use of "diagnostic events" in ethnographic analysis, see Sally Falk Moore, "Explaining the Present: Theoretical Dilemmas in Processual Anthropology," *American Ethnologist* 14 (1987), pp. 727–736.

7. Sources on Karo kinship include Masri Singarimbun, *Kinship, Descent and Alliance among the Karo Bataks* (Berkeley: University of California Press, 1975); Rita S. Kipp, "Terms for Kith and Kin," *American Anthropologist* 86 (1984), pp. 905–24; "Terms of Endearment: Karo Batak Lovers as Siblings," *American Ethnologist* 13 (1986), pp. 632–645; Rodney Needham, "Classification and Alliance among the Karo: An Appreciation," *Bijdragen tot de Taal-, Land- en Volkenkunde* 134 (1978), pp. 116–148. The classic work on this type of kinship system is Edmund Leach, *Political Systems of Highland Burma* (Boston: Beacon, 1965).

8. These problems inform the work that later resulted from my time in Karoland. See Mary Steedly, *Hanging without a Rope: Narrative Experience in Colonial and Postcolonial Karoland* (Princeton: Princeton University Press, 1993).

9. John Comaroff and Jean Comaroff, *Ethnography and the Historical Imagination* (Chicago: University of Chicago Press, 1992), p. 31. For a "non-redemptive" approach to the historical fragment, see Gyanendra Pandey, "In Defense of the Fragment," *Representations* 37 (1992), pp. 27–55.

10. Cf. Joan Scott, "Gender: A Useful Category of Historical Analysis," in Joan Scott, *Gender and the Politics of History* (New York: Columbia University Press, 1988), pp. 27–50; Gayatri Spivak (with Ellen Rooney), "In a Word: Interview," in Gayatri Chakravorty Spivak, *Outside in the Teaching Machine* (New York: Routledge, 1993); Joan Scott, "The Evidence of Experience," *Critical Inquiry* 17 (1991), pp. 773–797.
11. I owe this insight to Svetlana Boym.
12. Cf. James Clifford and George Marcus, eds., *Writing Culture* (Berkeley: University of California Press, 1986); Lila Abu-Lughod, "Writing against Culture," in Richard G. Fox, ed., *Recapturing Anthropology: Working in the Present* (Santa Fe: SAR Press, 1991).

3

Custody Battles

Marjorie Garber

"I scorn to distinguish between culture and civilization."

—Sigmund Freud, "The Future of an Illusion"

Ideas won't keep. Something must be done about them. When the idea is new, its custodians have fervor, live for it and, if need be, die for it.

—Alfred North Whitehead, *Dialogues*

Sed quis custodiet ipsos Custodes? [But who is to guard the guards themselves?]

—Juvenal, *Satire 6*

"The wholeness of the human problem," wrote a celebrated author in exile to the dean of a prestigious academic institution in his former country, "permits nobody to separate the intellectual and artistic from the political and social, and to isolate himself within the ivory tower of the 'cultural' proper."

The author in voluntary exile was Thomas Mann; the institution was the Philosophical Faculty of Bonn University; the occasion was his name's being removed from the roll of honorary doctors; the year was 1937.

"Cultural" in Mann's dignified letter of reproof meant "the intellectual and artistic" as contrasted with "the political and social." Yet in today's debates about the humanities, "cultural" is very often "the political and social" rather than "the intellectual and artistic." Race, ethnography, identity politics, feminism, Marxism, postcoloniality, queer theory: these categories of analysis and critique, which are crucial to the practice of cultural studies, are often described as intrinsically inimical to aesthetic judgment and literary merit.

It would have been hard to imagine, a few years ago, that "culture" would become such a loaded word; that the national and international press, and many American scholars, would be engaged in what are now routinely described as "culture wars." To paraphrase one of Freud's titles slightly, "Why Wars?" What's to fight about?

Is it a custody battle? Sometimes modern cultural critics are accused of throwing the baby out with the bathwater: the baby of literature, presumably, or of "high culture" and aesthetic value, out with the bathwater of "culture"—oh, those dirty rings. Or is it a battle of the books? The names chosen by the combatants in these "culture wars" tell the same tale of territory and labeling: the conservative National Association of *Scholars*; the liberal Teachers for a Democratic *Culture*.

"Literary intellectuals at one pole—at the other scientists…. Between the two a gulf of mutual incomprehension." This was C. P. Snow, writing some thirty-five years ago in a book called *The Two Cultures and the Scientific Revolution* (1959). We've come a long way from that moment—or have we? Culture, or cultures, again threaten to divide us, not so much by disciplines (literature and science—like literature and economics, literature and medicine, literature and law—are no longer strange bedfellows) but instead by approaches. The "gulf of mutual incomprehension," if there is one, stretches between proponents of "Culture" and proponents of cultures.

Now it wasn't so very long ago—1988, to be exact—that the Harvard postgraduate humanities center, a center founded to foster interdisciplinary studies, changed its name from the Center for Literary Studies, the name it had borne since its founding in 1984, to the Center for Literary and Cultural Studies, the name it bears today. The executive committee of the center made the decision—after considerable deliberation—to reflect the nature of the work our seminars were then producing. Among these seminars were "American Literature in International Perspective," "Cross Cultural Poetics and Rhetoric," "Eighteenth Century Literature and Culture," and "Women in the Renaissance and Reformation."

The center's board and its seminar leaders met and discussed the question, and agreed on the new name—a decision we forwarded to the dean for his approval. The January 1988 newsletter of the center thus announced, quite simply:

> Note: With this issue the Center for Literary Studies expands its name to the Center for Literary and Cultural Studies, to reflect the diversity of work being done in its Seminars.

It is perhaps worth reporting, given the publication of a massive tome called *The Western Canon* by one of literature's most passionate defenders, that the same issue of the newsletter listed, under "Future Events" sponsored by the center, the second series of Harold Bloom's Charles Eliot Norton Poetry

Lectures on "Milton," the "Enlightment and Romanticism," and "Freud and Beyond." Bloom's year as Norton professor was spent at the CLCS; we were his host and sponsor.

In a long article in *The Chronicle of Higher Education* heralding the publication of his book on the canon, Bloom was quoted describing cultural studies succinctly as *hazarai*, perhaps the first time that deliciously dismissive Yiddish word had ever appeared in the august pages of the *Chronicle*. Bloom told a fascinated reporter from *Newsweek* that at NYU, where he teaches part of the year, he was surrounded by "professors of hip-hop." If Todd Gitlin is right to say that "we live in a sound-bite culture," this is one cultural trend Bloom has clearly, and deftly, mastered.

What is culture? What are cultures? What is the difference between these two questions?

"Culture," in the collective, referential singular, seems frequently to refer to the arts, to literature, music, and dance, to so-called high culture (like Shakespeare in our time) and so-called low culture (like Shakespeare in his time).

"Culture in all its early uses was a noun of process, the tending of something," wrote Raymond Williams in *Keywords*. At first used for activities such as farming ("agri*culture*") it became by the sixteenthth century a process of human development. Thus Williams cites Thomas More: "to the culture and profit of their minds"; Francis Bacon: "the culture and manurance of minds" (1605); Thomas Hobbes: "a culture of their minds" (1651); and Dr. Johnson: "She neglected the culture of [her] understanding" (1759). The interesting if apparently inadvertent gendering of this little sequence, which ends up with a singular female subject who *neglects* culture, is excerpted by Williams, without comment, from the OED, from which he takes all of these quotations.[1]

Enlightenment historians came to use "culture" as a kind of synonym for "the historical self-development of humanity." The next "decisive innovation," according to Williams, can be traced to the proto-Romantic Herder, the champion of the folk spirit, who in the late eighteenth century apostrophized "Men of all the quarters of the globe," warning them that "the very thought of a superior European culture is a blatant insult to the majesty of Nature." This is the late eighteenth century; the speaker is not a rabid postmodern relativist multiculturalist. Nonetheless what Herder implied, and what constitutes for Raymond Williams that "decisive innovation," was the necessity of speaking "of 'cultures' in the plural: the specific and variable cultures of different natures and periods, but also the specific and variable cultures of social and economic groups within a nation."

Culture and cultures. In archaeology and anthropology, the material traces of civilization; in history and cultural studies, systems of signs and signification.

But things get really interesting when "culture," and what Williams calls "the important adjective cultural," begin to mean something like our current "high culture," or what Matthew Arnold famously referred to, in *Culture and Anarchy*, as "the best which has been thought and said."

Williams notes that "Hostility to the word *culture* in English appears to date from the controversy around Arnold's views. It gathered force in the late nineteenth century and the early twentieth century, in association with a comparable hostility to *aesthete* and *aesthetic*. Its association with class distinction produced the mime word *culchah*.... The central area of hostility has lasted, and one element of it has been emphasized by the recent American phrase culture-vulture. It is significant that virtually all the hostility...has been connected with uses involving claims to superior knowledge (compare the noun Intellectual), refinement (*culchah*) and distinctions between 'high' art ('culture') and popular art and entertainment. It thus records a real social history and a very difficult and confused phase of social and cultural development."

Culture-vultures, aficionados and practitioners of culchah, where are you now? The culture-vulture of Williams's world was a collateral relation to the culture maven of mine.

If "culture" is an aesthetic or artistic entity or attribute—the sort of thing students used to come to places like Harvard to "get"—then "cultures," in the plural, are potentially something else. "Cultures" are societies or "communities" or lifestyles: French culture, black culture, gay culture, skinhead culture, youth culture. (Even more dangerous are "subcultures," which is how some of these entities are better described.) In *The Closing of the American Mind,* Allan Bloom can talk despairingly of rock music and MTV as "*the* youth culture." ("Picture a thirteen-year-old boy sitting in the living room of his family home doing his math assignment while wearing his Walkman headphones or watching MTV.") For Bloom this image is the end of a kind of civilization. "It is *the* youth culture," he laments. "Some of this culture's power comes from the fact that it is so loud." Bloom deplores "rock music" as "a nonstop, commercially prepackaged masturbational fantasy." (He thinks this is a bad thing; you are free to make your own judgment.) Let a thousand Blooms flower.

But even secure monuments of culture may be cause for alarm. Consider— as it is my profession and my pleasure to do—the case of Shakespeare, the classic of classics. Shakespeare is the apotheosis of "culture," and even of "high culture." Harold Bloom calls him "the largest writer we will ever know"—and, twenty pages later, "the most original writer we will ever know," and, twenty pages later, the "Center of the Canon," and, thirty pages later, the canon itself: "Shakespeare is the Western Canon." As one who has spent an entire academic career teaching and reading Shakespeare, I am not disposed to disagree.

But which Shakespeare?

Shakespeare, of course, began as popular culture, not as high culture. Plays in the late sixteenth century were not "works" to be published in folio form (that happened only with the presumptuous Ben Jonson and later with the—significantly, dead—Shakespeare: death even then was a kind of prerequisite for literary immortality). Shakespeare's plays were printed in quartos, the instant books of their day, and Elizabethan playhouses were built outside the city limits because players, and playing, was so disreputable. Theater was *not* high art, even though the queen, and later the king, attended performances. It was only in the eighteenth century that the myth of "Shakespeare," and the reified Shakespeare text, began to be invented. Shakespeare in this sense is an eighteenth century author.

Or a twentieth-century author, again breaching the boundaries of "high" and "low," "popular" and "learned," "culture" and "cultural studies." All summer on the Internet, Shakespeare scholars buzzed with excitement about perceived analogies between the O. J. Simpson trial and *Othello*. (When Judge Lance Ito warned prospective jurors to stay away from bookstores, he presumably did not anticipate—though perhaps he should have—a rush to obtain copies of Shakespeare's play.) During the Clarence Thomas hearing, the Senate Judiciary Committee made persistent, if somewhat unreliable, reference to Shakespeare.[2] In the Fall of 1994 the New York City Bar Association heard an appeal in the case of *People v. Hamlet* in which the prince's conviction on six charges of homicide was challenged by celebrated lawyers (in an evening, according to the *New York Times*, marked by "bombast, wit, and erudite daffiness") on the grounds of sovereign immunity, jurisdiction, and victimology. A Shakespeare scholar (Jeanne Roberts) sat on the panel of judges; the *Times* noted, commenting on the appropriateness of the occasion, that in his own time "Shakespeare's most enthusiastic audiences included jurists from the Inns of Court, the Elizabethan residential law schools."[3]

Meantime on another page of the *Times*—not the theater page, the op-ed page—Shakespeare makes constant cameo appearances. On the first day of one academic term, which was, as it happened, the first day of my Shakespeare lecture course, not one but two *Times* columns included Shakespeare in their headlines: conservative William Safire's column was titled "Haiti: Much Ado About Something," and on the same page, liberal columnist Anthony Lewis's piece, also on Haiti, was titled "If it were done...." The column ended, "We could take advice from an unlikely source, Macbeth: "If it were done when 'tis done, then 'twere well it were done quickly."

Is this the politicization of literature? Or the acknowledgment of common cultural touchstones, fragments shored up against our ruins? (We might note in passing that Macbeth in this speech is talking about the planned assassination of Duncan, not necessarily a recommended political move.)

To note the popularization of Shakespeare has become a commonplace. On television I saw an advertising spot for home heating insulation that began with a portentous voice-over: "Whoever said, 'Now is the winter of our discontent' must not be using our products." (It seemed pretty clear that the intended audience was expected to recognize the fame of the quotation, but not its proximate source, Richard III.) My telephone bill arrived adorned with a picture of Shakespeare—the familiar portrait engraving from the First Folio—festooned with the inscription, "To beep or not to beep... That is the question." The answer, it seemed, was "selective call waiting." (To which, as always, Shakespeare himself offers the perfect reply: "But will they come when you do call for them?") In America today Shakespeare has become a common cultural language, a kind of secular Bible. Shakespeare, in short, turns out to be a process, as well as a monument. A culture, we might say, as well as a literature.

I point out to my students that no one today ever really reads Hamlet for the first time; we've heard it all before in bits and pieces, cultural bricolage, to beep or not to beep. Does this hurt Shakespeare, whatever "Shakespeare" is? Not a bit.

I said that Harold Bloom was one of literature's most passionate defenders. But who are its attackers? I know no one whose critique necessitates the deprecation of literature or literariness. No colleague, no student, has ever said to me, "Why do we waste our time with Chaucer and Shakespeare and Dickens and Dickinson?" What I want to suggest is that to accept this polarization is to be positioned rather than to take a position.

A colleague once passed along to me a letter he had received from a new organization of literary scholars and critics, urging him to join. The letter was clearly by people of discrimination, since, being forced to type (or rather, word process) instead of sign their names at the bottom of the page, they began their invitation, with somewhat ungainly precision, "We, the undernamed." What the undernamed persons had founded was a new professional association for the study of literature, which they envisaged as determinedly "inclusive" and "open to all those with a genuine interest in the study of literature." (A *genuine* interest in the study of literature.) The "current deficiencies" of "contemporary literary studies" were so well known, the letter said, that it was needless to rehearse them. So they didn't. What was needed was an organization that would stand for a "general faith in the validity of the literary imagination and in the value of literary studies." (Unlike which of us?) The signators were, many of them, scholars well known to me, scholars whose academic work I admire.

The letter's recipient, addressed as "Dear Colleague," was urged to participate because his agreement to do so would "serve to signal more cautious colleagues that the Association is well-founded, in the mainstream, and secure in its principles." It was not, they reiterated, "political." "While accepting support from individuals, institutions, and foundations that share its concerns, it is not and will not be identifiable with any ideological position or political agency." This strikes me as an extraordinary political document.

What is culture? What are cultures? It seems in a way to be a question about what are often called values and what is often called relativism—about aesthetics and politics, greatness and representativeness. Contemporary curmudgeons sometimes would seem to claim that it is, indeed, "Literary *or* Cultural Studies." That one must make a choice—or that modern scholars do choose—between the study of literature and the study of culture, or, to put the matter even more polemically, between aesthetic pleasure and the pursuit of social justice. This is a not only a false dichotomy, it is also, I believe, potentially a meretricious one. "Literary and Cultural Studies" is not an oxymoron. The best critics, and certainly the best teachers, are and have always been those who love literature (though it has become somewhat unfashionable, perhaps, to say so).

An aesthetic engagement with literature—or painting, or music, or theater—need not preclude a concern for social justice in the world nor an awareness of political and historical resonances within the text. And a concern about the cultural production of texts and artifacts need not—and with strong scholars does not—preclude an awareness of, and a deep, abiding, pleasure in, the aesthetic properties of a work of art—or, to use a very contested word, its greatness. This, as I say, is simply a false dichotomy. Scholars and students in the humanities choose to study *Schindler's List* or the all-male Cheek by Jowl production of *As You Like It* or the paintings of Cy Twombly or Mark Tansey or Deborah Kass—even to devote our lives to studying them—because they move us. To tears. To laughter. To rage. To vehement argument and dispute.

Art is not about correctness—political or any other kind. Art, as writers from Sophocles to Marlowe to Baudelaire to Joyce to Woolf to Morrison have always known and shown, is about transgression and daring and engagement. And pleasure. Literary study is concerned with boundaries and border crossings: between high and low, between classical and popular. But the now-classical was once "popular": Greek theater, Elizabethan drama, "classic" film. And the now "high" was once "low" and indeed thought threatening to "culture": impressionist painting, film noir, jazz, the music of Wagner. Today's Salon des Refusés is often—though there's no guarantee—tomorrow's benchmark; today's young turk is all too often tomorrow's oldtimer or curmudgeon or "traditionalist." MTV or hip-hop or soap operas may be tomorrow's "culture." It is probably shortsighted to be smug about these things. If a classic is, as Mark Twain famously remarked, "a book which people praise and don't read," a book praised as an "instant classic" is not, perhaps, such a good sign for its author—or for the times. We should be careful about feeling that we can judge "greatness," for greatness, like the canon, is always belated.

During the 1988 presidential campaign Democrat Michael Dukakis shied away from the word "liberal," allowing it to become, in his opponents' mouths, a word of deprecation rather than of pride. "Liberal" became, almost overnight, an epithet rather than a self-description. Let us not let that happen to the word "cultural." (Or even, I might add, the word "political.") Humanistic scholars today *are* "literary and cultural" critics, committed to analysis and interpretation, to understanding how texts create culture, and culture creates texts. Committed, that is, to literature *and* culture. This seems to me, I have to say, a very good thing.

NOTES

1. Raymond Williams, *Keywords: A Vocabulary of Culture and Society*, rev. ed. (New York: Oxford University Press, 1983), pp. 87–93.
2. See Marjorie Garber, "Character Assassination: Shakespeare, Anita Hill, and *JFK*," in *Media Spectacles*, ed. Marjorie Garber, Jann Matlock, and Rebecca L. Walkowitz (New York: Routledge, 1993), pp. 23–39.
3. Jan Hoffman, "People v. Hamlet: A Case of Infinite Jest," *New York Times*, October 18, 1994, B1–2.

4

Identity
Political Not Cultural[1]

Kwame Anthony Appiah

In my dictionary I find as a definition for "culture": "The totality of social-ly transmitted behavior patterns, arts, beliefs, institutions, and all other prod-ucts of human work and thought."[2] Like most dictionary definitions, this one could be improved. But it surely picks out a familiar constellation of ideas. In fact, it captures the sense in which anthropologists commonly use the term nowadays. The cultures of the Ashanti or the Zuni comprise, for the anthropologist, every object they make—material culture—and every-thing they think and do.

The dictionary could have stopped there, leaving out the talk of "socially transmitted behavior patterns, arts, beliefs, institutions" because these *are* products of human work and thought. They are mentioned because they are the residue of an idea of culture older than the anthropological one, some-thing more like the idea of a civilization: the "socially transmitted behavior patterns" of ritual, etiquette, religion, games, arts; the values that they engen-der and reflect; and the institutions—family, school, church, state—that shape and are shaped by them.[3] The habit of shaking hands at meetings belongs to culture in the anthropologist's sense; the works of Sandro Botticelli and Martin Buber and Count Basie belong to culture also, but they belong to civilization as well.

There are tensions between the concepts of culture and of civilization. Nothing requires, for example, that an American culture should be a totality in any stronger sense than being the sum of the things we make and do.

American civilization, on the other hand, must have a certain coherence. Some of what is done in America by Americans would not belong to American civilization because it is too individual (the bedtime rituals of a particular American family); some would not belong because it is not properly American, because (like a Hindi sentence, made in America) it does not properly cohere with the rest.

The second difference between culture and civilization, connected to the first, is that civilization takes values to be more central, in two ways. First, civilization is centrally defined by moral and aesthetic values, and the coherence of a civilization is primarily the coherence of those values with each other and, then, of the group's behavior and institutions with its values. Second, civilizations are essentially to be evaluated: they can be better or worse, richer or poorer, more or less interesting. Anthropologists, on the whole, tend now to avoid the relative evaluation of cultures, adopting a sort of cultural relativism, whose coherence philosophers have tended to doubt. And they do not take values to be more central to culture than are, for example, beliefs, ideas, and practices.

The move from "civilization" to "culture" was the result of arguments. The move away from evaluation came first, once people recognized that much evaluation of other cultures by the Europeans and Americans who invented anthropology had been both ignorant and biased. Earlier criticisms of "lower" peoples turned out to involve crucial misunderstandings of their ideas; and it eventually seemed clear, too, that nothing more than differences in upbringing underlay the distaste of some Westerners for unfamiliar habits. But to proceed from recognizing certain evaluations as mistaken to giving up evaluation altogether is a poor move, and anthropologists who adopt cultural relativism often preach it more than they practice it. Still, this cultural relativism was a response to real errors. That it is the wrong response doesn't make the errors any less erroneous.

The arguments against "civilization" were in place well before mid-century. More recently, anthropologists began to see that the idea of the coherence of a civilization got in the way of understanding important facts about other societies (and, in the end, about our own). For even in some of the "simplest" societies, different values and practices and beliefs and interests are associated with different social groups (women, for example). To think of a civilization as coherent is to miss the fact that these different values and beliefs are not merely different but actually opposed. Worse, what had been presented as the coherent, unified worldview of a tribal people often turned out, on later inspection, to be merely the ideology of a dominant group or interest.

There is another important distinction within the idea of culture. We customarily refer to the small-scale, technologically uncomplicated, face-to-face societies, where most interactions are with people whom you know, as traditional. In many such societies every adult who is not mentally disabled speaks the same language. All share a vocabulary and a grammar and an accent. While there will be some words in the language that are not known by everybody—the names of medicinal herbs, the language of some religious rituals—most are known to all normal adults. To share a language is to participate in a complex set of mutual expectations and understandings. But in such societies, much more than linguistic behavior is coordinated through universally known expectations and understandings. People will share an understanding of many practices—marriages, funerals, other rites of passage—and will largely share views about the general workings of the social and the natural worlds. While ethnographers may sometimes have overstated the extent to which basic theories of nature are universally believed in a society, even those people who are skeptical about particular elements of belief will nevertheless know what everyone is supposed to believe, and they will know it in enough detail to behave very often as if they believed it, too.

A similar point applies to many of the values of such societies. Some people, even some groups, do not share the values that are enunciated in public and taught to children. But, once more, the standard values are universally known and even those who do not share them know what it would be to act in conformity with them and probably do so much of the time.

In such a traditional society we may speak of these shared beliefs, values, signs, and symbols as the common culture; not, to insist on a crucial point, in the sense that everyone in the group actually holds the beliefs and values, but in the sense that everybody knows what they are and everybody knows that they are widely held in the society.

What I have called the common culture is what a social group has socially in common: it is what people teach their children in order to make them members of their social group. By definition, a common culture is shared; it is the social bottom line. It includes language and table manners, religious ideas, moral values, and theories of the workings of the natural and social worlds.

The citizens of a nation need not have a common culture, in this sense. There is no single shared body of ideas and practices in India or in most contemporary African states.

I think it is fair to say that there is not now and there has never been a common culture in the United States, either. The reason is simple: the United States has always been multilingual and has always had minorities who did not speak or understand English. It has always had a plurality of religious traditions; beginning with Native American religions and Puritans and Catholics and including now many varieties of Judaism, Islam, Buddhism, Jainism, Taoism, Baha'i, and so on. And many of these religious traditions have been quite unknown to each other. Americans have also always differed significantly even among those who do speak English, from North to South and East to West, and from country to city, in customs of greeting, notions of civility, and a whole host of other ways. The notion that what has held the United States together historically over its great geographical range is a common culture, like the common culture of a traditional society, is not sociologically plausible.

The notion that America has no national culture will come as a surprise to many: observations about American culture, taken as a whole, are common. It is, for example, held to be individualist, litigious, racially obsessed. I think each of these claims is true, because what I mean when I say that the United States has no common culture is not what is denied by someone who says that there is an American culture.

Such a person is describing large-scale tendencies within American life that are not necessarily participated in by all Americans. I do not mean to deny that these exist. But for such a tendency to be part of what I am calling the *common culture* they would have to derive from beliefs and values and practices (almost) universally shared and known to be so. And *that* they are not.

At the same time, it has also always been true that these United States had a dominant culture. It was Christian, it spoke English, and it identified with the high cultural traditions of Europe and, more particularly, of England.

This dominant culture included the common culture of the dominant classes—the government and business and cultural elites, but it was familiar to many others who were subordinate to them. And it was not merely an effect but also an instrument of their domination.

Whatever other languages American children know, they mostly know English; and they watch many of the same television programs and listen to much of the same music. Not only do they share these experiences, they know that they do, and so they can imagine themselves as a collectivity, the audience for mass culture. In that sense, most young Americans have a common culture based in a whole variety of kinds of English, but it is no longer that older, Christian, Anglo-Saxon tradition that used to be called American culture. All also belong to smaller groups than the American nation, with narrower common cultures—subcultures, so to speak—of their own.

It would be natural to assume that the primary subgroups to which these subcultures are attached will be ethnic and racial groups (with religious denominations conceived of as a species of ethnic group). It would be natural, too, to think that the characteristic difficulties of a multicultural society arise largely from the cultural differences between ethnic groups. I think this easy assimilation of ethnic and racial subgroups to subcultures is to be resisted.

First of all, it needs to be argued, and not simply assumed, that black Americans have a common culture—values and beliefs and practices that they share and that they do not share with others. This is equally true for, say, Chinese Americans; and it is *a fortiori* true of white Americans. What seems clear enough is that being an African American or an Asian American or white is an important social identity in the United States. Whether these are important social identities because these groups have shared common cultures is, on the other hand, quite doubtful, not least because it is doubtful whether they *have* common cultures at all.

With differing cultures, we might expect misunderstandings arising out of ignorance of each others' values, practices, and beliefs; we might even expect conflicts because of differing values or beliefs. The paradigms of difficulty in a society of many cultures are misunderstandings of a word or a gesture; conflicts over who should take custody of the children after a divorce; whether to go to the doctor or the priest for healing.

Once we move from talking of cultures to identities, whole new kinds of problems come into view. Racial and ethnic identities are, for example, essentially contrastive and essentially relate to social and political power; in this way they are like genders and sexualities.

Now it is crucial to our understanding of gender and sexuality that women and men and gay and straight people grow up together in families, communities, denominations. Insofar as a common culture means common beliefs, values, and practices, gay people and straight people in most places have a common culture; and while there are societies in which the socialization of children is so structured by gender that women and men have radically distinct cultures, this is not a feature of most "modern" societies.

What does this have to do with education? The short answer is: understanding may not help with problems that do not arise from *mis*understanding. What is often required, in dealing with identity conflict, is not understanding of cultures but respect for identities. A curriculum that takes seriously the cultural works of African Americans may be helpful here, even if it does not communicate a deepened understanding of African American culture.

I have insisted that we should distinguish between cultures and identities, but ethnic identities are distinctive in having cultural distinctions as one of their primary marks. Ethnic identities are created in family and community life. These—along with mass-mediated culture, the school, and the college— are, for most of us, the central sites of the social transmission of culture. Distinct practices, beliefs, norms go with each ethnicity in part because people *want* to be ethnically distinct; many people want the sense of solidarity that comes from being unlike others. In modern society, the distinct ethnic identity often comes first and the cultural distinction is created and maintained because of it, not the other way around. The distinctive common cultures of ethnic and religious identities matter not simply because of their contents but also as markers of those identities.

Culture in this sense is the home of what we care about most. If other people organize their solidarity around cultures different from ours, this makes them, to that extent, different from us in ways that matter to us deeply. In sum: Cultural difference undergirds loyalties. As we have seen repeatedly in recent years, from South Africa to the Balkans, from Sri Lanka to Nigeria, from South Central Los Angeles to Crown Heights, once these loyalties matter, they will be mobilized in politics and the public square, *except to the extent that a civic culture can be created that explicitly seeks to exclude them.*

A shared political life in a great modern nation is not like the life of my ideal typical (and thus, in a sense, imaginary) traditional society. It can encompass a great diversity of meanings. When we teach children democratic habits through practice in public schools, what we are creating is a shared commitment to certain forms of social behavior. We can call this a political culture, if we like. But the meanings citizens give to their lives, and to the political within their lives, in particular, will be shaped not only by the school, but by the family and church, by reading and by television, in their professional and recreational associations.

Maybe, in the end, there will be a richer American common culture; maybe it will lead to a consensus on the value of American institutions. Certainly cultural homogenization is proceeding apace. But it has not happened yet. And, so far as I can see, it doesn't have to happen for us to live together. Competing identities may be having a hard time living together in new democracies. But in this, the oldest democracy, so long as our institutions treat every significant identity with enough respect to gain its allegiance, we can muddle along in the meanwhile without a common culture. That, after all, is what we have been doing, lo, these many years.

NOTES

1. I owe the idea for this title to Kendall Thomas; he bears no responsibility, however, for any of these ideas!

2. *American Heritage Dictionary III for DOS* (Third Edition) (Novato, CA: Wordstar International Incorporated, 1993).

3. The distinction between culture and civilization I am marking is not one that would have been thus marked in nineteenth-century ethnography or (as we would now say) social anthropology: culture and civilization were basically synonyms, and they were both primarily used in the singular. The distinctions I am marking draw on what I take to be the contemporary resonances of these two words.

5

Productive Discomfort

Anthropological Fieldwork and the Dislocation of Etiquette

Michael Herzfeld

An ethnographer of Greece faces liabilities that provide a perspective, at once personal and political, on defining "culture" at the close of the twentieth century. These liabilities are an outcome of the history that the independent Greek nation-state shares with the discipline of anthropology—a history of Eurocentrism that today torments the nation and embarrasses the discipline. For a nation intent on realizing its geopolitical autonomy, the sorry tale of its subordination to Western European criteria of cultural hierarchy is a lasting reminder of its humiliation. For an anthropology grown critical of its colonial origins, years of complicity in the project of European domination have left a dismal legacy of preconceptions that undercut each new theoretical development. Yet nothing is to be gained by hoping that these meanspirited ghosts will simply fade away. On the contrary, as a constant reminder of the civil disabilities under which, as the eighteenth-century philosopher Giambattista Vico insisted,[1] nations and scholarly traditions both labor, such complications are a necessary irritant. They are the source of a productive discomfort.

The parallel between anthropology and nationalism is valuable precisely because it *is* so disconcerting. As such, it exemplifies the critical use—as opposed to the solipsistic self-indulgence—of reflexivity. At a time when journalists and others dismiss the resurgence of Balkan nationalism as anachronistic, Greece—a Balkan country where issues of European identity, modernity, and the role of history are the daily focus of public debate and self-examination—acquires a special importance.

What, then, to return briefly to the realm of personal reflection, are the specific liabilities of being an anthropologist working in Greece? First, they face the resentment of some (but, importantly, not all or even necessarily most) Greek intellectuals for allegedly treating Greeks in the same terms as non-European peoples. Second, diehard nationalists often express profound irritation that anthropologists would dare to expose the presence of officially nonexistent minorities or comment upon aspects of Greek culture that somehow do not belong to the canon of "civilization." These matters are clearly related to my theme.

But it is outside Greece, in a far less dramatic and more commonplace experience, that the dreary magnitude of the conceptual terrain becomes apparent. What I have in mind is the reaction that I often get in the U.S. when I say that I am an anthropologist working in Greece. It is the automatic assumption that I must be an archaeologist. Vague visions of ancient ruins and buried gold, flickering around the edges of the conversation, falter fast when I describe my work with shepherds, peasants, artisans, bureaucrats, and, yes, nationalists. When one speaks about a country that requires the prefix "modern" simply to remind educated sophisticates of its continuing existence, such intimations of contemporaneity are evidently discourteous.

This apparently trivial type of encounter is the immediate symptom of two false assumptions: that serious anthropologists do archaeology, and that archaeology is the only thing worth doing in Greece. These assumptions transformed my personal development, although it was not clear where the change would lead. As a disaffected former archaeology student hesitantly attracted to social anthropology by the desire to make a profession out of my enthusiasm for the modern culture and people of Greece, I found the taxonomic imperatives of academe ineluctable. Offered the chance to teach American undergraduates in Athens a course in Greek ethnography because my studies in prehistoric archaeology and modern Greek folklore made me an "anthropologist," and guided to a delightful international conference by a friend who said I must go if I wanted to *call* myself an anthropologist, I found myself tracing in my own life the fault lines of a more global taxonomy: the politics of nationhood, empire, and epistemology mapped the banal reasons for one student's career moves.[2]

Plunging ahead, I eventually discovered that many professional anthropologists were no clearer about what an anthropologist should do in a European country than were other sophisticates. By working in Greece, one was on the very edge of Europe, which might just be exotic enough; those who attempted to defamiliarize the cultures of the North and West were in a distinctly more perilous position. But this in turn, while perhaps comforting for novice anthropologists anticipating the search for respectability and employment,[3] posed correspondingly disturbing political questions about the status of the Greeks—these people to whom "Europe" supposedly owed its illumination. If anthropologists could legitimately study the Greeks only by exoticizing them, does this not validate Greek complaints about not being taken seriously as "civilized Europeans"? And then again: given the palpably racist implications of that question, why should we even want to answer it?

Of course, the question is offensive only if one takes "European civilization" as the measure of humanity. Yet it is this very criterion to which critics of earlier forms of anthropology, and especially of Victorian evolutionism, have rightly objected, tracing its persistent bias in ever subtler disguises even in the work of some of the most explicitly antiracist writers of our times.[4] The predicament thus created for the anthropologist is a prime example of what I mean by "productive discomfort." It might lead us to subtler and more responsible ways of addressing such phenomena as the cultural defense of genocide, historical revisionism, and human rights violations, those shoals on which liberal versions of relativism have been so badly damaged.

That intellectual nationalism may share some of the conceptual capital of anthropology is by now quite clear.[5] Indeed, this may help to explain why Greek nationalists are so angry with anthropologists. For, to the extent that anthropologists both criticize official Greek denials of minority rights and emphasize the diverse origins of the present-day Greek culture, are they not undercutting both the unity and (what amounts to the same thing) the pure ancestry on which Greek nationhood has always been predicated? And does this not mean that they are complicit in the ways in which Western hegemony constantly changes the rules, forcing Greece to define itself in terms of Classical tradition but then laughing derisively when Greek officials make geopolitical claims (concerning the name of Macedonia, for example) on the basis of that same tradition?

Recognizing these historical entailments does not mean that one condones their consequences. When a journalist, in attempting to deny minority status to Slavic-speaking people in Greek Macedonia, charges that the discipline that so acknowledges them—anthropology—was implicated in the origins of Nazism,[6] this neither allows us simply to ignore the historical grounds for such charges (however biased they may seem) nor mandates any endorsement of the journalist's own nationalistic agenda. Either option means accepting a totally deterministic view of history—which is, of course, what nationalism's "manifest destinies" are all about. An anthropology that is seriously committed to the battle against racism, for example, will not chimerically try to become something else—cultural studies, for example—by sloughing off its own history. That is a course of pure self-deception. Rather, it will try to reinvigorate itself, and other disciplines that fall under the cultural studies rubric, by pursuing the productive discomfort of its own historiography.

For anthropologists working in Greece, this means confronting the terrifying implications of the carefree phrase: "What fun it must be to dig things up in Greece!" Such snippets are, at one level, the legacy of Lord Elgin. The debates over whether the Elgin Marbles—which many Greeks often understandably prefer to call the Acropolis Marbles—should be returned to Athens have largely ignored a crucial point: that these objects have become a symbol of Western imperial predation at the Greeks' expense. Returning them would be a long overdue acknowledgment of an unequal history. Yet neither side has injected this particular proposition into the argument: Greek nationalists, we may suppose, are unwilling to see the country's independence as so conditional, while British traditionalists prefer to represent their past role as that of "protectors" rather than as predatory. And meanwhile—for such is the lingering force of highly educated ignorance—the only socially conceivable reason for a scholar to go to Greece is to dig up yet more romantic ruins.

Thus, the local nationalist conservatives and the old cultural imperialists are complicit in maintaining the image of a modern land that is interesting only because of its ancient associations. There is, in fact, a vocal and diverse intellectual opposition to this alliance both in Greece and abroad; it is the vantage point from which I now write, for example, and it has a lively presence in some influential newspapers. But, as a demonstration of the self-reproducing dynamics of cultural hegemony, the case of modern Greece is hard to beat.

All this has a certain interest for the small and contentious international community of scholars concerned with modern Greek culture. But why should it interest anyone else? The answer, I suggest, lies in the very need to ask the question.

Greeks take pride in a presumed centrality to European culture and affairs that constant international humiliations belie in actual experience. This means that the idea of a "Western cultural canon," so identifiably hostile to anything defined as "Other," is especially pernicious in and—as we shall see in a moment—for the land credited with its creation.

It is the centrality of "the Greeks" in Eurocentric humanism that has, in some senses, been the undoing of the Greeks of today. I say "in some senses" because one could (and indeed I would) argue that an independent Greek nation-state as we know it could never have emerged without the spur of the Classical vision.[7] But such compromised independence is severely limiting both culturally and politically, at least while the relationship of dependence is also sustained by internal political inequalities.

This is abundantly clear in the continuing play of ideas about Greek identity. The nineteenth-century European disregard for the Greeks' own views of their origins finds an ironic echo in both the marginalization of modern Greece to its glorious past and a rather more overdetermined one in Greek national leaders' steadfast disregard for local populations' ideas about where they came from.[8] Caught in the hegemonic logic of Western contempt, many Greeks—mindful, too, of the conventional parallels that nationalism has drawn between Greece's ancient and modern roles as the bastion of occidental civilization—are outraged by Martin Bernal's attribution of Greek culture to African and Semitic origins. The debate over Bernal's *Black Athena* in Greece has become mired in the essentializing discourse of national identity—a period dominated in the realm of constitutional law, which affects the treatment of minority interests, by a legal philosophy derived from common academic traditions in nineteenth-century Germany as the demand for an ancient Greek culture free of any African or Semitic taint.[9]

The refusal of European (especially German) philologists to take the ancient Greeks' accounts of their own origins seriously, as Bernal shows, indexes a cultural ideology that has had calamitous consequences for the modern world (Nazi "Aryanism," for a start). The occlusion of Greece—often, indeed, simply through the use of the name "*modern* Greece"—reproduces the same cultural hierarchy and has correspondingly threatening implications for current cultural debates. The issue is not solely that modern Greek culture did not seem to have been taken very seriously in the formative years of "classic" anthropology, but also that similar arguments can be made for most other cultural disciplines.[10] If anthropology has committed sins of omission, the whole panoply of critical theory in the West may be similarly implicated.

I am not suggesting that all cultural theorists should become instant experts on Greece. Superficiality is already a complaint often, and sometimes justly, leveled at foreign scholars by some Greek colleagues. It would be a major advance simply to recognize what the "Greek lacuna" portends. It offers an embarrassing perspective on the exclusivistic construction of social and cultural theory in countries that are also geopolitically powerful, especially when reflexive and sometimes self-accusatory styles are all the rage. For Greek national independence was originally a grudging gift, offered to the Greeks in defense of Great Power interests in the region. If Greek studies are now marginal to a supposedly self-critical academic canon, not much has been gained.

Here I return to Vico, because what happened to his ideas offers a sobering warning of the essentializing hegemonies that the best-intentioned critiques can also represent. Vico was used by Italian *risorgimento* nationalists as well as by their less benign successors to demonstrate the inevitability of Italian unification and national discipline. The writer who had warned that awareness of contingency was the basic precondition for true knowledge became the apostle of a romantic, absolutist epistemology; the critic of civic disability became the prophet of the Italian state. Such retrospective appropriations—the hagiography, as it were, of "Western canonization"— are familiar in academic as much as in geopolitical practice. In anthropology, it was Edmund Leach who tried to discipline Vico's ideas about the human capacity for creative imagination into a precursor of a highly formalistic structuralism.[11]

Now there is nothing *necessarily* wrong with either nationalism or struc-turalism. The trouble is that they easily change direction.[12] Nationalism often first emerges as a liberation movement, but turns to repression once there is a victory to consolidate. Structuralism presents itself as a universalist theory, yet the Lévi-Straussian discrimination between "cold" and "hot" societies reproduced the earlier hierarchy of "primitive" and "civilized" in ways that inhibited the application of conventional anthropological techniques to the latter. The recent emergence of an anthropology of bureaucracy and party politics not only turns the tables more drastically, I suggest, by placing "us" in the range of cultural comparison, but also rescues what is distinctively anthropological before it can be crushed between the mutually counterposed charges of exoticism and anecdotalism.[13]

This perspective allows us to pick up recent challenges in creative and pro-ductive ways.[14] The recognition that we are all very much part of what we study—Vico noted long ago that the terms of "the cultivated arts and arcane sciences are of peasant origin[15]—means that no cultural comment is itself culture free.[16] Clifford has suggested that "ethnographic authority" is based on exclusivistic claims to "having been there"—that is, in the "field" of "fieldwork." This does not *necessarily* mean that such authority is exercised irresponsibly; Clifford notes that modern ethnographic authority is frag-mented and diffuse, so that many research styles may legitimately be called ethnography.[17] By the same token, anthropologists' accountability is no less contingent upon cultural values than are the various forms of blame and responsibility that they study "in the field." Evans-Pritchard's concern with blame directed his analysis of the logic of feuding, but it also raised the then quite revolutionary possibility of alternative rationalities: when a granary fell on a person, was it "because" termites had eaten away the foundations (as "we" might say), or "because" another Zande individual had used witchcraft to make the granary fall down *at that particular time* (Evans-Pritchard 1937)? Clearly, accountability is socially constructed. In any society, what matters for all practical purposes is not who caused what to happen, but who can be *held responsible* for the course of events.[18]

Thus, the reflexive posture in anthropology—precisely because it is an ethical alibi of sorts—may mask a refusal of responsibility. This especially applies when we are asked to deny our historically embedded identity as anthropologists. In this sense, the structuralist Rodney Needham's slightly precious prophecy that anthropology would eventually dissolve in an "iridescent metamorphosis" seems less tendentious—because more recognizant of a sedimented history—than Said's ingenuous puzzlement at anthropologists' "optimism" that their discipline had a future. Surely an anthropology capable of chagrin at its own involvement in the sorry tale of "modern Greece" offers greater cause for optimism than a formulaic invention of "new" intellectual forms denying all connection with—and responsibility for—the ailments of the past?[19]

By accountability, I mean here a refusal to duck the burdens of past history. Much of what has been written about anthropology's entailment in colonialism, nationalism, or even fascism is persuasive, and, because it is persuasive, it is also acutely discomfiting. Refusal of an anthropological identity would only constitute escapism from such awareness.[20] Surely this is why the so-called crisis of representation in anthropology did not destroy it but refreshed and renewed its commitment to fieldwork—whose radical experiential dislocation was, after all, the origin of anthropologists' most productive discomforts. In the process, moreover, it has become clear that claims to representing *the* disenfranchised are as problematic as writing about *the* Nuer or *the* Greeks.[21] Respecting "the Greeks'" sensibilities may entail disrespect for *some* Greeks' interests, whether these be of ethnic or religious minorities or of politically marginalized populations. And so one chooses: accountability will not simply go away. Our own histories—the front line of reflexivity—are entailed in larger cultural formations. However much I cringe when I am told how much fun it must be to dig up Greek ruins, such ill-informed silliness presents me with a task I cannot evade: to explain why digging up ruins is not what I do, and, what is harder, why such misunderstandings *are* part of what I do.

Such retorts are hardly polite. But what, after all, *is* etiquette but a set of labels (French *etiquettes*), taxonomic devices, grounded in the same history of manners that represents itself as the apogee of high culture,[22] and that considers the excavation (and perhaps the theft) of Periclean glories the only reason to acknowledge the existence of Greece? If knowledge is what happens when taxonomic certainties are disturbed and categorical imperatives challenged, then knowledge creation is never polite. It is the reverse of sophisticated ignorance. It is what comes out of the defamiliarizing labor of ethnographic fieldwork, out of the realization that barely literate shepherds can be highly stimulating social theorists. It is, in short, productive discomfort.

NOTES

1. Giambattista Vico, *Principij di Scienza Nuova*, 3d ed. (Napoli: Stamperia Muziana, 1744), book I: sections 2, 3–4. On this aspect of Vico's thought, see especially Michael Herzfeld, *Anthropology through the Looking-Glass: Critical Ethnography in the Margins of Europe* (Cambridge: Cambridge University Press, 1987), 189; Nancy S. Struever, "Fables of Power," *Representations*, 4 (Fall 1983): 123.

2. Note here the ethnographer's characteristic move. It is to trace in quotidian trivialities the passage of larger events, to study the meaning of cosmic happenings for particular social actors, and to understand the etymologies of global symbols through the uses to which those actors put them.

3. Michael Llewellyn Smith (*The Great Island: A Study of Crete* [London: Longmans, 1965], 2–3) invoked Claude Lévi-Strauss (*Tristes Tropiques*, translated by John and Doreen Weightman [New York: Atheneum, 1974], 40–41) to sanctify even a nonprofessional personal expedition to the island of Crete.)

4. For probing critiques of this phenomenon from a variety of perspectives, see Talal Asad, *Genealogies of Religion: Discipline and Reasons of Power in Christianity and Islam* (Baltimore: Johns Hopkins University Press, 1993); Johannes Fabian, *Time and the Other: How Anthropology Makes Its Object* (New York: Columbia University Press, 1993); Adam Kuper, *The Invention of Primitive Society: Transformations of an Illusion* (London: Routledge, 1988).

5. See, for example, Richard Handler, "On Having a Culture: Nationalism and the Preservation of Quebec's *Patrimoine*," in George W. Stocking Jr., ed., *Objects and Others: Essays on Museums and Material Culturen* (*History of Anthropology* 3 [1985]) (Madison: University of Wisconsin Press), 192–217. Loring M. Danforth ("The Ideological Context of the Search for Continuities in Greek Culture," *Journal of Modern Greek Studies* 2 [1984]: 53–87) cites Fabian, *Time and the Other*, to make this point explicitly about Greece and the production of otherness *within* the nation-state.

6. This charge was leveled by Sarandos Kargakos ("Ti simeni i iper Karakasidhou sinighoria?" *Ikonomikos Takhidhromos*, 30 September 1993, 33–34) in the context of a debate, in which he also clashed with me, over his questioning of another anthropologist's accuracy, patriotism, and motives. In general, such debates, while intellectually sterile, are of considerable *ethnographic* interest

in that they underscore the cultural persistence of stereotypical idioms of denigration.

7. See Douglas Dakin, *The Greek Struggle for Independence, 1821–1833* (London: Batsford, 1973); William St. Clair, *That Greece Might Still Be Free: The Philhellenes in the War of Independence* (London: Oxford University Press, 1970).

8. For a critique of relevant scholarship on ancient Greece, see Martin Bernal's richly controversial *Black Athena: The Afroasiatic Roots of Classical Civilization.* vol. 1. (New Brunswick, N.J.: Rutgers University Press, 1987). On self-perception by minority groups, see especially Anastasia Karakasidou, "Politicizing Culture: Negating Ethnic Identity in Greek Macedonia," *Journal of Modern Greek Studies* 11 (1993): 1–28; Muriel Dimen Schein, "When Is an Ethnic Group? Ecology and Class Structure in Northern Greece," *Ethnology* 14 (1975): 83–97; and A. J. B. Wace and Maurice Thompson, *Nomads of the Balkans* (London: Methuen, 1913).

9. On the essentializing proclivities of this tradition in current Greek legal debates, see especially Adamantia Pollis, "The State, the Law and Human Rights in Modern Greece," *Human Rights Quarterly* 9 (1987): 587–614; "Greek National Identity: Religious Minorities, Rights, and European Norms," *Journal of Modern Greek Studies* 10 (1992): 171–195.

10. Herzfeld, *Anthropology through the Looking-Glass*; Gregory Jusdanis, *Belated Modernity and Aesthetic Culture: Inventing National Literature* (Minneapolis: University of Minnesota Press, 1991); Vassilis Lambropoulos, *Literature as National Institution: Studies in the Politics of Modern Greek Text Criticism* (Princeton: Princeton University Press, 1988).

11. Edmund Leach, "Vico and Lévi-Strauss on the Origins of Humanity," in Giorgio Tagliacozzo and Hayden V. White, eds., *Giambattista Vico: An International Symposium* (Baltimore: Johns Hopkins University Press, 1969), 309–318. See also José Guilherme Merquior, "Vico et Lévi-Strauss: Notes à propos d'un symposium," *L'Homme* 10 (1970): 81–93. Just as Vico's antiobjectivist philosophy had been deployed in the service of a decidedly objectivist view of the national Mind ("national character" or even *mentalité*—again an idea with close historical ties to anthropology [see G. E. R. Lloyd, *Demystifying Mentalities* (Cambridge: Cambridge University Press, 1990)]), so Leach used Vico to give a respectable history to the universalist claims of structuralism.

12. See Bruce Kapferer, *Legends of People, Myths of State: Violence, Intolerance, and Political Culture in Sri Lanka and Australia* (Washington: Smithsonian Institution Press, 1988), on nationalism; Fabian, *Time and the Other*, p. 103, on structuralism and related theoretical perspectives. On the hot/cold polarity, see Claude Lévi-Strauss, *The Savage Mind* (Chicago: University of Chicago Press, 1966).

13. On bureaucracy, see Don Handelman, "Introduction: The Idea of Bureaucratic Organization," *Social Analysis* 9 (1981): 5–23; Don Handelman and Elliott Leyton, eds., *Bureaucracy and World View: Studies in the Logic of Official Interpretation* (St. Johns: Institute of Social and Economic Research, Memorial University of Newfoundland, 1978); Michael Herzfeld, *The Social Production of Indifference: Exploring the Symbolic Roots of Western Bureaucracy* (Oxford: Berg, 1992); Stacia E. Zabusky, *Launching Europe: An Ethnography of European Cooperation in Space Science* (Princeton: Princeton University Press, 1995). On political symbolism, see Marc Abélès, *Anthropologie de l'état* (Paris: A. Colin, 1990), and *Quiet Days in Burgundy: A Study of Local Politics*, trans. Annella McDermott (Cambridge: Cambridge University Press, 1991); Christopher A. P. Binns, "The Changing Face of Power: Revolution and Development of the Soviet Ceremonial System," *Man* (n.s.) 14 (1979): 585–606 and 15 (1980): 170–187; David I. Kertzer, *Ritual, Politics, and Power* (New Haven: Yale University Press, 1988). If anthropology forgets about those "other" societies where it originally developed the tools for such analyses, however, it will face the loss of its distinctive comparativism—the fundamental source of "productive discomfort."

14. James Clifford, "On Ethnographic Authority," *Representations* 2 (Spring 1983): 118–146; Edward Said, "Representing the Colonized: Anthropology's Interlocutors," *Critical Inquiry* 15 (1989): 205–226.

15. Vico, *Scienza Nuova*, book 2, section 2,2,1.

16. Said ("Representing the Colonized," 211) explicitly charges anthropologists with having inexplicably resisted this very point (but see also my *Looking-Glass*). Here it becomes especially pertinent to argue for the important distinction between self-indulgent and responsible reflexivity—much as Struever ("Fables of Power") contrasts the politically responsible etymologizing and conceptual archaeology of Vico and Foucault with the verbal acrobatics of Derrida.

17. This pluralism may be no more than a refraction of the generally splintered and volatile state of authority in the modern world; see Bruce Lincoln *Authority: Construction and Corrosion* (Chicago: University of Chicago Press, 1994). But it also shows how much more complex ethnographic accountability has become.

18. See J. L. Austin, "A Plea for Excuses," in Colin Lyas, ed., *Philosophy and Linguistics* (London: Macmillan, 1971), 79–101. The relevant studies by E. E. Evans-Pritchard are: *Witchcraft, Oracles and Magic among the Azande* (Oxford: Clarendon Press, 1937); *The Nuer: A Description of the Modes of Livelihood and Political Institutions of a Nilotic People* (Oxford: Clarendon Press, 1937). The perspective indicated here offers many advantages, not the least of which is the extent to which it permits us to transcend arguments about whether some cultures are more rational than others; see also Stanley J. Tambiah, *Magic, Science, Religion, and the Scope of Rationality* (Cambridge: Cambridge

University Press, 1990). This turns the spotlight of fairly conventional anthropological analysis on "our" culture(s). Martha Balshem (*Cancer in the Community: Class and Medical Authority* [Washington: Smithsonian Institution Press, 1993]), for example, has offered a stunning account of how epidemiological rhetoric can be turned back against the medical establishment by a working-class community disproportionately afflicted by cancer. In *The Social Production of Indifference*, I have similarly focused on Greek nationalism and national institutions to explore the conventional range of means for avoiding accountability.

19. Rodney Needham, "The Future of Social Anthropology," in *Anniversary Contributions to Anthropology: Twelve Essays* (Leiden: E. J. Brill, 1970), 46; Said, "Representing the Colonized."

20. Note again that it is central to Vico's philosophy that the seed of self-aggrandizement and eventual revolution is ignorance of the past, including its excesses and failures; Vico's own successive canonizations by brutally absolutist ideologies ironically point up the moral of his argument.

21. Fabian, *Time and the Other*, 80.

22. Norbert Elias, *The Civilizing Process*, trans. Edmund Jephcott (New York: Pantheon, 1982).

PART TWO

National Identities, Global Identities

6

Planet Rap
Notes on the Globalization of Culture

Henry Louis Gates, Jr.

Last February, I found myself in Outer Mongolia—Ulan Batar, to be exact—among a group of, well, Outer Mongolians. Now, Mongolia is just as remote, sparse, and isolated as you might imagine. And at that time of the year...let me just say that I will never complain again about a Chicago winter. You have to imagine me bundled up like an Eskimo, because it was 42 degrees below zero and *windy*, and I kept thinking that mother Africa did not make me for such a fate. But there I was, courtesy of a university program that sends members of the faculty to places like this one, addressing a group of denizens of this windblown icy region.

Naturally, I want to establish a sense of what cultural references we might have in common, and so I ask these good people: How many of you have heard of Al Gore? Raise your hand.

Nobody raises a hand.

How many of you have heard of rap?

Practically *everybody* raises their hands. Looking into their expectant eyes, I wondered if they expected me to break into some hip-hop refrain right then and there: LL Cool J with a Ph.D. I like to *think* there's a resemblance, myself. And Lord only knows what they expect from a traveling African-American.

But of course there's a simple explanation. It may be 42 degrees below zero and wind-blasted, but they still get MTV. CNN and MTV are what's available, and it may be that many of them watch the latter with more attention than the former. So when Public Enemy's Chuck D called rap black America's CNN, he didn't know how right he was.

In this essay, I want to talk a little about traveling cultures, and about how some of the ways that we conventionally talk about the phenomenon have failed us. What does it mean that the hip-hop nation is now multinational? What does it mean that you can get Coca-Cola in Burundi? Remember the group Milli Vanilli, the Marcel Marceau of pop music? One of the pair, I think it was Fab Morgan, once told a journalist about the time he went to Africa. He said: "I went to Africa once, and there was no soap, and there was no soda, but there was Milli Vanilli." Let's agree that something distinctive is happening today, something that isn't captured by the stale rhetoric of multiculturalism.

Multiculturalism is a shockingly uninformative word. *Multi*, many—got that part. *Cultural*—a little harder, one of those words we all think we know the meaning of, until we probe a little further. But then you get *ism*. And that's the really tricky part. Still don't know what to make of that *ism*, to tell you the truth.

So you get a vision of cultural complexity as analogous to a box of Whitman's Samplers: you know, those boxes of chocolates with each one in its own paper compartment, just awaiting the delectation of the connoisseur. Or else you get the Cuisinart alternative: cultural interaction reduced to a sort of gazpacho, a smooth, lumpless liquid—served cold.

Of course, neither one will serve us well.

And a similar problem bedevils our thinking about traveling cultures. On the one hand, we have this model of "cultural imperialism": once we conquered with the musket; now a Musketeers bar will do the trick. The effluents of Western civilization, as processed by mammoth corporations, are the teeth-rotting candy that's corrupting an otherwise macrobiotic world. Stay pure, we exhort these dignified Others: stay noble, stay innocent, stay…savage.

Well, that model of cultural imperialism turns out to be profoundly condescending, denying the volition of the people we would save not from us, ultimately, but from themselves.

At the same time, the people who want to focus our attention on capital and the technologies of mass media have part of it right. The trouble with academics like me is we think about the canon, this imaginary syllabus of the literary republic, and forget the very real circumstances in which our schools find themselves. We imagine the world as a library or bookstore. It's more like a shopping mall, with a lot of mayhem going down in the parking lot. And we've managed to dock ourselves in front of the B. Dalton's section for the Penguin classics…and soon we've forgotten that there's anything else in the mall.

So there's something to be said for anything that redirects our attention to the larger context in which these conversations take place. When I talk about traveling culture, I don't want to forget that real context of mass communication.

Hip-hop is actually an intriguing example here, because the form itself is so hybrid—it's what happens to an Afro-Caribbean base round aground in black metropoles like the South Bronx. The musical texture is often a literal collage of musical precursors. The rap group Jungle Brothers isn't terribly unusual in its range: it samples everything from Coltrane to field recordings of African so-called tribal chants. It's been said that minor poets borrow; great poets steal. Hip-hop, at any rate, has turned appropriation into an art, digesting and reconfiguring the great tracks of earlier eras, splitting choruses from hooks, lyrics from refrains. So what happens when the art of appropriation is itself appropriated?

(First, a digression. Literature profs often go to extremes when they start addressing popular culture: either it's all dross, or it's all gold. I used to hear that it's all dross: now I often hear it's all gold, although the wind may be shifting. But the truth is, 99 percent of the poetry that's published is lousy; why should rap be any luckier, in the long run? The trouble, if you're a literary academic, is that your way of taking something seriously is to write literary criticism about it, and the way we're trained to do that has the effect of magnifying the object beyond measure. And there's another aspect as well. Academics write criticism the way dogs spray fire hydrants: it's a way of staking out turf, a way of asserting territorial rights.)

But back to the globalization of hip-hop. Quite conveniently, for my purposes, the Warner record label Tommyboy has just released an album titled *Planet Rap*, which contains "world wide rap," including six different rappers from Italy. In Eastern Europe, the discontents of a new order are played out. The popular Czech group, Rapmasters, raps about what it's like to be young and poor and surrounded by rich Western tourists. The latest De La Soul album had a great success featuring a group of Japanese rappers. Meanwhile, French rap is taking off—not just in France, but in the United States. The French rapper MC Solaar, who's of Senegalese origins, has teamed up with the American rapper Guru from Gang Starr, in a bilingual song called "The Good, the Bad"/"Le Bien, Le Mal," which has made the regular MTV rotation. The Brits have specialized in various modes of fusion, combining hip-hop with reggae in a permutation known as ragga, or combining it with "house music" in a permutation known as hip-house. And the drive for mixing and matching has certainly come home to roost; the marriage between rap and other forms of music like heavy metal and alternative rock is now commonplace, as witnessed by the recent collaborations between such rappers and rockers as Run DMC and Living Colour, Ice T and Slayer, or Cypress Hill and Pearl Jam.

So the language of roots and branches won't do, either. The truth is, rap's homecoming to Africa was not an entirely felicitous occasion: it happened when LL Cool J brought his tour to Abidjan, in the Ivory Coast, and lasted about half an hour, when fisticuffs broke out among the huge audience.

But to me, anyway, one of the most intriguing cases is the instance of meta-meta-appropriation: the appropriation of the appropriator's appropriator— Vanilla Ice, in this case, and his devoted Indian disciple Baba Sehgal. It all started in 1991, when a group of investors started beaming MTV down to the subcontinent. Scrambling to become India's first rapper, Baba Sehgal superimposed his lyrics over Vanilla Ice's hit "Ice Ice Baby." The chant was now: "Thanda Thanda Pani, Thanda Thanda Pani." It means: "Cold Cold Water, Cold Cold Water." And it sold 100,000 copies in about three months, becoming the fastest-selling album in India. So let the literary studies crowd talk about a cultural palimpsest: here you've got Vanilla Ice, who already stands accused of cultural imposture as a white rapper, whose own song "Ice Ice Baby" isn't just borrowing its style from urban black America, but borrowing its riffs from David Bowie and Queen, now remastered by an Indian adept and rapped with different lyrics in the Hindi language, with the result that "Thanda Thanda Pani"—"Cold Cold Water"— becomes a national hit on the other side of the globe. So what happened here to "Ice Ice Baby," the Western model, in the course of transnational transposition? You might say it melted.

But if you really want to examine the structure of the globalization of culture, there's, well, there's Always Coca-Cola. Or, in its current rendering, a rather Jamaican sentiment: "always Coca-Cola."

But the interesting fact is: it wasn't until 1979 that Coca-Cola—the company that once wanted to "teach the world to sing"—decided that it could deliver its campaign to a global audience from a central location. No longer would it be dependent upon local agencies in foreign markets. As Marcio M. Moreira, the team leader and director of Coca-Cola International Advertising at McCann-Erickson, tells us, the initial impetus was economic. The fact that the America market was a mature one, crowded by a huge competitor in Pepsi, made foreign markets much more attractive as an area of growth. At the same time, it didn't seem obvious that the same advertising approach that suited this market was appropriate for the rest of the world, where, in many places, Pepsi had made only slight inroads. As Mr. Moreira recalled in an interview published in *Public Culture*:

> I looked at Coke on the one hand saying: "We need multicultural advertising." And I looked at this team of multicultural creative talents sitting in New York City. We brought the two things together—InterNational Team and Coca-Cola.[1]

Today, McCann's InterNational Team develops "multicultural advertising for Coca-Cola, Gillette, Goodyear, GM, UPS, Mennen, Martini, Unilever, you name it." But for our purposes, Coke is, indeed, It.

But in order to prepare the rest of the world for the simplicity of the slogan "Coke is It"—which was the slogan of the day—introductory lyrics had to be devised. For otherwise the slogan only raised eyebrows. What did it mean, "Coke is It"? The explanatory stanza runs as follows:

> It's a part of me and you,
> And all the things we like to do.
> Coca-Cola is there, part of all that we share,
> Always good, always real, always true,
> Coca-Cola is It!

To be sure, difficulties relating to lifestyle imagery arise in Moslem nations, but nothing that Mr. Moreira and his colleagues cannot easily surmount. A beach commercial is shot in Rio, with boys and girls in it wearing scanty bathing suits. Then the cameras are stopped, and the women are costumed up in long, flowing dress covering their arms and ankles. The men stay as they are, of course. So you double-shoot. And, voila, the Malaysian ad is filmed. As Mr. Moreira remarks, "Double-shooting, triple-shooting, and quadruple-shooting is something that all my producers are familiar with."

Sometimes other adjustments are made. At the time the rest of the world was being told "You can't beat the feeling," the ads in Japan said, in English: "I feel Coke." You can't beat the feeling is a mouthful in Japanese, apparently, whereas "I feel Coke" properly conveys the quality of Westernness that historically has helped position imports in the Japanese market. But things are changing. Previously, as Moreira said, "Leveraging the Westernness of the brand was moving the brand. Today, showing Japanese people enjoying it is what moves the brand. They no longer need to see Western people drinking it so that they feel it's all right to drink it. On the contrary, they now want it to belong, to be part of their lives." I understand that Coke's earlier slogan—Have a Coke and a Smile—was similarly shelved for the Korean market: some limited measure of local variation was permitted.

Best of all, though, is that they've discovered you can shoot a black commercial for Africa in Amsterdam, so long as you have the right cast. Mr. Moreira again: "Coke is more about values and relationships and the social catalyst role that the product has and its appropriateness at various times of day and with food…. So it's no problem. Once I learned that lesson, that it wasn't so much putting Coke into a black world, but putting black people into a Coke world, we were off and running." I suppose the gods *must* be crazy.

Mr. Moreira balks at the notion of "Coca-colonization": "All the thing wants to do is to refresh you, and it is willing to understand your culture, to be meaningful to you and to be relevant to you. Why is that called Coca-colonization?"

Why indeed? In all fairness, I don't think that the model of cultural imperialism is useful here, and for reasons I've alluded to. But it does help keep something in focus, which is that corporate multiculturalism is not merely a technique of diversification but of homogenization as well.

And it is this paradoxical development that we might, for convenience, dub *Coca-Culturalism*, a mode of market penetration that in part alters local environments and in part conforms to them, in a process of mutual adaptation.

Here I would advert to those lyrics I quoted earlier, with particular attention to the strongly universalizing rhetoric:

> It's a part of me and you,
> And all the things we like to do.
> Coca-Cola is there, part of all that we share,
> Always good, always real, always true…

No relativism here! I always knew Allan Bloom was wrong to think that relativism was overtaking our culture, and here's proof. Now, you may ask: How does something achieve the status of a transcultural value? The answer is, you *make* it transcultural. You "teach the world" to sing…Coca-Cola jingles.

And notice that when the corporation decided to update its slogan, it was toward even greater universalization: "Always Coca-Cola." A slogan declaring that even as their marketers conquered the barriers of space, so too the product would survive the impediments of time. And so they assert a temporal dominion to accompany their spatial one.

What I have elsewhere termed the Benettonization of the world, what complainants call the commodification of ethnicity, clearly does play into this. But must the global circulation of American culture always be identified as imperialism, even if imperialism by other means? In an era of transnational capital, transnational labor, and transnational culture, how well is the center-periphery model holding up?

The distinguished anthropologist Arjun Appadurai has drawn our attention to that "uncanny Philippine affinity for American popular music": "An entire nation," he writes, "seems to have learned to mimic Kenny Rogers and the Lennon sisters, like a vast Asian Motown chorus." All this, in a former U.S. colony racked by enormous contrasts of wealth and poverty, amounting to what he describes as "nostalgia without memory." Unfortunately, an American-centered view of the world blinds us to the fact that America isn't always on center stage, whether as hero or as villain. As Appadurai writes,

> it is worth noticing that for the people of Iran Jaya, Indonesianization may be more worrisome than Americanization, as Japanization may be for Koreans, Indianization for Sri Lankans, Vietnamization for the Cambodians, Russianization for the people of Armenia and the [former] Baltic Republics. Such a list of alternative fears to Americanization could be greatly expanded, but it is not a shapeless inventory: for the polities of smaller scale, there is always a fear of cultural absorption by polities of a larger scale, especially those that are nearby. One man's imagined community is another man's political prison.[2]

Someone, I believe it was Tatyana Tolstaya, has said that if she had to choose between nationalism and imperialism, she would choose imperialism. She had been brooding, she said, on the deleterious effects of resurgent, raging nationalisms in the former Soviet Union and in Eastern Europe. Yet the contrast between nationalism and imperialism, and in fact the usual vocabulary of nationalism in these contexts, is terribly misleading. For nationalism in its modern sense, the sense it has had since its advent in the eighteenth century, *is* a form of imperialism: it represents the consolidation of smaller political and cultural entities. The idea of a unitary "French" or "English" or "German" or, Lord knows, "Italian" identity requires the subordination or even erasure of such earlier identifications as "Gascon" or "Savoyard," say; or "Cornish" or "North Umbrian," say; or "Hessian" or "Hanoverian"; or whatever the adjectival form is of Schleswig-Holstein or Saxony. "Nationalism" has historically been the banner under which the annihilation or conquest of ethnic particularity has proceeded.

In his *Notes Toward a Definition of Culture*, T. S. Eliot asserted that "the invocation of a possible 'world culture' should be of particular interest to those who champion any of the various schemes for world federation, or for a world government; for obviously, so long as there exist cultures which are beyond some point antagonistic to each other, antagonistic to the point of irreconcilability, all attempts at political-economic affiliation will be in vain." But one can be skeptical, as Eliot of course was, of the prospect of both such things and still recognize the value of some measure of intercultural tolerance.

Certain things have changed since Eliot's day. The truth is, what unifies—and divides—America is less the wisdom of John Locke, or Alain Locke, than the culture of the marketplace. It's MTV more than Montaigne, Viacom more than Voltaire. David Rieff remarks that "the more one reads in academic multiculturalists' journals and in business publications, the more one contrasts the speeches of CEOs and the speech of noted multicultural academics, the more one is struck by the similarities in the ways they view the world." At the end of the day, most of what proceeds under the heading of multiculturalism—our gussied-up versions of identity politics—may be a less important source of cultural fragmentation than those five hundred channels of television the cable companies have promised. In the late twentieth century, we are consumers first, citizens second. If you're really worried about social fragmentation, never mind about the canon debates: you're better off attending to the growth of niche marketing.

A blindness to the pervasive influence of consumer culture afflicts even those who ought to know better. For example, probably the best-known attempt to engineer a measure of cultural unity was E. D. Hirsch's *Cultural Literacy*, whose democratic and anti-elitist impulses aroused only suspicion from many of its natural allies. Hirsch's central argument, as I understand it, was that by establishing a base of common knowledge, our schools can better produce citizens able to participate on an equal footing in the common polity. The primary beneficiaries of his approach were to be the relatively underprivileged, whose backgrounds tended to exclude them from the "dominant" culture and thus from the exercise of power: students, in short, for whom the school environment is the main site of transmission of "cultural literacy," which is, by stipulation, also political literacy.

What political advantages are conferred by cultural literacy—a knowledge of the common core? There are more and less elaborate explanations, but the short answer is that it's a matter of "catching the references." As anyone who learns another language is repeatedly reminded, a crude word knowledge isn't sufficient to properly understand a text; you need to know something of the rich texture of conventional allusions—"to be or not to be," that sort of thing. Catching the references, the argument runs, is necessary to being an informed citizen.

For better or worse, however, the patterns of references have changed significantly from Lincoln's day, and, unless Daniel Patrick Moynihan is your model of a typical politician, Hirsch's notion of political discourse embarrasses by its flattery. At one point during the last presidential campaign, then–Vice President Quayle announced that the campaign would really be

about *character*. It quickly turned out that what he meant was *characters*—
The Waltons, Bart Simpson, Murphy Brown. There's nothing very new here.
About all that most of us can remember of the 1988 presidential campaign
are George Bush's reference to *Jake and the Fat Man*, and Michael Dukakis's
to Joe Isuzu. Now, Hirsch was widely lambasted when he explained that to
attain cultural literacy, you didn't actually have to read any of Shakespeare's
plays, just recognize the allusions to them. Strangely, no one seemed alarmed
when Bush conceded he'd never seen *Jake and the Fat Man* and when Dan
Quayle admitted that he hadn't yet watched an episode of *Murphy Brown*,
thus taking the Hirschian principle to an anchorite extreme.

If the 1992 presidential campaign was in any way typical of national politics, it must be said that one waited in vain for the allusion to Shakespeare
or his characters. Somehow we managed to discuss the vacillating Ross Perot
with nary a mention of Hamlet, Governor Clinton with no side-glance at
Romeo, and Bush with scarcely a thought of King Lear. (Granted, those
Clarence Thomas–Anita Hill hearings were an exception to this pattern,
being a veritable orgy of Shakespeareana: somehow "Othello" loomed dark
and inescapable in the minds of more than a few senators. But this I take
to be the exception that proves the rule.) Otherwise, high art surfaces in
public consciousness only if it has been denied a grant from the National
Endowment for the Arts. For better or worse, that is, the idealized image of
political colloquy many of us nurture comes up short before the all-pervasive
flux of mass culture.

From an anthropological perspective, at least, the statistics that over 96 percent of American households own a television set is a better index to cultural cohesion than the tendency of our seventeen-year-olds to confuse James
Garfield and James Garner. Curiously enough, there's powerful resistance to
this news. It's the result of a systematic confusion between culture in the all-
encompassing anthropological sense (a sense whose English usage is usually
dated to E. B. Tylor's writings in the 1870s) and culture in the normative and,
as it were, Arnoldian sense, designating a body of intellectual and artistic
achievement. Needless to say, one would be ill-advised to consult the pro-
gramming of subscription symphony concerts for indices of social fragmentation, and equally misguided to suppose that assigning Zora Neal Hurston
rather than Ernest Hemingway (or vice versa) significantly contributes to
the "broken polity."

The last time I pointed this out, a friend of mine, a well-known theater
director, complained that high art had few enough supporters as it was and I
wasn't helping any. I pointed out that high art is only slighted when forced to
subserve the objectives of social engineering. In this respect, it seems to me
that the insistence on the left that art support (and perhaps be appraised by its

adherence to) utopian social objectives is fueled by the unreflective conservative rhetoric that, in a similar way, insists on high art's centrality in the maintenance of social order. Then it's William Bennett versus Adorno. The debate then becomes about what social order you like: the assumption that art provides the appropriate battlefield for this struggle doesn't get questioned. But as I've said, surely there's something wrong with a vision of literature that imagines Henry James as the preferred reading of the power elite; or imagines that replacing Hemingway with Hurston can solve substantial social ills.

I suppose the real problem is that most of us have hopelessly confused the clamorous debate over diversity with the diversity being debated. It's like looking at a whirling, snarling ball of fur that used to be two dogs: the misdeeds of one are freely attributed to the other. Cultural pluralism doesn't entail when-in-Rome relativism: it forbids it. For relativism is finally a way of not taking other cultures seriously. Pluralism doesn't entail the elevation of "difference" over commonality: it rejects it. For such cultural pluralism seeks to broaden the constricted vistas of ethnic absolutism. Finally, pluralism doesn't entail the proliferation of vulgar identity politics: for an honest account of ethnic dynamism gives full weight to the forces of assimilation and convergence as well as those of differentiation and divergence. Vanilla Ice may land in Bombay, but he does not emerge unscathed or unchanged.

And once we manage to sort things out, we might be able to retrieve a viable vision of cultural pluralism as an antidote to the ever alluring perils of ethnocentrism and cultural chauvinism. After all, we haven't just entrusted to schools the task of reproducing the democratic polity: we've asked that they improve it, too. I want schools to teach, as increasingly they do, the story of America as a plural nation, with people from different lands who had different and shared experiences, not simply as a tale of Pilgrim Triumphalism. But I also want elementary schools to inculcate civic virtues: I want them to discourage youngsters from smoking, accepting candy from strangers, and hating brown-skinned people.

That's not to call for distortion in the name of celebration: the truth will serve very well, thank you. Cathy Davidson, president of the American Studies Association, recently wrote: "Multicultural representation? Gender equity? Diversity? Forget it! Just give me *good* history (whether social or literary history), a far more dangerous proposition." As she notes, this was a continent "inhabited by various American cultures long before the Puritans made their way to these shores. Slaves and immigrants built much of the country, a country that extends far beyond New England. Roughly half of the population has always been female, not all of it was ever heterosexual, and relatively little of it (any gender, racial, or immigrant group) has been rich." With this kind of history, who needs special pleading? It may well be that such special pleading is not the province of multiculturalism, but the denial of multiculturalism. And that's because we have been multicultural all along; we cannot even imagine a culture that is not multiple in its roots and its branches.

There are no shortcuts to ethnic harmony, to be sure. And those who look to multiculturalism or whatever next year's shibboleth will be to provide a cheap fix for expensive problems are bound to be disappointed. Enlightened pluralism isn't a magic wand that would alleviate the ethnic strife in the world: hostile ethnic identities are as often the outcome of such strife as their cause. Even so, our task is clear: we must learn to live without the age-old, deleterious dream of purity—whether purity of bloodlines or cultural inheritance—and learn to find comfort, solace, and even fulfillment in the rough magic of the mix, however imperfect and mutable. I don't claim that the multicultural truth shall set us free. But, like democracy, it seems to enjoy a decided edge over the alternatives.

I realize that some people dream of the world as a cultural museum, in which mixing is eschewed as contamination: or else, if such intercultural contact is allowed, the flow must be one-way from them, the Exotic Other, to us, the corrupted metropole. But the truth is, there are no one-way flows. I don't want to throw cold water—Cold Cold Water, as Mr. Sehgal would have it—on these dreams, but we can no longer pretend to deny the realities of the world in which we live. The tumultuous emergence of mass culture, a development we can usefully date to the 1920s, now pulses in media that would have been undreamed of by our ancestors. An electronic net of computer terminals drapes over the globe with digital avenues like bitnet and telnet, avenues broader than any sixteen-lane highway in Los Angeles. A new generation of interactive media has commanded impressive backing and resources, and stands poised to revolutionize our very relation to mass media and reconfigure the architectures of information to which we're now accustomed. And there is no hiding place.

Which brings us back to Outer Mongolia. The point isn't that entertainers may excite more attention than political leaders. I think it would have surprised Mozart to learn that relatively few of those who know and admire his work today could confidently name the monarch and archbishop he so devotedly served. Now, I'm certainly not comparing Michael Jackson, say, to Mozart—not at all. I mean, Mozart couldn't Moonwalk to save his life. I'm just saying that we shouldn't be so quick to judge the priorities of other people in other places. So here we are, back on the frozen tundra of Outer Mongolia, somewhere not too far from the Gobi Desert, the world's coldest: and Western culture has a black face. Now quite likely I was, strictly speaking, the only black person in the country at that time, but in a larger sense, I was surrounded by a multitude of my countrymen. And as I traipsed my way out of the hall in the frozen weather, wondering, as I say, what this lost child of Africa was doing at this elevation and longitude and latitude, it suddenly flashed to me: somebody was trying to tell me something. They were trying to say: Welcome to the twenty-first century.

Tell you the truth, I'm still not sure if that's a warming thought.

NOTES

1. Sometimes, perforce, local talent has a role to play. For example, in Argentina, by law, advertising must be produced locally with Argentinean talent, doubtless reflecting a laudable desire to protect the integrity of its own cultural tradition. But it just so happens, the U.S. team leader explains, "that Coca-Cola Argentina loves the pattern advertising that comes out of InterNational Team. As a result, they take our work and give it to an Argentine director, and he reshoots it frame by frame. Exactly what we did, even the wardrobe looks the same. The consumer could not tell the difference."

2. Arjun Appadurai, "Disjuncture and Difference in Global Cultural Economy," *Public Culture* 2 (Spring 1990).

7

Violence and Interpretation
Enzensberger's "Civil Wars"

Beatrice Hanssen

The events that took place in Central and Eastern Europe in 1989 seemed to confirm Hannah Arendt's prophetic words that the twentieth century would come to be known as "a century of revolutions."[1] The nonviolent mass demonstrations in the East German cities of Leipzig and Dresden for a while at least appeared to reestablish confidence in the power of the people, as well as prove the possibility of peaceful revolutions and new beginnings. Commenting on these events in June 1990, Jürgen Habermas, however, was quick to draw attention to the "mutually exclusive interpretations" to which these revolutionary upheavals had been subjected, ranging from Stalinist, Leninist, and reform-communist revisions to postmodern, anticommunist and liberal models of explanation.[2] One of the better known interpretive models was Francis Fukuyama's "The End of History?," which gained international notoriety not only for the confidence with which it established the demise of communism as the "unabashed victory of economic and political liberalism,"[3] but also for the curious anachronism with which the events of 1989 were said to present the triumph of the "modern liberal state," whose principles of liberty and equality Hegel would have hailed in the 1806 Battle of Jena.[4] Similarly, conservative historians and politicians in Germany—foremost among them Ernst Nolte—celebrated the revolutions of '89 as the definitive overcoming of "the global civil war started by the Bolsheviks in 1917."[5] Among Germany's left-liberal intelligentsia, by contrast, the collapse of the GDR, together with the utopian potential of an alternative "middle way" democratic socialism, was to lead to a profound cultural crisis or to what Helmut Dubiel, in a much noted article in *Merkur*, would call "left-wing melancholia."[6] Habermas's position, finally, proved to be more cautionary. Already in 1990 he referred to the changes in Eastern Europe as "revolutions of recuperation," which, in spiraling back to the bourgeois revolutions of the West not only abandoned totalitarianism for constitutional democracy but, on a negative note, uncritically espoused a market economy and consumerism. Rejecting both the jubilant triumph of liberalism and the left-wing melancholia of Wolf Biermann and others, he instead ascribed a critical role to socialism, which was to function as the necessary corrective to liberalism.

Today, these divisive, irreconcilable debates about collapse or regeneration, progressive democratization or the failure of a "middle way" democratic socialism, while not abated, appear to have shifted grounds as politicians and cultural critics seek to come to terms with the new nationalisms, ethnic violence, and xenophobia that followed the end of the Cold War bipolar world order. In a recently translated collection of essays, *Civil Wars*,[7] which has garnered much critical attention in Great Britain and the United States, German author and essayist Hans Magnus Enzensberger describes the wave of violence to have marked the postrevolutionary age as the explosive encounter between "the unprecedented" and the "atavistic."[8] Promising to make sense of a widespread cultural malaise, Enzensberger presents the eruptions of neonationalist and ethnic violence in postrevolutionary Europe as but part of a more global turn to violence and civil war. If in an earlier essay, "Ways of Walking" (1990), Enzensberger could still hail the East German revolution as the radical defeat of Marxist utopianism and as the decisive victory of civil society over state socialism,[9] *Civil Wars* paints a more somber picture, pronouncing the end of revolutions altogether. On this reading, the age of revolutions has been swept away by a new era of violence. Only since the end of the Cold War would it have become possible to lift the mask of so-called revolutionary uprisings and national liberation wars to recognize them for what they really are: civil wars in disguise. Thus, if Ernst Nolte established 1989 as the year that marked liberalism's victorious overcoming of the "global civil war," initiated by Bolshevism, Enzensberger instead seems to defend a radical cultural pessimism when he *globalizes* civil strife. It can hardly come as a surprise, then, that Fukuyama recently took exception to the nihilism that permeates *Civil Wars*, much as his *The End of History* decried the pessimism of the twentieth century.[10]

Starting from the observation that more than "30 to 40 civil wars [are] being waged openly around the globe,"[11] Enzensberger proceeds to stretch the term "civil war" beyond its customary meaning to advance it as a conceptual grid with which to capture such culturally diverse phenomena as interethnic strife, urban unrest, and the gang warfare of inner cities. Whether it be ethnic cleansing in the former Yugoslavia, the 1992 race-related unrest following the Rodney King verdict in South Central L.A., or the resurgence of xenophobia in postunification Germany—all are said to be palpable manifestations of a global, molecular civil war. Not only does the postrevolutionary era signal the return to the "primary form of all collective conflict," whose original account is to be found in the *History of the Peloponnesian Wars*,[12] but it also introduces a *new* type of civil war, marked by the absence of clear political goals, plans, or ideas,[13] and by an all-pervasive autism on the part of its perpetrators. Using a language that at times would seem remarkably close to Daniel Bell's pronouncements on the end of ideology, Enzensberger contends that such violence has divorced itself from all ideological foundations. As such, global violence not only announces the end of politics, but it signals the end of all political models that in the past have sought either to interpret or change the world, from Hegel's struggle for recognition to the Marxist class struggle. What remains instead is naked, "valueless" strife, or the lapse into a Hobbesian state of permanent (civil) war. "[A]ll political thought, from Aristotle and Machiavelli to Marx and Weber, is turned upside down."[14] All that remains, Enzensberger writes, is a negative utopia or "the Hobbesian ur-myth of the war of everyone against everyone else."[15]

Enzensberger's model of the new civil wars is a seductive one, for it not only promises to make sense of random violence, whose manifestations indeed seem to have become ever more prevalent, but it also purports to combine the soundness of what are offered as anthropological observations with claims to newness and historic periodization. It further speaks the language of return and of the encounter between barbarism, primitivism and modernity, whose entwinement, as anthropologists such as Benedict Anderson have noted, constitutes one of the persistent paradoxes of nationalisms. Further, that violence and fratricide should belong to the ur-myths of mankind is something Hannah Arendt already observed when in *On Revolution* she suggested that the eighteenth-century conception of the *status naturalis* counts as a "theoretically purified phrase" for the mythical insight, laid down in the tales of Cain and Abel, Romulus and Remus, that "in the beginning was a crime."[16] However, Enzensberger's popularizing discourse of a globalized violence lacks the astuteness of these theoretical models. Not only does it speak to a kind of eschatological cultural pessimism, whose manifestations seem to have become increasingly pronounced as we reach the end of the millennium.[17] But his account also mobilizes a quasi-anthropological[18] foundationalism, essentialism, and primitivism that can no longer acknowledge structural, political, or cultural differences, linked as it is to the contention that the new civil wars portend the end of ideology. With the urge to label a new historic era comes the leveling of all conceptual or political distinctions between revolutions, riots, upheavals, urban unrest, liberation wars, and uprisings—all rendered as local outbreaks of a vast, molecular civil war. To be sure, this is not to dispute the urgency of what currently is called the "war on violence," or to deny the disquieting number of civil wars in the geopolitical arena, and, even less, to condone the use of violence. Rather, what also warrants critical attention, I would submit, is the ease with which a globalizing discourse on violence, of the sort proposed in *Civil Wars*, tends to erase all structural difference, at the expense of an ability to implement political analysis. Indeed, as I hope to show by placing *Civil Wars*, first, in a German, then in a larger, comparative context, such a globalizing discourse can function as a screen for what are thought to be the flaws of exceedingly multicultural or multiethnic societies.

When seen in a German cultural context, Enzensberger's essay must first of all raise questions with regard to the ease with which right-wing incidents, such as the murders of Turkish immigrants in Mölln and Solingen, are presented as symptoms of a global turn to violence. Not only does his analysis remain vulnerable to charges that it follows the conservative strategies used in the former West German Republic and in postunification Germany to progressively normalize and rectify the image of Germany's so-called *Sonderweg*.[19] But his cavalier observations about German neo-Nazism are, if not reminiscent of the technique of historical analogism mobilized during the historians' debate of the eighties,[20] then at least questionable for the haste with which they foreclose political analysis. In light of such a lack of critical acuity it should come as no surprise that the French philosopher André Glucksmann has seen Enzensberger's plea for a return to national and purely German concerns, together with his rejection of an ethics of "universal responsibility"—sustained by the gruesome images of global media news coverage—as the very shirking of historic accountability.[21] As such, Enzensberger's intellectual biography—from his infatuation with the communist revolution in the sixties to his current defense of a strong state—has been read as part of the turn to the right that recently, in the figures of such renowned authors as Martin Walser and Botho Strauß, has profoundly shaken German cultural life.[22]

Insofar as civil wars pit neighbors against neighbors, they always have counted as a significant threat to the body politic.[23] They also form the political limit into which any revolution may threaten to lapse. Civil wars thus put at risk legitimate violence, traditionally the monopoly of the liberal nation-state, as Walter Benjamin suggested in his "Critique of Violence." Enzensberger would seem to imply as much when he observes: "Where the state can no longer enforce its monopoly then everyone must defend himself."[24] Thus, the inability of current governments to cope with civic feuding is said to have been caused by "the retreat of the state."[25] But if in the past, terror was still "the monopoly of totalitarian regimes," then "today it returns in a denationalized form [*in entstaatlichter Form*]."[26] In fact, the global civil war in Enzensberger's account becomes a sort of free-floating violence, which, like a "political retrovirus,"[27] at any point may spread across national borders. Enzensberger's metaphorical language here is problematic not only because of the register of disease, which, toward the end of the essay, will be matched by an ethics of *triage*, suggesting that there may be no cure for the sick body politic, only a reasoned, strategic coping with immediate demands. Equally worrisome, however, is the phantasm of the nineteenth-century nation-state, which would seem to form the essay's underlying countermodel. Civil war is said to be devoid of the rationality that still typified the classic warfare between nation-states, whose laws and logistics have been laid down in Clausewitz's *On War*. As such, it spells the end of an "old-style European nationalism,"[28] which, in spite of its imperialist legacy, is primarily defended here as the harbinger of human rights.

Enzensberger's skewed justification of nineteenth-century nationalism is perhaps less puzzling when seen for what it really is, namely, a covert critique of multiculturalism. To be sure, Enzensberger seems acutely aware of the pressing civic, political, and cultural difficulties that face many European nations, including Germany, as governments have proved increasingly incapable of responding adequately to global migrations and demographic changes. Thus, the essay "The Great Migration" convincingly argues at points that it would be erroneous for states to distinguish between economic and political refugees or to propagate a "preventive migration policy." Other passages, however, suggest that the state of civil war fundamentally is the result of a fall from "culture," from whose definition Enzensberger seems to expect an answer to the many problems posed by multiculturalism. Indeed, one may well wonder to what extent the *theoretical model* of civil war serves as a screen for what are perceived to be the conflictual, contentious claims of multicultural societies. In a review of potential explanations for the surge in global violence, Enzensberger seems to give credence to the thought that the alleged return to the state of nature may have been brought on by claims to ethnic and cultural identity, which, with their competing demands for recognition, have proliferated beyond the frame of reasonableness. Worldwide terrorism and religious fundamentalism that seek the enforcement of recognition through the use of violence are but the more extreme manifestations of a fundamental corrosion that has befallen the political concept of recognition, spawning the primitive struggle of all against all.[29] Enzensberger's account in this respect differs radically from Fukuyama's *End of History*, which optimistically celebrated political and economic liberalism as the universalization of recognition. Influenced by the Hegel scholar Kojève, who drew renewed attention to the "struggle for recognition" at the center of the master-slave dialectic, Fukuyama proposed to read the end of communism as the absolute validation of "universal and reciprocal recognition,"[30] guaranteed by the basic rights of liberal democracy. *Civil Wars*, by contrast, establishes the exhaustion of the Hegelian paradigm: "[T]he desire for recognition, first in cities and then across the whole world, has gathered a momentum that a certain philosopher in 1806 could never have dreamed of."[31] If at this point Frantz Fanon is invoked, it is not, however, to take stock of the significant modification to which the Antillean psychiatrist and activist had subjected the Hegelian dream of recognition,[32] nor is it to query the limits of what essentially remains a Western perspective. Instead, current eruptions of violence are linked to the self-destruction, aggression-turned-inward, and tribal warfare that marked the first stage of African decolonialization, and whose dynamics are presented as a transitory phase in *The Wretched of the Earth*. Fanon's discourse on counterviolence thus is merely adduced as objective proof that the claim to recognition indeed counts as an anthropological given.[33]

Significantly, the category of recognition has been at the core of recent political and philosophical discussions concerning multiculturalism, from Charles Taylor's proposal for a more hospitable liberalism that practices a politics of equal respect without "homogenizing difference"[34] to its thematization in the practical philosophy of Frankfurt School theorists such as Habermas, Honneth, or Benhabib.[35] But while these theorists have tried to modify the category profoundly, seeking to strip it of its apparent claims to symmetry or of its potential power dynamics, *Civil Wars* implicitly rejects these solutions on the grounds that the demand itself never can be fully gratified. Enzensberger thus introduces an infinity to the modality of recognition, whose needs are such that they cannot be satisfied as communities produce ever more inequalities. More is at stake here than simple pessimism. By rejecting recognition as an idealistic trope, never to be fulfilled, Enzensberger again implicitly forecloses the kinds of practical, political solutions offered by Habermas and others, who, in their interventions in the asylum and multiculturalism debates or in their comments on antiforeigner violence, have emphasized the need for *judicial* or *legal* recognition. In his dialogues with Charles Taylor, for example, Habermas asserts that no fundamental contradiction exists between individual rights and the recognition of collective identities once one has "a democratic understanding of the actualization of basic rights."[36] This presupposes that one uphold a strict difference between ethics and judicial recognition, that is, between "the ethical substance of a constitutional patriotism" and "the legal system's neutrality vis-a-vis communities that are ethically integrated at a sub-political level."[37] Applied to the German situation, this means that only when the Federal Republic becomes a genuinely legal rather than an ethnic community can it take leave of the prepolitical conception of nationhood that marred the unification.[38] Only when the Federal Republic changes its citizenship laws, which are still largely determined by the so-called 1913 blood laws,[39] and repeals the restrictions placed on asylum rights by the 1993 amendment to the Basic Law will it be able to guarantee recognition through legal equality. In effect, Germany would then reach "a national self-understanding that is no longer based on ethnicity but founded on citizenship."[40]

Clearly, this is not the last word on the issue of legal recognition. Despite the accomplishments of civil rights and other social struggles, formal legal rights cannot automatically safeguard against exclusionary or discriminatory applications of the law. Nor does racial justice prevent discrimination—a point driven home by the Critical Race Theory group in its reflections on the 1992 upheavals in South Central L.A. Apart from suggesting that the frame-by-frame breakdown and disaggregation of the Rodney King video can be seen as an allegory for the ways in which questions of power, law, and interpretation are still largely dissociated from one another in our society, the group's analysis also demonstrates that much is at stake indeed in whether the incidents that occurred are called "riots," following the dominant cultural narrative, or, alternatively, "insurrections," as the counternarrative had it, that is, "as a communal response to a much larger set of issues of social power."[41]

As unquestionably as these events resulted in violence, they are to be read, then, not as outbreaks of a global civil war but perhaps as symptomatic of "our nation," as Cornel West has suggested. To be sure, West rejects both the labels "race riot" and "class rebellion" for the L.A. incidents, qualifying this "monumental upheaval" instead as "a multiracial, trans-class, and largely male display of justified social rage."[42] Yet, much like the Critical Race Theory group, West focuses on the incidents' symbolic representation and narrative interpretation. For despite deep-seated ideological differences, he argues, the dominant cultural narratives mostly singled out "the problems of black people" rather than "the flaws of American society," thus failing to understand "that the presence and predicaments of black people are neither additions to nor defections from American life, but rather *constitutive elements of that life*."[43] The true challenge the L.A. upheavals fundamentally presented was "whether a genuine multiracial democracy can be created and sustained in an era of global economy and a moment of xenophobic frenzy."[44]

As the political complexity of these and other incidents demonstrates, it will not do simply to reduce such foundational rifts to irrational outbreaks of rage or violence, as *Civil Wars* inadvertently seems to imply. If anything, Enzensberger's text still begs the question of the interpretational grid within which disparate political and social events are placed. Even if we may not quite have managed to change the world significantly, neither should we stop examining the way we interpret it.

NOTES

1. Hannah Arendt, *On Revolution* (London: Penguin Books, 1990), 18.

2. Jürgen Habermas, "Nachholende Revolution und linker Revisionsbedarf. Was heißt Sozialismus heute?" in *Die nachholende Revolution. Kleine Politische Schriften VII* (Frankfurt a.M.: Suhrkamp, 1990), 179–204; translated as "What Does Socialism Mean Today? The Revolutions of Recuperation and the Need for New Thinking," in Robin Blackburn, ed., *After the Fall: The Failure of Communism and the Future of Socialism* (London, New York: Verso, 1991), 25–46.

3. Francis Fukuyama, "The End of History?" in *The National Interest* 16 (Summer 1989), 3.

4. Francis Fukuyama, *The End of History and the Last Man* (New York: The Free Press, 1992), xi and 64.

5. Habermas, "What Does Socialism Mean Today?" 30. Habermas's reference is to Ernst Nolte's article, "Nach dem Weltbürgerkrieg? Erhellung der Vergangenheit durch die Gegenwart," which appeared in *Frankfurter Allgemeine Zeitung* (February 17, 1990).

6. Helmut Dubiel, "Linke Trauerarbeit," *Merkur* 496 (June 1990): 482–91.

7. Originally published in German as *Aussichten auf den Bürgerkrieg* (Frankfurt a.M.: Suhrkamp, 1993). An excerpt, titled "Ausblicke auf den Bürgerkrieg. Hans Magnus Enzensberger über den täglichen Massenmord und die überforderte Moral," appeared in *Der Spiegel* (June 21, 1993): 170–76. In the United States, the collection appeared under the title *Civil Wars: From L.A. to Bosnia* (New York: The New Press, 1994); in Great Britain, however, it was published as *Civil War,* translated by Piers Spence and Martin Chalmers (London: Granta Books, 1994). All references will be to the American edition. Unless otherwise indicated, the main focus of the following analysis will be on the collection's title essay, "Civil War."

8. Enzensberger, 12.

9. Hans Magnus Enzensberger, "Ways of Walking: A Postscript to Utopia," in Robin Blackburn, ed., *After the Fall: The Failure of Communism and the Future of Socialism*, 18–24.

10. See Fukuyama's book review of Enzensberger's *Civil Wars*, "The New World Disorder," in the *New York Times Book Review* (October 9, 1994), 12–13. As he notes: "Given that the post-cold war world presented in this book is in many respects much better than its predecessor, the question remains why its author and other Europeans like him are so pessimistic."

11. Enzensberger, 14.

12. Enzensberger, 11.

13. Enzensberger, 18.

14. Enzensberger, 31.

15. Enzensberger, 31. The English translation omits the term "negative utopia." See Enzensberger, *Aussichten auf den Bürgerkrieg*, 36.

16. Arendt, 20.

17. For a discussion of the widespread cultural malaise that marks the end of the present century, see Andreas Huyssen, *Twilight Memory: Marking Time in a Culture of Amnesia* (New York and London: Routledge, 1995).

18. Enzensberger's use of "anthropology" as a final category or the endpoint of reasoning, is also evident in his "Ways of Walking," where he justifies the end of utopianism by asserting that "utopian thinking is by no means an anthropological constant" (20).

19. See Habermas's lecture, "The Asylum Debate," in which he discusses Arnulf Baring's attempt to reverse the *Sonderweg* hypothesis, and specifically the latter's argument that Germany "after unification is […] once again the old one." Jürgen Habermas, "The Asylum Debate," in *The Past as Future*, translated and edited by Max Pensky, foreword by Peter Hohendahl (Lincoln & London: University of Nebraska Press, 1994), 137. On these strategies of progressive normalization, see particularly Andreas Huyssen, "After the Wall: The Failure of German Intellectuals," and "Nation, Race, and Immigration: German Identities after Unification," in *Twilight Memories*.

20. On the use of historical analogy in the *Historikerstreit*, see Charles S. Maier, *The Unmasterable Past: History, Holocaust, and German National Identity* (Cambridge and London: Harvard University Press, 1988).

21. André Glucksmann's comments originally appeared in *Globe Hebdo* and are reprinted as "Ein neuer Vogel Strauß. Der Philosoph André Glucksmann antwortet Hans Magnus Enzensberger," in *Der Spiegel* (September 13, 1993), 247–49.

22. See Enzensberger's interview with André Müller, "Ich will nicht der Lappen sein, mit dem man die Welt putzt," *Die Zeit* (January 27, 1995), 13.

23. See Arendt, 34.

24. Enzensberger, 46.

25. Enzensberger, 46.

26. Enzensberger, 27.

27. Enzensberger, 30.

28. Enzensberger, 22.

29. Enzensberger, 38.

30. Francis Fukuyama, *The End of History and the Last Man*, xviii.

31. Enzensberger, 38.

32. See Frantz Fanon's "The Negro and Recognition," in *Black Skin, White Masks*, translated from the French by Charles Lam Markmann (New York: Grove Weidenfeld, 1982), 210–22.

33. Enzensberger, 37ff.

34. Charles Taylor, "The Politics of Recognition," in Amy Gutman, ed., *Multiculturalism: Examining the Politics of Recognition* (Princeton: Princeton University Press, 1994), 61.

35. See K. Anthony Appiah's response to Taylor, "Identity, Authenticity, Survival: Multicultural Societies and Social Reproduction"; Jürgen Habermas, "Struggles for Recognition in the Democratic Constitutional State," in Amy Gutman, ed., *Multiculturalism: Examining the Politics of Recognition;* Axel Honneth, *Kampf um Anerkennung* (Frankfurt a.M.: Suhrkamp, 1992); Seyla Benhabib, "In Defense of Universalism—Yet Again! A Response to Critics of *Situating the Self,*" in *New German Critique* 62 (Spring/Summer 1994): 173–89.

36. Habermas, "Struggles for Recognition," 116.

37. Habermas, 134. As he puts it: "The neutrality of the law vis-a-vis internal ethical differentiations stems from the fact that in complex societies the citizenry as a whole can no longer be held together by a substantive consensus on values but only by a consensus on the procedures for the legitimate enactment of laws and the legitimate exercise of power" (135).

38. See also Jürgen Habermas's "The Asylum Debate," in *The Past as Future*, e.g., 129.

39. See Rogers Brubaker, *Citizenship and Nationhood in France and Germany* (Cambridge and London: Harvard University Press, 1992), 165ff.

40. Habermas, "Struggles for Recognition," 148.

41. Kimberlé Crenshaw and Gary Peller, "Reel Time/Real Justice," in Robert Gooding-Williams, ed., *Reading Rodney King, Reading Urban Uprising* (New York & London: Routledge, 1993), 56–70.

42. Cornel West, "Introduction: Race Matters," in *Race Matters* (New York: Vintage, 1994), 3.

43. West, 6.

44. West, 13.

8

OUR AmeRíca

Doris Sommer

Las palabras se hacen fronteras, cuando no nacen del corazón
hablemos el mismo idioma y así las cosas irán mejor.
[Words can become barriers when they don't come from the heart
Let's speak the same language, and that way things will go better.]

—Gloria Estefan and Emilio Estefan, Jr.

"Universalism is not what it used to be," quipped Werner Sollors after hearing "Hablemos el mismo idioma."[1] The song is translated as "Let's Speak the Same Language" in the bilingual booklet that comes with the CD, an apparently ecumenical accompaniment to make good on the lyric's call for racial rainbows and musical mixes (*colores de un arcoiris, acordes de un mismo son*). But there is no denying that Gloria Estefan's monolingual appeal to get beyond differences is pitched to decidedly Latin locutors. You see, after the title (which means, figuratively, "Let's get together") and the undiscriminating plea of the first few lines, the song narrows its focus and disinterpellates some of us who may want to sing along. The "us" in the refrain turns out to be *"nosotros hispanos."*

Gloria Estefan rehearses here the pitch for pan-Hispanic solidarity already intoned in this country by other recording stars, including Puerto Rican Willie Colón, Panamanian Rubén Blades, and Cuban Celia Cruz. They too may be saying, with some relief for never having fit into the milky homogenization, that universalism is not what it used to be. But universality has a renewed hope—Seyla Benhabib, among others, can remind us—in an America tuned in to the dissonance that signals political gaps, gaps that can promise the kind of open space needed for negotiations.[2] Discord locates the gaps that make up the empty political space of democratic negotiation. Unbreachable differences give some universalists pause; but pause is not a bad thing, it lets one listen to others.[3] Universalism makes sense today, Judith Butler cautiously agrees, as a site of translation,[4] of the contests and moving mixes in which Homi Bhabha locates modernity in general.[5]

My work lately has been about pauses and residues from translation, about the ethical and political limits of comprehension (which still means grasping, owning). I want to play on those themes using Bhabha's concept of lagtime, which names the temporal gaps between an already existing center and peripheries that cannot (or will not) catch up. This does some urgent work of underlining the asymmetries and complicating the notion of empty or homogeneous modern time that Bhabha attributes to Walter Benjamin (although we should say that Benjamin named the bourgeois temporal tidiness in order to blast it apart with the interruptions of *Jetztzeit*).[6] Time-lag decries inequalities, against the drone of pluralism and multiculturalism. But for me, here, the notion will serve less as a critique than as an engaging musical notation, a particular asymmetry of quotidian counterpoints. Despite, or even contra Bhabha, I'll attend to the rhythmic variations in speech when we speak the same language, when we defer a stress, or delay apprehension of meaning, when we skip a beat in conversation as if it had the rhythm of a joke; time-lag can be the signature of one language through the medium of another. Skewed rhythms and dissonant notes, as in "Hablemos el mismo idioma" (with its universalist theme and its particularist appeal)[7] are not noise, but are the very conditions of possibility for liberal improvisation. We share a polity, after all; differences coexist in time as well as through time. Blockage comes, instead, from rushing to fill in the gaps, through understanding or through empathy; these play in a treacherous strain toward easy harmonies that neutralize unfamiliar sounds.

Signs of difference and of contingent translations are everywhere, unless we continue to ignore them. The gesture that first made me pause was Rigoberta Menchú's peculiar insistence that she was keeping secrets in her 1983 testimony about Guatemala's war on Indians. Why proclaim her own silence, I wondered, as if declaring secrets mattered more than the ethnographic data? With all those secrets, no amount of information could establish a mood of intimacy and collaboration. Perhaps that was the point, I began to think; it was to engage us *and* to interrupt our universalizing habit of identifying with the writer, sometimes to the point of replacing her. A formidable lesson. Still illiterate, the young woman who spoke a newly learned, halting, Spanish managed to turn an ethnographic interrogation into a plat-form for her own irreplaceable leadership. The stunning move made me think of other books that interrupt universalizing mastery. Among them were slave narratives commissioned by abolitionists, the Inca Garcilaso's chronicles, Toni Morrison's *Beloved*, Elena Poniatowska's novelized testimonio, stories about blacks told by self-consciously incompetent whites, even the accom-modationist memoir of Richard Rodriguez, in his refusals of intimacy with readers. The examples that drew me back and brought me up short are almost arbitrary. Anyone can think of others. The point is that some ethnically marked writing refuses to keep universalizing time. It halts, syncopates, and demands cautious engagements.

1995 is an auspicious year for tuning in to the counterpoints of Our Americas.[8] The year commemorates at least three centennials. One is the death of Sor Juana Inés de la Cruz, a nun who was too brilliant and too bold to fit inside Mexico or her seventeenth century. Another is Jorge Isaacs, that universal but unhomogenized figure for the nineteenth century. He was a fissured, mosaic star, a Colombian Jew, and the century's only Latin American novelist to thrill readers far beyond his own country. But Isaacs's Hebraic habits made him almost unassimilable at home.[9]

And the third centennial commemorates José Martí, author of many works including the Cuban War of Independence and the essay "Our America" (1891). What "Our" means in his celebration of indigenous and African strains in New World Hispanism is a problem, for two reasons. First, the possessive pronoun neutralizes internal differences and claims ownership in monocultural ways that now seem unproductive. Martí's nineteenth-century nationalism needed to focus on victory by squinting at Cuba, compressing its complexity into a thin but homogenous *Cubanidad*. The other problem is that the discriminating pronoun "Our" is so shifty, so available for compet-ing positions and equivocal meanings. This is not to miss Martí's obvious meaning of danger to America's politically and culturally enabling differ-ences, the danger when one country threatens to override distinctions between us and them. He was right, of course, to mistrust "The descendants of the pilgrims...they are no longer humble, nor tread the snow of Cape Cod with workers' boots. Instead they now lace up their military boots aggres-sively and they see on one side Canada and on the other Mexico."[10] Worry can be a continuing border occupation almost anywhere. The problem is not only how to fix borders against aggression; it is also how to define the dif-ferentiated territories that the borders demarcate. And in a New World where commercial, cultural, and political border crossings define so many lives, boundary words like here and there, mine and yours, are hardly stable sign-posts. They are, as always, shifters. Merely to translate the possessive claim to

"Nuestra América," for example, as "Our America" is to hear the claim deformed by the treachery of displacement. It is to move from a defensive position right into the enemy's camp.[11]

Strategists will know that mobility is not only a cause for worry; it is also an opportunity to gain ground. Perhaps Nuestra América, in the genre of Estefan's solidarity song, has a future history here, up North. Translation, of course, literally means switching ground. And since Puerto Ricans have become quite expert at this, they can be our guides here. Following particular guides is an important precaution, if we hope to avoid the muddle of mistaking the category "Hispanics" in this America as an easily generalizable group. The very rhythm of repeated efforts in music and other media to promote solidarity, sometimes for particular political goals, is a cue to the division among constituencies usually identified by national origin.[12] Puerto Rico presents a strong case of a nation that maneuvers along the faultline of grammatical shifters, in the space between here and there, Our America and theirs.

It is a case of an entire population that stays on the move, or potentially so, so much so that Luis Rafael Sánchez makes a hysterical joke about Puerto Rican national identity being grounded in the guagua aérea (air bus) shuttling across the Atlantic puddle.[13] Literally a nation of Luftmenschen, half is provisionally on the Caribbean island, and half on and around that other mad-hatter island, which has become a homeland of sorts for new nationals. Tato Laviera calls them, and himself, *AmeRícan* in the title of a brilliantly bilingual book of poetry.[14] His genius is to read aloud the English sign for America with an eye for Spanish. Anyone who reads Spanish properly can tell that the sign looks like "América;" because without a written accent mark on the "e" to give the word an irregular stress, America would use a default, unwritten, accent on the "i." So Laviera's hyper-corrected reading of the arbitrary English name changes its stress by displacing the logic of diacritical marks from one language to another. The alleged omission of an accent mark then becomes an opportunity, an invitation to read the country with facetious correction in order to pronounce AmeRíca, a new sound whose visible signs reform the country's look, too. With a foreign stroke if you read it in English (just as superfluous and incorrect a mark for pedantic Spanish), and with an intrusive capital "R" that fissures and then fuses a conventional name into a convincing compound, Laviera's orthographic encroachments push both standard languages slightly out of bounds. The result is a practically providential metaphor: AmeRíca transforms what for English or Spanish is just a word into a *mot juste* in Spanglish. It proclaims doubly marked mainland Ricans as the most representative citizens we've got.

Puerto Rican independentists resent the doubling, and they resist being taken for endless rides in the guagua aérea. They have been saying "no" even before the 1917 U.S. decision to confer, or to force, "American" citizenship on the island. At that time, José de Diego published a protest simply and unequivocally titled "No." "Crisp, solid, decisive as a hammer blow, this is the virile word that should inflame our lips and save our honor in these sad days of anachronistic imperialism."[15] "Yes" may be useful for some things, he coyly admits after this first sentence, but

> in political evolution, in the struggle for freedom, it is...always deadly.... We must learn to say NO: arch the lips, relax the chest, tense up all the vocal muscles and powers of will, and shout out that O of the NO! It might resound through America and the world, and to the very heavens, more effectively than the roar of guns.[16]

De Diego had good reason to be confident; Puerto Ricans had in fact already armed themselves against one empire, successfully, by simply saying "no." I know this from Antonio S. Pedreira, a 1930s ideologue who otherwise deplored Puerto Ricans' "passivity." But he celebrates it for two incidents when unaggressive patriots struck their unmovable pose; both occurred when Spain tried to draft Puerto Ricans into wars, first to stop the liberators of Venezuela and then to punish the patriots in Santo Domingo. The nationally legitimating effect of nay-saying in both cases is reported in Pedreira's lapidary *Insularismo*, where the incidents make up a chapter wisely and paradoxically called "Afirmación puertorriqueña."[17]

But I want to suggest another reason for so highly esteeming the simple slogan, an unspoken reason behind de Diego's reasoning about NO being the only word with real political purchase. It's that the value of "no" doesn't get lost in translation from Spanish to English. De Diego suggests as much by pausing to consider the alternative "sí," its brevity and harmony in Romance languages contrasting with the clumsier Latin equivalents (131), and presumably with the cacophonic "yes" in English. From Spanish to English the words of affirmation do not match up, and the asymmetry opens up a space, a trench like the one we might notice between NAFTA (North American Free Trade Agreement)—sounding so explosive in European languages—and its Mexican counterpart, TLC (Tratado de Libre Comercio)—so misleadingly friendly in American English. When a Spanish speaker hears the English "yes," does s/he sometimes wonder at the insistent sibilant "s" at the end, where it might have stayed discreetly underpronounced in Spanish, wonder if the word might be a hiss of disapproval or the totemic sound of a serpent stalking its prey? And is it possible that an English listener might hear in a Spanish "sí" not a simple endorsement but an invitation to look at something unsettling? "No," by contrast, is as smooth and hard, as virile as a bullet; it may in fact be the only politically significant word that is so firm a sound and a substance, so impervious to interpretation, that it alone can safely be used. "No" is not vulnerable to ventriloquism, nor is it a traffic problem in the endless translations of Puerto Ricans from one place and language to another. Mercifully, one word, one possession at least, doesn't tarnish on the trips. NO remains intact and unambiguous.

Is it really so safe, though? The very coherence of the word, its traveler-friendly usage, is a kind of betrayal. The problem with "no" is precisely that it translates so easily, that it is as natural here as it is there, and floats effortlessly between its linguistic homes. The very word that refuses intimacy with empire produces that intimacy. "No" is a weapon of self-defense that turns out to be a deconstructive trap, a roar of virile resistance that begins to sound like the moan of irresistible seduction. "No" treacherously turns around, and its supplementary message, despite de Diego's painstakingly pronounced refusal to collaborate, is its own translatability, the essence of a supple and pragmatic war of positions. And the equivocal positions may not be a political disorder at all, but rather a strategy for staying afloat that de Diego's rival called "posibilismo"[18]

To consider the possibilities of what American or AmeRícan may mean, is first to hear where the accent falls. Does it name exceptionalism, in a paradoxically repeatable project from one American country to another, like the project American Studies celebrates for the USA, and the one José Vasconcelos consecrated in *La raza cósmica* (1925) as Mexico's synthetic mission to the world? Or is AmeRícan part of *La raza cómica*, as my Puerto Rican friend Rubén Ríos suggests, a people whose hilarity shows up missions as madness?[19] And once we learn to hear local accents and sometimes purposeful mispronunciations, we may also want to notice that the tail end of America can sometimes turn up as a male signifier, an aggressive agency. Américo is the name, after all, of the father of Chicano studies, who in 1958 warned Texan readers, "with his pistol in his hand," that they were on shifty ground, a land alternately called the Southwest and el Norte.[20]

Ambivalent naming wavers between cause and effect in American history. For nineteenth-century founding fathers in the Southern Cone, America meant a project because it was everything they wanted to overcome: it was the indigenous Pampa, emptiness, desert, an impossible grounding for a *república*, that would first have to be filled before it could bear modern values.[21] "Gobernar es poblar" was the slogan of generations, to govern you first need to populate the territory.[22] But the word Pampa, according to El Inca Garcilaso's seventeenth-century chronicle, means public space itself, and the public women who create a hub of erotic and economic interest in the suburbs of ancient Incan cities.[23]

Reading Peru's bilingual chronicler of the oxymoronic Quechua Castilian name, we may wonder what it is that we *do* know about America. It is next to nothing of indigenous cultures, but also embarrassingly little even about the Europeans' "discovery." In 1484, begins Garcilaso, after multiple prologues and admonitions against underestimating our own ignorance, an obscure sailor got blown off course from the Canaries to the Caribbean. And barely alive back in Spain, the victim of his uninvited voyage is cared for and questioned—to death—by a shrewd Columbus.

Who, then, are the heroes of American history? How many histories is it? El Inca Garcilaso wrote one as commentary or supplement to standard Spanish versions. Adding el Inca to his Spanish name was already a daring supplement to monolingual monopolies on worth, an emblem of the dangerous doubling that monolingualism makes possible while it insists that we speak the same language. Translation produces excess, as in the possessive pronoun that shifts belonging from Nuestra América to Ours, and even the simplest NO of uncompromising refusal can get stuck in the slime of translation's surplus. But for English and Spanish speakers to avoid translation is, of course, simply to imagine a cultural emptiness on the other side of an Imperial language, to erase public space from the populated Pampas, and to mistake New York (Nous York, in an Air Canada advertisement) as unusably foreign. Ambiguous translation is not only a limit of understanding; it is also a beginning that stops squinting and starts winking at the enabling contradictions of AmeRícan negotiations.

Ambivalence keeps alive what ethicist Emannuel Levinas calls the Saying, that is, the mystery and transcendence of social intercourse; it doesn't allow language to kill the desired other by getting his meaning right. The ambivalence, for example, of hoping to speak the same (Latino) language and issuing a bilingual booklet suspends the copula between the speaker and her identity, so that American cannot yet "be" any essentialized, definitive, or dead thing. It remains a range of simultaneous belongings, desired, virtual, but wisely and prophylactically unconsummated connections; they safeguard Saying Our America, in all its rhythmic accents, shifty attributions, and impossible refusals.

NOTES

1. "Hablemos el mismo idioma" is song no. 10 on Estefan's very successful CD *Mi tierra*; music and lyrics are by Gloria Estefan and Emilio Estefan, Jr., and the 1993 copyright is held by Foreign Imported Productions and Publications Inc. I played the song during the first session of a course called "NAFTA Literatures," which I co-taught with Werner Sollors and Marc Shell in the fall of 1994, precisely in order to raise questions of inclusion and exclusion in language.

2. See Seyla Benhabib, *Situating the Self: Gender, Community and Postmodernism in Contemporary Ethics* (New York: Routledge, 1992).

3. Jean-François Lyotard, "The Other's Rights," in *On Human Rights: The Oxford Amnesty Lectures 1993*, ed. Stephen Shute and Susan Hurley (New York: HarperCollins, 1993) 136–147. 142: Aristotle said: "The master speaks and the pupil listens. For that moment, the status of *I* is forbidden to me…. The suspension of interlocution imposes a silence and that silence is good. It does not undermine the right to speak. It teaches the value of that right."

4. Judith Butler, in Seyla Benhabib, Judith Butler, Drucilla Cornell, Nancy Fraser, and Linda Nicholson, *Feminist Contentions: A Philosophical Exchange* (Routledge, 1995), 130.

5. Homi K. Bhabha, *The Location of Culture* (New York: Routledge, 1994). See especially 32, 242. Translation is the favored strategy for keeping the promise of modernity usably alive.

6. Bhabha, *The Location of Culture*, 95. But he will give Benjamin credit for the critique in "Translator Translated: W. J. T. Mitchell talks with Homi Bhabha" in *Artform #7*, March 1995, 80–119, 110.

7. Performative contradictions (as in Habermas's critique of Foucault) are an opportunity for discourses to be jostled (perhaps an image from Benjamin's essay on Baudelaire).

8. The reference is to Fernando Ortiz, *Contrapunteo cubano del tabaco y azúcar* (originally Havana, 1941). Since then, the metaphor of counterpoint has been standard in discussions of cultural conflict and conflictual creativity in Latin America.

9. *María* (1867) is the classic novel by Jorge Isaacs. It is the most widely read, pirated, and imitated novel of nineteenth-century Latin America. Required reading in Colombian high schools, it is also on standard syllabi in many other countries.

10. José Martí, *Obras completas* (Havana: Editorial de Ciencias Sociales, 1963–65), pp. 205–206. Quoted in, and translated by, José David Saldívar, *The Dialectics of Our America: Genealogy, Cultural Critique, and Literary History* (Durham: Duke University Press, 1991), 9.

11. Waldo Frank titled his book about the entire hemisphere *Our America* (New York: Boni and Liveright, 1919). Translated in references as *Nuestra América*, it was, for example, an inspiration and model for José Carlos Mariátegui, the major theorist of a particularized, Peruvian marxism. "En Waldo Frank, como en todo gran intérprete de la historia, la intuición y el metodo colaboran…. Unamuno modificaría probablemente su juicio sobre el marxismo si estudiase el espíritu—no la letra—marxista en escritores como el autor de *Nuestra América*…. Diré de que modo Waldo Frank es para mí un hermano mayor." *El Alma matinal y otras estaciones del hombre de hoy* (Lima: Amauta, 1972), 197,

192. Mariátegui's piece is from 1929.

12. In "Do 'Latinos' Exist?" in *Contemporary Sociology* 23:3 (May 1994): 354–56, Jorge I. Domínguez reports this observation from two books under review: Rodolfo O. de la Garza, et al., *Latino Voices: Mexican, Puerto Rican, and Cuban Perspectives on American Politics* (Boulder, CO: Westview Press, 1992); and Rodney E. Hero, *Latinos and the U.S. Political System: Two-Tiered Pluralism* (Philadelphia: Temple University Press, 1992). "Very large majorities of Mexicans, Puerto Ricans, and Cubans identify themselves by their national origins, not as 'Latinos' or Hispanics." Domínguez, 354.

13. Luis Rafael Sánchez, "La Guagua Aérea: The Air Bus," translated by Diana Vélez in *The Village Voice*, January 24, 1984.

14. Tato Laviera, *Amerícan* (Houston: Arte Público Press, 1985).

15. José de Diego, "No," in Iris Zavala and Rafael Rodríguez, *Intellectual Roots of Independence* (New York and London: Monthly Review Press, 1980), 131–33; 131.

16. de Diego, 131–33.

17. Antonio S. Pedreira, *Insularismo: Ensayos de interpretación puertorriqueña* (San Juan: Biblioteca de Autores Puertorriqueños, 1942, originally 1936).

18. *Puerto Rico Cinco siglos de historia*, 644. "Muñoz Rivera, el más moderado de los líderes unionistas, convenció a sus correligionarios de que no abandonaran la autonomía. Gracias a su intervención, el Partido aceptó dicha fórmula como medida detransición hacia la independencia.

El principal partido puertorriqueño había dado de pronto con esta acción un giro hacia al izquierda. El resultado inmediato fue la división de las filas unionistas entre *nuñocistas* y *dieguistas*. Muñoz Rivera seguía favoreciendo la reforma del régimen colonial, con o sin ciudadanía norteamericana…. Él líder siempre gragmatico combatía, por lo tanto, la resistencia a la ciudadanía estadounidense procedente del ala independentista del Partido diriida por de Diego."

19. Rubén Ríos Avila, "La Raza Cómica: identidad y cuerpo en Pedreira y Palés," in *La Torre*, núm. 27–28 (julio–diciembre 1993), 559–76.

20. I am, or course, referring to Américo Paredes and his classic book *With His Pistol in His Hand: A Border Ballad and Its Hero* (Austin: University of Texas Press, 1958).

21. The most obvious reference here is to Domingo Faustino Sarmiento, *Facundo: Civilización y barbarie*, first published in 1845 and subsequently a standard work for the continent.

22. The slogan comes from Jaun Bautista Alberdi's *Bases*, 1851, the basis for Argentina's post–civil war constitution and an inspiration for many other legislators throughout Spanish America.

23. Garcilaso de la Vega, El Inca, *Royal Commentaries of the Incas and General History of Peru*, trans. Harold V. Livermore, foreword by Arnold J. Toynbee

(Austin: Texas University Press, 3d paperback printing 1994, originally 1609 and 1616), pp. 216–17.

It remains to say something of the public women, which the Incas permitted to avoid worse consequences. They lived in the fields, in poor cabins, each by herself and not together. They were forbidden to enter the towns lest they communicate with other women. They were called *pampairuna*, a word that indicates their dwelling-place and trade, composed of *pampa*, "open place" or "field" (it has both meanings), and *runa*, which in the singular means "person" (man or woman) and in the plural means "people." Putting the two words together, if the sense of "open field" is taken, *pampairuna* means "people who live in the field, because of their wretched trade"; if the sense of "marketplace" is taken, it means "a person or woman of the marketplace," implying that as the place is public and receives all those who go to it, so do they. In short, it means "public woman."

9

Are We Post-American Studies?

Lawrence Buell

The one-word answer to the question posed by the title would have to be "no." As one fellow Americanist has written, "Cancellation-by-prefix more often than not preserves as connection what it pretends to erase as sign."[1] I doubt that we shall ever truly become post-American studies, however earnest our resolves, until or unless the United States ceases to be a unit of jurisdictional and curricular organization, and neither is likely to happen soon. But this much at least is certain: what for the last half-century or more has called itself American studies surely *will* change and indeed is changing fast.

The challenge for us who work in this area is to define what will follow the current age of revisionist awakening. That's more or less where we have been since circa 1970, when the first and perhaps the only "school" ever to dominate American studies—the so-called myth-symbol approach—began to come under serious attack both methodologically (for liberties taken in selection and interpretation of historical evidence) and theoretically (for its consensus approach to American history, its tendency to posit *a* "mainstream" of American thought). Academic research then began to assimilate what had been overlooked by the classic consensus narratives of American culture's internal teleology generated during the previous several decades. They were too male, too high-canonical, Eurocentric, exceptionalist, perhaps even imperialist in their framing of American culture. Or so that earlier dispensation today increasingly called "Cold War criticism" has come to seem.[2] Never mind that the contemporary critique, in order to make its own countercase, is bound to oversimplify the internal complexity and intellectual range of that formative epoch of American studies. It is incontestible that around 1970, just as the coordinates of American culture seemed mapped, the project started to come undone, never to be reassembled as it was before the rise of feminist and African-American revisionism. "Conflict" or "dissensus" replaced consensus as the preferred metaphors.

Even after a quarter-century, Americanists are still processing the results, because the various revisions in American culture studies have not come all at once but in waves, and because they have come symbiotically with such developments as the increasing percentage of important contemporary writing in the United States produced by non-WASPS, and the movement within academic theory to question whether literary texts should remain the main objects of literary study. A quarter-century of ferment and fission has left practitioners of American studies feeling that the field needs remapping but that their basic cartographical instruments will no longer serve the purpose. In particular, the most fundamental category, "American," seems more problematic than ever before. Not only must our research and teaching reflect the awareness that "America" is pluriform, not monolithic; it must be equally attentive to the parochialism of American studies' traditional equation of "America" with "United States." If we continue to disregard that our two master terms—the cultural entity and the political unit—are not the synonyms that American studies (as practiced in the United States, anyhow) has traditionally taken them to be, we risk lapsing into what increasingly looks like an uncritical nationalism, or at least being thought to have so lapsed.[3] For most Americanists in the United States, this contemporary problematization of "America" requires a conceptual shift as fundamentally significant as feminist theory's critique of the generic male pronoun a generation ago.

How must we then reconceive American studies, given the directions that history, literature, and academic discourse are taking? In particular, how should we reconceive American studies in the light of the hemispheric and indeed global character of "America," taking into account its full range of origins, interdependencies, and effects?

1. Our theories about American culture must adjust themselves to a theory of nationhood something like this: that nations are utopian social fictions[4] that are at once epistemologically suspect, economically obsolete, politically potent (since world order continues to recognize the sovereign nation as primary unit), territorially determinate (except in wartime), and culturally porous. In short, nation and culture aren't coextensive, but neither are they disjunct.

2. Given that national interdependence is increasing in the main if not uniformly, American studies will preoccupy itself increasingly with boundary-crossing phenomena of all sorts, such as: (a) diaspora studies that trace patterns of "dissemi-nation" (as Homi Bhabha wittily calls it);[5] (b) so-called border studies that reimagine the culture (or cultures) of the United States as hemispherically interlinked;[6] and (c) the placement of the United States within (trans)hemispheric circulation of cultural formations, whether generated from within the United States or circulating through the United States from some external point of origin.[7] Henry Louis Gates, Jr., and Doris Sommer have done distinguished work in areas (a) and (b).[8] My own interest lies especially in area (c): for example, in how "(post)colonial" formations like pastoral nationalism have influenced cultural self-definition in the United States.[9]

3. I have already suggested that the focus on national borders and border erasure follows logically from the multiculturalist thrust that was in good part responsible for the displacement of the older-style consensualism of the classic myth-symbol school. African diaspora studies, Asian-American studies, and especially Latino studies have been the bridge. This refocus will quicken the shift we are already seeing away from now-familiar debates about national identity vs. cultural particularism, toward the issue of whether a model of cultural identity at any level can hold its ground against a model of cultural hybridization or syncretism. If the increasingly complicated ethnic composition of the student body at major universities today is a fair litmus test, the answer is certainly no.

4. Insofar as self-identified American Studies projects continue to center on the United States (and most undertaken within this country probably will), practitioners must guard against reinstating versions of older-style totalization. New historicist analysis of American ideological formations, like much recent work on the culture of United States imperialism, too easily rigidifies into the mirror of the consensualism it rejects. Indeed, Americanists (i.e., United States-ists) of all persuasions—I certainly plead guilty to this myself—seem chronically tempted to define the meaning of America, which always gets us in hot water. In this we repeat ancient traditions of Americanist discourse, such as essentialism, didac-

ticism, and utopianism—ringing moralistic *procunciamentos* whose cogency depends more on rhetorical will than on evidentiary base to call what we described into being. (The foregoing sentence, of course, demonstrates my own irretrievable colonization by that genre.)

5. Though contemporary transnationalism and cultural theory require us to forgo older myths of national distinctiveness and question the solidity of nation as category, that does not bar us from adopting motifs distinctive to United States history as central reference points. On the contrary, it might be a healthy thing if the American studies faculties of every university where such programs exist held periodic retreats at which they collectively drew up and pondered lists of historical/cultural traits that are arguably distinctive to the United States: the percentage of residents who claim they believe in God and hell, the institution of the liberal arts college, the United States's status as the first modern ex-colony to win independence, the hyperspecificity of its race law (in certain states, particularly), the national homicide rate compared to the rates of other industrialized nations, the percentage of autobiographical writing in both the traditional *and* the expanded literary canons, or the size of this country's land mass that lies within the temperate zone. On the basis of such empirically specifiable traits as these, perhaps we might be able to arrive at a more faithful set of generalizations about the culture of the United States than have been formulated. In short, I still see a place for projects like the quite good 1990 multidisciplinary Oxford conference published under the title of *Is America Different?: A New Look at American Exceptionalism*. Provided, that is, that the section of libraries devoted to Americanist symposia with interrogative titles also includes such works as *Do the Americas Have a Common Literature?*—an equally meritorious compendium of contrary thrust, emphasizing intrahemispheric circulation rather than national distinctiveness.[10]

6. Americanists whose field is *literature* may stand especially to benefit from my hypothetical motif inventory, for two reasons. One is literary study's skittishness about empirical procedure. At the fall 1994 meeting of the *PMLA* Editorial Board, I was struck (though not surprised) to find that the call for papers for a special issue on the use of evidence in literary studies had been unusually slow in generating contributions that were even close to passing muster. From conversations since, and such desultory reading on the subject as I have managed, I am convinced that the editors of *Questions of Evidence*, a compendium of *Critical Inquiry* sympsosia, are quite right—at least with respect to literary studies—in asserting that "it is extraordinary how little direct attention [the topic of evidence] has received."[11] To the extent this bespeaks tribal disinterest

in empiricism as a dimension and calibrator of theory, studies of the literary history of the United States need to take on more ballast. This need is especially compelling in light of a second consideration: that the argument for literary distinctiveness on the basis of language is largely denied us, since U. S. literature is so overwhelmingly Anglophone— albeit vernacularized here and there.

The case for American literature's autonomy has therefore always rested much more on claims about subject matter than about aesthetic form: on broad sociohistorical claims about the impact on the creative imagination of the ideology of individualism, the frontier experience, etc. The more decentered so-called American literary studies becomes, the more suspect the category of nation as a putative cultural unit, and the more likely United States literature specialists may be to oscillate between clinging to discredited assumptions about national distinctiveness vs. throwing ourselves wholly, *amor fati*-like, on the pyre of postnationalism (in a kind of subdisciplinary suttee). Whereas if we're truly rigorous in trying to get to whatever empirical bedrock underlies those assumptions while at the same time remaining attentive to the distinction between culture and nation (and with this the promise of border, diaspora, and global culture studies), then we will be faithful to our posts as post-American Americanists, whatever the outcome of the culture wars.

NOTES

1. Carolyn Porter, "What We Know That We Don't Know: Remapping American Literary Studies," *American Literary History*, 6 (1994): 476–77.
2. Americanist Cold War criticism was first significantly characterized as such in several of the contributions to Walter Benn Michaels and Donald E. Pease, eds., *The American Renaissance Reconsidered* (Baltimore: Johns Hopkins University Press, 1985), particularly Pease's essay, "*Moby-Dick* and the Cold War," as well as Jonathan Arac, "F. O. Matthiessen: Authorizing the American Renaissance." Matthiessen and Perry Miller, the most seminal figures in premodern American literary studies, have understandably been singled out for special scrutiny. On Miller, cf. Amy Kaplan's reading of him as an intellectual Cold Warrior in "'Left Alone with America': The Absence of Empire in the Study of American Culture," *Cultures of United States Imperialism*, ed. Amy Kaplan and Donald E. Pease (Durham: Duke University Press, 1993), pp. 3–11. For a good diagnosis of what is at stake in Cold War criticism diagnostics, see David Suchoff, "New Historicism and Containment: Toward a Post–Cold War Cultural Theory," *Arizona Quarterly*, 48 (1992): 137–61.
3. Hence, for example, Sacvan Bercovitch's introduction to *The Cambridge*

History of American Literature (New York: Cambridge University Press, 1994) is careful to emphasize the contributors' engagement with "nationality as a problem" and their awareness that "'America' in these volumes designates [geographically] the United States, or the territories that were to become part of the United States." "America" from this standpoint conceptually refers to "a declaration of community, a people constituted and sustained by verbal fiat," and hence "a semiotics of exclusion, closing out not only the Old World but all other countries of the Americas" (1: 3).

4. Benedict Anderson, *Imagined Communities* (London: Verso, 1983), is the seminal text from which recent, more nuanced discussions of nation as fiction have sprung.

5. Homi Bhabha, "DissemiNation: Time, Narrative, and the Margins of the Modern Nation," in Bhabha, ed., *Nation and Narration* (London: Routledge, 1990), pp. 291–322. Several other essays in this post-Anderson collection are also exemplary. See also the journals *Diaspora*, *Callalloo*, and *Transition*.

6. In the field of history, for example, see for example Ramón Gutierrez's study of Pueblo-Hispanic (and eventually also Anglo) contact in New Mexico, *When Jesus Came, The Corn Mothers Went Away: Marriage, Sexuality, and Power in New Mexico, 1500–1846* (Stanford, CA: Stanford University Press, 1990); and David J. Weber, *The Spanish Frontier in North America* (New Haven: Yale University Press, 1992). In literary studies, see for example José David Saldivar, *The Dialectics of Our America: Genealogy, Cultural Critique, and Literary History* (Durham and London: Duke University Press, 1991), which experimentally remaps North American literary culture with Havana as its center.

7. The variety of conceptual frameworks is rich. For example, Kaplan and Pease (note 2 above) operates from a U.S. hegemony approach; Frederick Buell, *National Culture and the New Global System* (Baltimore: Johns Hopkins University Press, 1994), operates from a more decentered global culture approach; Jean-Philippe Mathy, *Extrême-Occident: French Intellectuals and America* (Chicago: University of Chicago Press, 1993), updates a more traditional "European Invention of America" approach; Richard Slatta, *Cowboys of the Americas* (New Haven: Yale University Press, 1990), takes an intrahemispheric/comparatist approach.

8. I especially have in mind Gates, *The Signifying Monkey* (New York: Oxford University Press, 1988); and Sommer, *The Foundational Fictions of Latin America* (Berkeley: University of California Press, 1991).

9. Cf. "New World Dreams and Environmental Actualities," *The Environmental Imagination: Thoreau, Nature Writing, and the Formation of American Culture* (Cambridge: Harvard University Press, 1995), pp. 53–82, which discusses forms of pastoralism in (Anglophone) settler culture and indigenous culture (e.g., Négritude). See also Renata Wasserman, *Exotic Nations: Literature*

and Cultural Identity in United States and Brazil, 1830–1930 (Ithaca: Cornell University Press, 1994), an extended triangulation of the history of "edenic" thinking in Europe and two "new world" (post)colonies.

10. Byron E. Shafer, ed., *Is America Different?: A New Look at American Exceptionalism* (Oxford: Oxford University Press, 1991); Gustavo Pérez-Firmat, ed., *Do the Americas Have a Common Literature?* (Durham: Duke University Press, 1990).

11. James Chandler, Arnold I. Davidson, and Harry Horootunian, "Introduction," *Questions of Evidence: Proof, Practice, and Persuasion across the Disciplines* (Chicago: University of Chicago Press, 1994), p. 1.

PART THREE

National Literatures in a Global World?

10

Don Quixote and the National Citizenship of Masterpieces

Mary Malcolm Gaylord

In the year 1615, a European writer sends the second half of his major work to his patron, prefaced with a dedicatory letter in which he reports that the already published first half has proven so universally popular that the author has received an invitation from no less a personage than the Emperor of China, begging him to send his book right away. According to his emissary, the great ruler means to found a college where the author's native language will be taught using the best-selling novel as primer and principal textbook, with the author himself as rector of the college. Unfortunately for the chosen candidate, the emperor's enthusiasm for founding academic centers and the talent-scouting of his headhunters have gotten ahead of their fund-raising efforts. When the rector-designate asks whether the flattering offer includes travel expenses, it turns out that such practical details have not crossed his would-be employer's mind. At this point the dream-bubble bursts, the prestigious appointment evaporates, and the whole affair is unmasked as a pretext for offering thanks to a longstanding patron for commute-free employment at home.

The episode acts out the dream of every writer, perhaps of every literary academic. It reads like a David-Lodgean fable of continent-hopping, fame-seeking, field-founding, with a bit of pedagogical activity thrown in on the side. And, of course, it *is* a writer's dream, the fictionalized dream of a real writer, in whom you may already have recognized Miguel de Cervantes Saavedra. If *Don Quixote*'s creator was letting his fantasies get ahead of the book's actual circulation, subsequent centuries of international literary history have made him a prophet. Even in 1615, the tale was not all fantasy: it takes off from the historical realities of the publication of Part One of Don *Quixote*, with instant success inside and outside of Spain, multiple reprintings and translations into a host of other tongues—of which the official censor takes note in his approbation of Part Two, and of which the Don himself will learn in its opening chapters.

Still, the passage is uncanny for its sheer prescience. After all, *Don Quixote*'s author *is* in fact revered today, almost four hundred years later, as the greatest writer of the Spanish language and its transforming architect (in one of the most brilliant instances of adaptive reuse that literary construction has even seen), as creator of national icons and universally symbolic characters, as founder of the modern novel, as a super-writer read in schools and universities everywhere in dozens of languages.

Was Cervantes psychic? Did he have what his Mad Knight longed for— the long view back from the future to a present desired as always already past? Probably not. It seems much more likely to me that the author is here ironically associating his own hopes for Fame with Don Quixote's. Cervantes's dream of being rescued from poverty and old age (in 1615 he would have been sixty-eight) to carry the Castilian tongue around the globe as its chief defender and practitioner might have been drawn from the fictional stores of his famous protagonist. It replicates—in the arena of cultural embassy and foreign-language pedagogy—the Ingenious Gentleman's vision of himself as a knight-errant called to the service of his monarch, as universal savior of the oppressed, as pre-scriber of his own life and pre-scripter of his own Fame. The author's script for himself echoes the proclamation of the humanist grammarian, Antonio de Nebrija, in 1492, that Language had ever been and would ever be the handmaiden of Empire, a retrospective prophesy that he placed at the service of the messianic projects of the Catholic kings, Isabel and Fernando. The scripts of both the novelist and his character act out the fantasies of Spanish churchmen and conquistadors, one of whose obscure objects of desire was the legendary kingdom of the Great Khan, from whom Marco Polo had earlier taken a similar invitation to European teachers to bring Christian learning to his court.

None of these scripts was unrelated to the realities of their day: their apparently fanciful particulars take aim as much at the vainglory of Castilian cultural imperialism as at either the author or his fictional protagonist. What is striking for my purpose here is that when Cervantes writes the great novel of origins, he wraps it up in an exquisitely ironic fable of *destinies*—his character's, his book's, his own, that of his language and his culture's imperial expansion. When he does this, he thinks his writing simultaneously from the outside in and from the inside out, gathering up a fictionalized past and projecting it fictionally into the future, imagining his book already as the national and universal icon it has become. This prophetic, self-monumentalizing gesture makes *Don Quixote* an ideal text to plunge us headlong, *in medias res*, into the question of the national citizenship of literary masterpieces and their "proper" place in humanities curricula of our time.

To whom does a masterpiece belong? To the national language and culture that produces it? To the local literary tradition that culminates in its appearance? Or to subsequent currents that flow from its founding force? Is it the property of its author's fellow (cultivated) native speakers, whose linguistic and literary tools enable them to appreciate its contribution to their shared literary language? Is it the domain of fellow citizens of the historical world fictionally represented in it, who can reap the greatest harvest of meaning from its referential gestures, or whose past and future seem symbolically to be at stake in the book's message? Or since masterpieces by definition stretch beyond the particulars of their own plots, referential orbits, and original languages, toward Aristotelian universal truths, are they not more freely and more fully appreciated from somewhere outside the historical and linguistic boundaries of a particular time and place? And who was Cervantes writing for, anyway? Who were his ideal readers, and what did he want to say to them? Does it matter four hundred years after the fact? Do the answers to these questions have anything to teach us? Do they particularly have anything to teach us about the *ways we teach*, and about the way we organize the study of literature?

In Spanish, master*piece* becomes master*work (obra maestra)*. Castilian preserves the etymological force of the term of "mastery," from the Latin *magister/magistra*, meaning "teacher." In Cervantes' anecdote, alongside a bit of well-deserved self-congratulation, lies an intuition about the teaching role of the masterwork, about the exemplary force of both its vision and its concrete textuality. Masterpieces such as *Don Quixote* are, in fact, taught everywhere. The greatest Spanish novel's presence in books, articles, and syllabi in Spanish seems natural enough, although I will be arguing that even that assumed "naturalness" deserves scrutiny. But more than one hefty chapter in a history of the text's migrations, translations, and expatriate residences could be filled with particulars of its extended sojourn in Western (i.e.,

European and postcolonial North and South American) scholarly agendas
and academic curricula. The Don's book has long since been "naturalized"
into the research and teaching agendas of non-Hispanophone professors of
English, of comparative literature, of literary theory. Indeed, in this country it is probably taught at least as often in English as in Spanish. In critical
and theoretical writing, "outsiders'" claims for the novel's importance have
been no less sweeping than those that might be advanced by the most patri-
otic Spaniard. Cervantes is widely credited with having, with this one bold
stroke, (1) laid the foundation and drawn the blueprint for modernity's preferred literary form, the novel; (2) hit upon an infinitely generative formula
for the fictional representation of reality; (3) made major contributions to
the fictional exploitation of pseudo-documentary, dialogue, the language of
gesture, authorial irony, self-reflexivity; and (4) created in the figure of the
mad knight one of Western literature's greatest symbolic characters, who has
been seen to incarnate—fictionally—everything from the *volksgeist* of
Spanish culture to a panoply of intellectual and spiritual enterprises, including perfect Christian chivalry, Renaissance Utopianism, and the Romantic
quest for ideal virtue and beauty.[1] In the late twentieth century, symbolic
appropriations of *Don Quixote* have culminated with the transformation of
book and character into eloquent figures of no less riveting a concern than
the work of verbal signification and of written representation. Implicit in
these uses of the classic is homage to the sheer power of Cervantes' construct, which is seen as transcending the particulars of history, nation, and
culture, and as lending its generative energy not only to the making of meaning but to illuminating how we make words mean.[2]

Is there anything wrong with this? Isn't it a measure of Cervantes' dream
fulfilled? Shouldn't Spaniards and readers of Spanish rejoice at his success,
even if they don't agree with particular appropriations? More to the point, do
Hispanophone scholars and teachers of literature do better by their Number
One classic writer? Clearly, they do differently by him. The massive corpus of
studies written in Spanish, or in other languages by readers of Spanish, offers
access to the miraculous fecundity and subtlety of Cervantes' own Castilian.[3]
They reveal his rich literary culture in Spanish, Italian, Portuguese, the classics;
his knowledge of lesser genres, of nonliterary texts; his immersion in the concrete literary-theoretical problematics of the turn of the seventeenth century.
They bring to light his close attention and sometimes slippery responses to
the burning political and ideological questions of his day; to his full engagement with the social, economic, and military histories of the Spain of Philips
II and III. The fact that much of this important work, written in Spanish and
by students of Spanish literature, has not always succeeded in transcending
its linguistic and disciplinary borders represents a great loss for scholars out-

side academic Hispanism. But it has to be acknowledged that the *Cervantismo* of Hispanists "on the inside" has not altered the thrust of universalizing readings from "the outside" as often as we might like.

Could either group be doing something different, even something better, that might bring the generalists' and the Hispanists' readings together? Keepers of foreign languages often claim that they are the ones who hold the surest key to competent reading, and that others should work to obtain it. (I could recommend Harvard's Spanish A, or Ax for those who aim at reading knowledge.) But I think it is worth asking at least whether we might not change something about the way we do our pedagogical business in literature courses, something that might bring the inside and the outside of reading *Don Quixote* closer, something that might help us get at why Cervantes so confidently imagined his novel being read both at home and in far-flung continents and cultures.

As a member of the Spanish section of a Romance languages and literatures department, I am mindful of how often we bring disciplines together, only to separate them internally. This happens not only for the modern children of Vulgar Latin, but for areas within each of what were once the "national" languages: French and Francophone, Portuguese and Brazilian, Spanish Peninsular and Latin American. Our official faculty "slots" are heavily marked by geography, our graduate fields and exams are separated by continents and "worlds," and most of our courses follow suit, as do the divisions of the Modern Language Association and other organizations. This is in no way to deny that many individuals work to transcend those divisions. But in the postcolonial world, with formerly imperial parent countries held in disfavor by intellectuals and bodies politic, such efforts struggle against powerful currents. As a sixteenth- and seventeenth-century scholar, I am keenly aware of the Atlantic chasm that has kept academically separated the two spheres of Hispanic writing in the early modern period. We have been accustomed to calling these two spheres "Golden Age literature" on the one side, and "Latin American colonial literature" on the other. With respect to the sixteenth century and the early part of the seventeenth especially, a *de facto* division of labor has kept the two fields apart: to the Golden Age is assigned literature, poetry and poetics, art for art's sake, fiction about fiction; to the colonialists goes history.

What does this have to do with the way we read Cervantes' greatest novel? I believe that the Atlantic divide has encouraged many readers (both insiders and outsiders) to assume that *Don Quixote* is principally a fiction about the making of fictions, and to look for its intertextuality in relation to other European works of imaginative literature. Moreover, since the majority of its references to concrete places, events, persons, and books that lie beyond its fiction point to Spanish, European, Mediterranean contexts, it has been taken for granted that the *Quixote* is an Old World book. It even seems quintessentially so: neither the knight nor his author ever crossed the Ocean Sea; they only dreamed of conquering islands or holding bureaucratic posts in the Indies.[4] As a result, a major repertory of texts that is gaining currency outside of Spanish-speaking circles in the wake of the Quincentenary, the "chronicles" of the American experience, have most often been studied in courses and frames separate from the life of the Ingenious Hidalgo. Having only recently been granted provisional status as literary texts, as distinct from documents, they have been read with a different set of questions and criteria. Written by navigators, soldiers, priests, and official historians, the chronicles are still framed as history. Even when they are judged unreliable or admired as narrative construction, their authors' representational energies are assumed to have been expended on something real—and something American. Consequently, they offer a mirror image of *Don Quixote*, an Old World book, whose historiographic tropes are no more than pseudo-history, whose engagement with serious history is assumed to be a joke.[5]

An unscheduled experience of filling a gap in the colonial curriculum gave me an idea of what we might be missing by keeping the two apart. Teaching simultaneously separate semester courses on the New World chronicles and *Don Quixote*, I found myself reading, as it were, two sides of the same page. What I confronted were writers of history, on the one hand, and a writer of prose fiction on the other, all wrestling with the same demons: the same chivalric and epic models, the same rhetoric of historical authority, the same paradoxes of representation. Although Cervantes' text makes direct mention of America only rarely (some dozen times), the novel shares a truly staggering number of its themes with the Conquest literature: exploration, discovery, naming and mapping, styles of combat, rituals of honor, just war, good government (especially of islands), epistolary diplomacy and notarial bureaucracy, acquisition of wealth and titles, religious conversion, slavery, the rebelliousness of native vassals, barbarity, wilderness, multilingualism, the search for new spaces of personal freedom, visions of Utopia, truth in telling, the writing and uses of history—even the appearance in battle of Santiago the Moorslayer! It is not necessary to document actual textual influences in order to establish that these subjects, literally and insistently foregrounded in the chronicles, would necessarily have had a powerful New World resonance in Cervantes' day. They *cannot not* have put his readers in mind of the Hispanic experience in the Western hemisphere, as reported by chroniclers and historians, in letters from American relatives, or by *indianos*, who were not Native Americans but returning Spanish émigrés who often brought wealth and who always brought stories—true and false.

Although he mentions conquistador authors only twice—Alonso de Ercilla, author of the Araucanaid (I.6), and Hernán Cortés (II.8)—Cervantes evidently had America on his mind and would have been a keen observer of the fallout in Spain of the question of the Indies. And he was clearly steeped in the lore that went into the *Books of the Brave*, as Irving Leonard so aptly termed them; so steeped that he knew that imitating Amadis of Gaul was a national pastime and a program for empire. At least one official chronicler of the Indies, Gonzalo Fernández de Oviedo, and perhaps even the Emperor Charles V, wrote romances of chivalry, the former while in America and the latter while planning real-life war games. I believe it can be demonstrated that Cervantes was familiar with a significant amount of the chronicle literature and with the issues of the New World polemic, to the point of being able, in the *Quixote*, to critique in very concrete detail the discursive practices of Spain's transatlantic empire, putting the very words of conquistadors and chroniclers in his characters' mouths.[6] But you don't have to accept all of that in order to concede that, after hearing its New World resonances, we cannot quite so comfortably talk about *Don Quixote* as an Old World book about Old World books.

Are there significant ways in which this contextualization might alter the most generative of the "outsider" readings? I am convinced that there are. Several possibilities suggest themselves to me:

- that Bakhtin's location of *heteroglossia* in Cervantes' masterpiece has to do not only with books but with the mixing of languages in the world;
- that Harry Levin's quixotic principle of "Art embarrassed by Nature" and Robert Alter's perception of a new "world of mirrors" in the first modern novel will take on bolder relief in a two-world backdrop;
- that Austin's infelicities illuminate communicative isolation not only within speech communities but between them;
- that Cervantes' understanding of mimetic desire (as described by René Girard) had as much to do with the political world of his time as with the delusions of one reading fool;
- that even Foucault's brilliant intuition, that *Don Quixote* stands as the major literary marker of a brave new world of representation, can be historicized through a fuller understanding of the work's intertextual reach; and finally
- that the Western search for new understanding of the workings of fictional representation is absolutely bound up with the dramas of New World historiography, which faced every day the problem of how to make "things never before heard or seen" real to the European imagination.

What does this mean for teachers of the humanities in an American university? For those who teach Spanish texts, this perspective on *Don Quixote* suggests that we are certain to gain greater access to all of the works we study by restoring to our curricula the unity of the early modern Hispanic speech community. As a more general principle, I submit that, like Cervantes, we need to keep thinking about our work simultaneously from the inside out and from the outside in, whether our inside is Golden Age studies, Latin American colonial literature, Hispanism as a whole, comparative literature, literature, or history.[7] *Don Quixote's* author would doubtless smile to see his book-child thus (re)nominated as cultural ambassador within our Small World.

NOTES

1. Among the important "outsider" readers of Cervantes in this century are Eric Auerbach, *Mimesis: The Representation of Reality in Western Literature*, trans. Willard Trask (Princeton: Princeton University Press, 1953); Robert Alter, *Partial Magic: The Novel as a Self-Conscious Genre* (Berkeley: University of California Press, 1975); Harry Levin, "The Quixotic Principle: Cervantes and Other Novelists," in *The Interpretation of Narrative*, ed. Morton W. Bloomfield (Cambridge, Mass.: Harvard University Press, 1970), pp. 45-66; Ian Watt, *The Rise of the Novel* (Berkeley: University of California Press, 1957); Mikhail Bakhtin, *The Dialogic Imagination*, trans. Caryl Emerson and Michael Holquist (Austin: University of Texas Press, 1981); René Girard, *Mensonge romantique et vérité romanesque* (Paris, 1961); Michel Foucault, *Les mots et les choses* (Paris: Editions Gallimard, 1966); Gyorgy Lukács, *The Theory of the Novel*, trans. Anna Bostock (Cambridge, Mass.: MIT Press, 1971). For a polemic history of symbolic appropriations of the novel before the twentieth century, and especially the German Romantics, see Anthony Close's *The Romantic Approach to Don Quixote* (Cambridge: Cambridge University Press, 1978).

2. Here, of course, I am thinking of Mikhail Bakhtin's use of Cervantes' novel as an emblem of novelistic *heteroglossia*, and especially of Michel Foucault's appropriation of Don Quixote as a theoretical icon of Representation. J. L. Austin also invokes Don Quixote as classic performer of infelicitous speech acts in *How To Do Things with Words* (Cambridge, Mass.: Harvard University Press, 1962).

3. Among the major Hispanist readers of *Don Quixote* are John Jay Allen, *Don Quixote: Hero or Fool?* 2 vols. (Gainesville: University of Florida Press, 1969-79); Américo Castro, *El pensamiento de Cervantes*, ed. Julio Rodríguez-Puértolas (Barcelona and Madrid: Noguer, 1972); Ruth El Saffar, *Distance and Control in "Don Quixote"* (Chapel Hill: University of North Carolina Studies

in Romance Languages and Literatures, 1975), and *Beyond Fiction: The Recovery of the Feminine in the Novels of Cervantes* (Berkeley: University of California Press, 1984); Stephen Gilman, *The Novel According to Cervantes* (Berkeley: University of California Press, 1989); Carroll Johnson, *Madness and Lust: A Psychoanalytical Approach to "Don Quixote"* (Berkeley: University of California Press, 1983); Francisco Márquez Villanueva, *Fuentes literarias cervantinas* (Madrid: Gredos, 1973), and *Personajes y temas del Quijote* (Madrid: Taurus, 1975); Maurice Molho, *Cervantes: raíces folklóricas* (Madrid: Gredos, 1976); Michel Moner, *Cervantès conteur* (Madrid: Casa de Velázquez, 1989); Luis A. Murillo, *The Golden Dial: Temporal Configurations in "Don Quixote"* (Cambridge: Dolphin Book Co., 1975); José Ortega y Gasset, *Meditaciones del Quijote* (Madrid, 1914), trans. as *Meditations on Quixote* by E. Rugg and Diego Marín (New York: W. W. Norton, 1961); E. C. Riley, *Cervantes's Theory of the Novel* (Cambridge: Cambridge University Press, 1961); Leo Spitzer, "On the Significance of *Don Quijote*," in *Cervantes: A Collection of Critical Essays*, ed. Lowry Nelson, Jr. (Englewood Cliffs, NJ, 1969); Edwin Williamson, *The Half-way House of Fiction. Cervantes and Arthurian Romance* (Oxford: Oxford University Press, 1984).

4. In a 1590 petition to Philip II, Cervantes tries to trade on his service at Lepanto and long Algerian captivity in order to garner a bureaucratic appointment in Guatemala or Mexico. See Luis Astrana Marín, *Vida heroica y ejemplar de Miguel de Cervantes Saavedra*, 7 vols. (Madrid: Instituto Editorial Reus, 1948-58); or the less unwieldy biography of Jean Canavaggio, *Cervantès* (Paris: Mazarine, 1986).

5. A very cogent and learned statement of this viewpoint is the classic article of Bruce W. Wardropper: "*Don Quixote*: Story or History?" in *Modern Philology* 63 (1965): 1–11.

6. Here I can only summarize one of the central theses of a book nearing completion, titled *Tropics of Conquest*, which looks at indirect reflections of the American experience in sixteenth- and seventeenth-century Spanish language and literature.

7. See Judith Ryan's wonderfully witty piece, "Skinside Inside: The National Literature Major versus Comparative Literature," in *Profession* 91: 49–52.

11

Russian Literature
Past, Present, Future

William Mills Todd III

Russian literary scholarship, a relative newcomer in the American university, has developed somewhat apart from other national literary fields. There are a number of explanations for this differential development, some of them related to the special status of literature in Russian culture, some of them concerned with great power relations that have little to do with literature at all. The striking and irreversible changes in Russian political and literary life over the past decade and the entry of Russia into the "global" postmodern world it had in many ways avoided invite, indeed compel, students of Russian literature to consider a series of new topics as the culture they have studied changes before their eyes.

Russian literature has figured in the curricula of many departments in American universities, including English, history, government, comparative literature, and, quite recently, women's studies. Since the 1950s it has increasingly come to be housed in departments of Slavic languages and literatures. Like other areas of the humanities that came to prominence as academic disciplines during the age of Romantic nationalism, Slavic philology set itself the goal of preserving and studying the language and cultural monuments of a set of peoples whose modern languages were thought to share a common origin. In the case of the Slavic peoples, who found themselves under the political domination of three multinational empires (Austro-Hungarian, Ottoman, and Russian), this philological mission encompassed not merely the preservation of written documents but sometimes the creation of them, as not all of the Slavic peoples had well-developed or longstanding written literary traditions.[1] Slavic philology found itself the willing servant of politics, then, in ways not unakin to those that animate the ethnic studies programs in modern American universities, and the prominent place of notable early Slavists in movements of national and Pan-Slavic self-determination testifies to the young field's vital cultural force. By the early twentieth century this had gained academic expression in the products of a normal discipline: serious scholarly monographs, bibliographical and publishing ventures, and university departments throughout Europe. The threefold mission to preserve, create, and study the documents of ethnic or national identity in turn found its place in American universities, although the third aspect has predominated. Nevertheless, the expansion of the Soviet empire into the former territories of the Austro-Hungarian and Ottoman empires lent a new urgency to the first and second aspects, preservation and creation, during the post-1945 period.

The orderly narrative of the migration of scholarship to the new world glides over a number of rough spots, among them the relationship of Russian studies to the study of other Slavic languages and the relationship of literary history to linguistics, as both literary study and linguistics moved in directions unforeseen by founders of the field. Meanwhile, the expansion of Slavic studies during the 1950s took place in an atmosphere of Cold War urgency that helped keep the young field somehow intellectually "out of phase" with its neighboring humanities departments. As other fields, especially English, were exploring the New Criticism and archetypal criticism, for example, Russianists were seriously examining the interaction of literature and politics in Russian culture, which, aside from isolated groups, had rarely entertained notions of the autonomy of the literary process. Later, as our colleagues in other fields discovered deconstruction and the decentering of the subject, Russianists, who received much of their initiation into Russian literature on exchanges in the Soviet Union, where they met and worked with both academic and dissident scholars, were joining with their Russian colleagues in constructing a highly centripetal model of Russian culture.

The outlines of this centripetal orientation are generally familiar to newspaper readers of the Cold War period: an autocratic or totalitarian government confronts the great writer who, in the words of one of Solzhenitsyn's fictional characters, constitutes a "second government," one lacking repressive state apparatuses, to be sure, but armed with moral force and "truth." The writer-witness—one recalls that "martyr" in Greek means witness—is persecuted by Tsarist or Soviet authorities, but the work lives on, and the writer enters the calendar of writer-saints celebrated by chroniclers as disparate as Pushkin, Herzen, and Roman Jakobson, Pushkin in his 1822 notes on Russian history, Herzen in his 1851 book on the development of revolutionary ideas in Russia, and Jakobson in his famous article "On a Generation that Squandered its Poets," first published in 1931. The writer works in harmony with a reading public of which the critic Belinsky began to dream in 1840: a public for whom literature would be "not relaxation from life's cares, not a sweet slumber in a soft armchair after a rich dinner…but a res publica, great and important, a source of lofty moral enjoyment."[2] Pioneering sociologists of literature, both pre- and postrevolutionary, both Russian and non-Russian, would slant their surveys to demonstrate the moral seriousness of the reading public, its demands for a literature purveying moral profundity and lessons for living. The Russian reader, unlike his or her Western equivalents, did not turn to "escapist" dross. The view of literature that accompanied this elevation of writer and public centered on great issues and central problems. Its canon, as Jeffrey Brooks has suggested, selected the great narratives and lyric poems of the nineteenth century, doing so in opposition both to a rising flood of popular fiction and to an elitist culture of high modernism.[3] The criticism that mediated between work and public also concentrated on current events and "burning questions," helping to constitute literary life as, in Habermas's terms, a "literary public sphere" in the midst of an autocratic state. Even the censors contributed to the centripetal nature of classical Russian literature, as their very presence strongly encouraged readers to translate the literary text into a veiled commentary on sociopolitical issues. The "surplus of the signifier," to resurrect a phrase from the 1970s, became negligible in the presence of such narrowly sociopolitical decoding.

The present reversal of forces in this variously centripetal institutionalization of literature at times defies belief for those who matured during the "epoch of stagnation." The wealth of new reading material on the tables outside a Moscow metro station offers a concise index of these changes in cultural life: native and translated detective fiction, first and foremost, and books on business management; multivolume editions of modernist poets of the early twentieth century, such as Mandelstam; classical philosophers, such as Vladimir Solov'ev; spiritual writing from the same period, Mme. Blavatsky, for instance; memoirs from the Stalinist period; pornography of breathtaking vulgarity; fiction by Nabokov and Solzhenitsyn, although overproduction has made them something of a drug on the market; dictionaries and grammars of English and German; historical romances; expensive art books for foreigners. The logic of this flea-market activity is, of course, the return of the repressed. Gogol once commented that "More events take place in Russia in ten years than occur in other states in half a century."[4] Here, on the booksellers' tables, we can see a similarly striking set of literary events as the Russian reader encounters nearly two centuries of suppressed culture—emigre, underground, prerevolutionary, Soviet. For anyone who can afford them, modernism, postmodernism, and mass culture swirl together with spiritual and practical guides, a heady mixture that only members of the cultural elite with Western friends could encounter before the advent of *perestroika*.

As heretofore dominant images in Russian culture fly apart centrifugally, and as Russia finds itself, willy-nilly, part of the "global world," research agenda spring to mind, projects for the future. All six projects that I will suggest can involve the multidisciplinary, comparative, and theoretical illuminations that a modern university has to offer, and I will list them in increasing order of remoteness from realization. Some of the projects will sound very familiar to scholars of other literatures, but I will try to avoid a "me too" mentality; because our colleagues in other literary disciplines are doing something is sufficient reason to be aware of it, not to pursue it. I must also add that in each case, the ground has begun to be broken, sometimes in American university research, sometimes in the former Soviet Union, sometimes before the fall of the Soviet Union or even before the coming of *perestroika*.

The first such project for the future would involve a series of detailed studies of the social construction of literary roles and discourses in Russian culture: it would study the centripetal model with particular attention to the roles of "author," "critic," "censor," and "reader." It would attempt to define the functions and aims of literature as these have been variously articulated during the postmedieval period, and in this regard it would find that institutionalization has produced strange bedfellows. As disparate as the fundamental cultural and political orientation of Lenin and Solzhenitsyn might be, such a project would discover a series of remarkable similarities between Solzhenitsyn's Nobel Prize acceptance speech (1972) and Lenin's famous essay on "Party Organization and Party Literature" (1905): contempt for entertainment literature, the use of "crisis" to legitimate controls on literature, distrust of individual experience, notions of the writer's social responsibility, rejection of any aesthetic of autonomous art.

A second general project for the future would address the literature that the centripetal narrative has excluded, namely popular literature, whether the proto-rapsters of the middle ages, the Skomorokhi; the chapbooks that constituted the bulk of Russian literature from the seventeenth century to 1917, when Lenin's new government closed down this trade; the penny dreadfuls and penny newspapers that became popular in the decades before the revolution; or the entertainment literature of the 1920s and 1990s. All of these eruptions, some of them precursors of our "global" mass culture, have called forth highly negative reactions, if not outright persecution—sometimes from the Russian Orthodox Church, sometimes from the state, and sometimes from the intelligentsia, whose centripetal vision of Russian literature these popular products seemed to threaten. Such investigations will investigate new media. Anyone familiar with contemporary Russian popular culture will be aware that the most captivating of these seems to be not our American *Santa Barbara*, but a Mexican soap opera, *Simply Maria*.[5] The provenance of these soaps suggests, in turn, a new comparative agenda: not only the traditional comparisons of Russian and Western European literatures, but now Russia and the United States, Russia and other countries undergoing cultural "globalization."

The third project for the future turns toward an area, that of private life and attendant topics involving sexuality and gender, which is almost terra incognita in Russian studies. The terms "privacy" and "private life" defy adequate translation into Russian, as Svetlana Boym has noted,[6] and topics that have obsessed scholars in other literary fields have barely begun to dent the Russian studies curriculum or research agenda. As literature's traditional role in constituting a public sphere in Russia yields much of its hegemony to television and the newspapers, and as elective politics assume a greater burden of the country's political energies, literature will likely focus more and more upon such domestic and intimate problems, as it has done in other modern cultures. The weakening of repressive state apparatuses in Russian life (the police, the censorship) will inevitably call increasing attention to forces that secure the replication of patterns of social domination, including ones of gender. The traditionally critical role of literature in Russian culture may find, and is finding, a large new arena in the intimate aspects of the private sphere.

A fourth project would address science and technology. Literary scholars can study in a serious way the relationships of literature and science during the past two centuries. In the nineteenth century most novels were published alongside scientific articles in the Russian journals. How did these discourses differ? How did they interact? How, in the Soviet period, did literary discourse address such problems as ecological disaster? How has imaginative literature helped produce the Russian sense of nature as, in large part, something to be tamed, a hostile, threatening, or indifferent force? How global in its orientation is the present ecological movement and how nationalistic?

A fifth project would involve cutting across the grain of a tendency that John Guillory has outlined in *Cultural Capital*, namely that processes of canon revision involve a shift in the syllabus from older works to modern ones.[7] The changes in Russian culture that we witness every day will, no doubt, bring a new set of works to the fore, many of them modern. Yet important questions remain to be asked of earlier periods of Russian literature, questions involving alternative forms of national identity, of literature's function, and of the possibility of subcultures. The present fragmentation and fragility of traditional cultural life invite us to find equivalent phenomena in the past. As we do so, we will discover entire critical traditions that have been neglected by both Soviet and Western scholarship: not so much conservative writers and thinkers (however we may define "conservative" in a Russian context), but ones in the middle, whose writing may have lacked the maximalist fire that carried the day in the nineteenth century and in most of the twentieth, but who constituted a sizable portion of the literary population as readers, writers, and critics. Not coincidentally, many of these literary people will turn out to be women. I suggest that we study the literature of neglected groups, including women, not because I am trying to impose American liberal pluralist politics on Russian culture, but because this fiction may show us that the centripetal version of Russian literary culture has obscured alternative thematics and ways of writing.

A final project would involve the role of the aesthetic in Russian culture. This is a phenomenon that I have not touched upon during the first parts of my paper, in large part because the images of Russian literature crafted by the nineteenth-century intelligentsia and by the Soviet educational system seem to have neglected it. The aesthetic is by its very nature notoriously difficult to define, and I will not do so here, except in a minimal way, as the sense of playfulness, experiment, artifice, and unpredictability that calls for correspondingly creative ideational activity on the part of readers. The aesthetic has been, in the centripetal vision of Russian culture, a minimal presence, often scorned or ignored. It has, in recent Russian literature and criticism, made something of a comeback, not only in the work of such older subversives as Abram Tertz, but also, prominently, in some of the best of contemporary writing. In an illuminating article on women's fiction, Helena Goscilo has demonstrated that the most striking examples of women's writing—by writers such as Tatiana Tolstoy or Ludmila Petrushevskaia—are those that have avoided direct political commentary, given free reign to unliterary obscenity, unstable focalization, multiple perspectives, and other subversions of literary tradition and the literary language.[8] It will be one of the ironies of an new literary history of Russia that the aesthetic, dismissed as reactionary or irrelevant by Russia's critical intelligentsia, should bear the burden of fostering a critical, illuminating vision of Russian society and culture. A heightened sense of the aesthetic, provoked by the advent of new literature and new media on the Russian cultural scene, might, in turn, be a positive consequence of Russia's recent participation in postmodern global culture.

NOTES

1. Alexander M. Schenker and Edward Stankiewicz, eds., *The Slavic Literary Languages: Formation and Development* (New Haven: Yale Russian and East European Publications, 1980).

2. V. G. Belinsky, "Russkaia literature v 1840 godu," *Sobranie sochinenii v deviati tomakh* (Moscow: "Khudozhestvennaia literature," 1976–82), 3: 195–98.

3. Jeffrey Brooks, "Russian Nationalism and Russian Literature: The Canonization of the Classics," in Ivo Banac, et al., eds., *Nation and Ideology: Essays in Honor of Wayne S. Vucinich* (Boulder, CO: East European Monographs, 1981), 315–34.

4. N. V. Gogol, *Polnoe sobranie sochinenii*, 14 vols. (Moscow: Nauka, 1937–52), 8: 369.

5. Alessandra Stanley, "Russians Find Their Heroes in Mexican TV Soap Opera," *New York Times*, March 20, 1994.

6. Svetlana Boym, *Common Places: Mythologies of Everyday Life in Russia* (Cambridge: Harvard University Press, 1994), 3, 73–88.

7. John Guillory, *Cultural Capital: The Problem of Literary Canon Formation* (Chicago: Chicago University Press, 1993), 15.

8. Helena Goscilo, "Domostroika or Perestroika? The Construction of Womanhood in Soviet Culture Under Glasnost," in Thomas Lahusen with Gene Kuperman, eds., *Late Soviet Culture: From Perestroika to Novostroika* (Durham: Duke University Press, 1993), 233–56. See also her earlier article, "Body Talk in Current Fiction: Speaking Parts and (W)holes," *Stanford Slavic Studies* 7 (1993), 123–44.

12

Shrunk to an Interloper

Judith Ryan

In one of my very earliest classrooms—it must have been at nursery school—
hung a large map of the world. In the lower middle part of the map, a big
reddish-pink island swam in a blue sea; at both upper corners small reddish-
pink shapes hovered like guardian angels on either hand; in the center a large
reddish-pink triangle pointed downward from an amorphous and multicol-
ored land mass; and the whole map was satisfyingly unified by patches of
ruddy color distributed over a substantial portion of its surface. I did not
know then that what I was experiencing was the aesthetics of Empire.

"Two souls, alas! reside within my breast," declares Goethe's Faust.[1]
Within my breast reside, however, not two, but at least three souls. Teaching
German and comparative literature would seem to place me equally on the
side of the "national" and the "global." Yet I also happen to be Australian.
The Australian self—my "third soul"—subverts conventional relations
between the smaller and the larger worlds.

Hence I've conceived this paper from the viewpoint of what Australia's
great poet, Ern Malley, has described as a "black swan of trespass on alien
waters."[2] In Australia, we were taught from the beginning to internalize a

Eurocentric view while at the same time defiantly creating an Australian one. When we learned French and German, we had to memorize the words for scores of trees, plants, and flowers, along with their English translations—but practically none of this vegetation actually grew in Australia. I still don't know what a nightingale sounds like—though the mere thought of its song is enough to move me quite profoundly.

To place myself as an Australian is to feel myself—again in the words of Ern Malley—"shrunk to an interloper,"[3] yet also conveniently located off to the side of an argument in which it is only too easy to take one side or the other. If you ask me whether "national literatures" should be eliminated in favor of "global" perspectives, I'm inclined to say "yes"—as long as I don't specifically think about Australian literature and its long and ultimately successful struggle for an identity of its own.

Let me talk now about some literary texts of our time in which a great writer has tried to come to grips with the problem of the national versus the global viewpoint. My first example is Thomas Keneally's novel *Schindler's List*,[4] of 1982; my second is Günter Grass's travelogue *Show Your Tongue*, of 1988; the third, Marguerite Duras's novel *The Lover*, of 1984.[5] In a more conventional presentation, I would have felt obliged to treat these works chronologically; but what interests me here is the gradation in complexity with which they explore the ways in which one's national identity affects the position one takes toward complex cultural relations. I will try to show that even in the apparently dualistic worlds of these works, another, more complicated "soul" leaves an important trace—a trace that might even be regarded as the principal message of these difficult and troubling texts.

Schindler's List is the story of a man who saves numerous Jews from the Nazi death camps for motives that are by no means unmixed and irreproachable. In the novel, as opposed to the movie, the ambiguous nature of Schindler's actions is highlighted at every turn. Schindler is a Faustian figure with two souls in his breast, genuinely caring, in some sense, about the Jews entrusted to his care, but at the same time driven by economic motives and his desire to succeed as a big businessman. After the war, the Jews Schindler saved from the Nazis are scattered over the face of the Earth among what the "Author's Note" at the beginning of the book describes as "seven nations— Australia, Israel, West Germany, Austria, the United States, Argentina, and Brazil."[6] The Schindler survivors, a nation in the psychological sense, are disseminated throughout a range of other nations in the political sense of the word. But this duality of psychological versus political nationhood is only one way of seeing what is at work in the formulation of the "Author's Note." This prefatory explanation also subtly disturbs most customary hierarchies, arranging the various nations neither alphabetically nor in order of their relative political power. In this list, Australia is named first.

Another important trace of a "third soul" occurs in this text at the point where Oskar Schindler decides to move his enamel factory from Cracow to Brinnlitz. On returning to Cracow from a preliminary visit to the Brinnlitz site, Schindler finds the charred wreckage of a downed Stirling bomber. The men in the plane, he discovers, were Australian. "If Oskar had wanted some sort of confirmation [of his plans to move away from Cracow], this was it. That men should come all this way from unimaginable little towns in the Australian Outback to hasten the end in Cracow."[7] Whereas the writer who names Australia first in his list of seven nations can only be an Australian, the speaker in this passage about the Stirling bomber shifts into the consciousness of someone for whom Australia is quite remote from the familiar. No Australian would speak of "unimaginable little towns in the Australian Outback"; even if we have never actually seen outback towns, Australians have no trouble imagining them. Keneally's novel, despite its subsequent entry into the "global world" by means of the Steven Spielberg movie, is nonetheless a text that secretly insists on its Australianness—while overtly distancing itself from Australia by treating World War II from a perspective that appears to transcend what might otherwise have seemed, to the "global" world, a far too limited one.[8]

The implications of *Schindler's List* for Australians go beyond the events of German racism in the nineteen-thirties and -forties, though this has rarely been noted in connection with the book. Most Australians would prefer, after all, not to think about their country's own racist past as exemplified in the notorious "White Australia" policy, the aim of which was to prohibit the immigration of Asians and Pacific Islanders into Australia and to deport workers of Asian origin from the sugarcane fields of Queensland. When the original bill (called the Immigration Restriction Act) was enacted in 1901, one newspaper wrote, for example, that the policy would save Australia "from the coloured curse" and from becoming "a mongrel nation torn with racial dissension."[9] The Immigration Restriction Act was not rescinded until 1973. Only those familiar with the history of Australian nationalism can fully understand the irony of that little scene in *Schindler's List* (the novel) where Australian bombers descend upon Cracow in an attempt to drop supplies for the partisans fighting against Nazism and where the charred remains of one pilot are found in the destroyed plane, still firmly clutching "an English Bible."[10] The novel's final sentence about Oskar Schindler, "he was mourned on every continent,"[11] thus acquires a peculiar resonance for readers from Keneally's homeland.

Günter Grass's *Show Your Tongue* is, as it were, the other face of *Schindler's List*. Written not from the point of view of an ex-colonial, but from that of a former colonizing nation, the book is contemporaneous with Grass's 1988 proposal for a Pan-European cultural union. In large measure, *Show Your Tongue* is about the crossing of borders and the partitioning of nations. Grass's visit to India—the ostensible subject of the book—also permits a side trip to Bangladesh, a divided country whose citizens repeatedly urge him to draw the comparison with Germany, which at the time of course was still divided. In Grass's view, only one thing unites the split Bengali nation: its admiration for its lost leader Subhas Chandra Bose. The novel opens with a discussion of a bronze statue of Bose in Calcutta,[12] and later notes the existence of statues of him in other cities. Traveling around the subcontinent, Günter and Ilse Grass learn the story of Bose's attempt to free India from British domination by allying himself in turn with Nazi Germany, Imperial Japan, and Stalinist Russia; they learn of the plane accident that caused his death and of his continued popularity in India and Bangladesh as a "Führer" and "holy man" who is thought to be hiding out in the hills and will reputedly return, at the age of one hundred, to rescue his fellow Bengali from their fate. In Grass's view, the numerous monuments to Bose crowd out memorials to his polar opposite, Gandhi, the "other soul"—to use my Faustian terminology—of the country the two Germans are touring.

Subverting this easy dualism are the narrator's repeated references to Ilse's uninterrupted preoccupation with the nineteenth-century German realist Theodor Fontane, whose novels she reads obsessively throughout their travels. The presence of this literary precursor in the minds of the two travelers gives an additional twist to their response to Indian cultural history. Fontane's comments on the Scottish regiments' defense of Calcutta during the Sepoy uprising,[13] which took place while he was living in Britain as press attaché for Prussia, the similarities between present-day traces of Victorian India and the nineteenth-century country estates described in Fontane's novels,[14] and finally Grass's embarrassed discovery of Fontane's "ironic, patronizing amiability when dealing with Jews,"[15] serve to cast an icon much cherished in the German literary tradition into a highly questionable light. Grass's book about India complicates the insider-outsider problematic of traditional travel writing by insisting on its Germanness and criticizing it at one and the same time, distinguishing between home and abroad, past and present while simultaneously conflating these seeming oppositions. An early note in the travelogue articulates the difficulties of this complicated perspective: "What I am flying away from: repetition that claims to be news; from Germany and Germany, the way two deadly foes, armed to the teeth, grow ever more alike; from insights achieved from too close up; from my own perplexity, admitted only sotto voce, flying with me."[16]

Marguerite Duras's novel *The Lover* is an even more complex attempt to deal with these issues. Narrated by a woman who, like Duras herself, grew up as the daughter of a French schoolteacher in Vietnam but has now reversed her parents' emigration and returned to live in France, it tells the story of an adolescent who moves among what seem at first to be three cultures: her French family, the Vietnamese world around her, and the young Chinese businessman who becomes the partner in her first erotic experiences. The intrusion of the Chinese lover troubles the fifteen-and-a-half-year-old's adolescent self-image, a deliberately ambiguous amalgam of apparent oppositions. We first see her dressed in gold lamé sandals and man's flat-brimmed hat, a privileged white girl on her way to school who nonetheless looks and acts in many ways like a child prostitute.[17] Dualisms of male and female, mother country and colony, educated and uneducated classes, age and youth—among others—are set up in this opening passage, only to be undermined by the Chinese lover, who cannot be identified by any of these conventional rubrics. Other elements in the novel also work to subvert the binary structures of colonialism: the narrator's retarded classmate, Hélène Lagonelle, who belongs to the privileged boarding-school world but can never be completely integrated into it; the narrator's mother, whose psyche combines activist ambitions with passivity and melencholia; and the violent older brother who is at once a wild beast in the Vietnamese jungle, a viciously oppressive representative of the male sex and the colonizing nation, and the ultimate symbol of the decline of empire and (conflated but not necessarily identical with it) the modern collapse of reason. Finally, the retrospective narration that comprehends the past not as a factual reality but as an imaginative and constantly metamorphosing construct that must continually be subjected to questioning, subverts the conventional autobiographical compact as it is usually described by literary theorists.[18] Couched in deceptively simple language, the novel increasingly gathers complexity. Its insistence on what is not said, not written, not photographed, is much more than a call for the reader to recover what has been repressed—or suppressed, according to one's perspective. Nor is it an attempt to hold oppositions in suspension by converting them first into ambiguities, and then, by sheer multiplication, into what is fashionably termed "indeterminacy." Rather, Duras's novel is quite literally a demonstration of the resistance put up by linguistic and cultural structures to representation when even an individual viewpoint can only be understood as inherently multiple.

Many of us who move easily between "national" and "global" traditions have tended to ignore what remains in our psyches of a colonial or otherwise subjugated existence. Rescued from its repression, this "third soul" can become a powerful tool to undermine an opposition between the "national" and the "global" that should long since have become outmoded. And yet it is surely an affront to those who have been more clearly and outrageously oppressed to suggest that a postcolonial like myself is peculiarly equipped to dissolve binarisms. For this reason, I do not propose that we should all adopt in some sense a position on the margins—that is precisely what my literary examples do *not* do. Rather, they show the complexities of contemporary cultural situations in which the opposition between center and periphery is no longer adequate. But neither is it enough, they imply, merely to activate a third perspective in addition to the familiar two. Rather, they suggest that we should experiment more freely with an array of different positions, discarding conventional dualisms, but also avoiding "indeterminacies" that swallow up fine distinctions and nuances that mark relational experience in all its exhilaration and despair. Even when the languages we speak and the traditions in which we move prevent us from freeing ourselves entirely from oppositional thinking, we should at least become more aware of the interplay of multiple perspectives that informs our understanding of culture and that makes it impossible for any individual, whatever his or her actual intention, to be reduced to a spokesperson simply for the "national" or the "global." Reading literary texts, and observing ourselves as we read them, is one of the best ways we have of understanding this intricate problem.[19]

NOTES

1. *Faust*, Part I, Act I, line 1112 (cited according to Goethe, *Faust I & II*, ed. and trans. Stuart Atkins [Cambridge, MA: Suhrkamp/Insel, 1984], p. 30).

2. "Ern Malley" was the pseudonym of two Australian poets, James McAuley and Harold Stewart. Under the name of Ern Malley, they submitted a modernist poem-sequence titled "The Darkening Ecliptic" to an Australian literary journal in 1944; only subsequently was the poem revealed to have been a hoax designed to expose what the two poets saw as the pretentiousness of modernist verse. Ern Malley has since become something of an Australian legend (see Michael Heyward, *The Ern Malley Affair* [St. Lucia: University of Queensland Press; and London: Faber and Faber, 1993]). The words cited, "the black swan of trespass on alien waters" form the last line of the opening poem, "Dürer: Innsbruck, 1495" (Ern Malley, *Collected Poems* [Pymble, NSW: Angus and Robertson, 1993], p. 25).

3. On first seeing Innsbruck, the speaker of "Dürer: Innsbruck, 1495" had not known of the picture referred to in the poem's title; only later does he discover its existence, remarking regretfully: "Now I find that once more I have shrunk / To an interloper, robber of dead men's dream" (Ern Malley, *Collected Poems*, p. 25).

4. The shift from the novel's original Australian title, *Schindler's Ark*, to its American title, *Schindler's List*, provides a miniature version of the debate about

different cultural perspectives that was at the heart of this conference.

5. For reasons of time, the section on *The Lover* was omitted from the version of my paper delivered at the conference.

6. Thomas Keneally, *Schindler's List* (New York: Simon and Schuster [Touchstone], 1993), p. 9.

7. *Schindler's List*, p. 288.

8. For an overtly "Australian" perspective on the Second World War, see David Malouf's important novel, *The Great World* (London: Chatto & Windus, 1990).

9. The Brisbane *Worker*, quoted by Manning Clark in *A Short History of Australia* (1963, revised illustrated edition Ringwood, Victoria: Penguin Books Australia, 1986), p. 176.

10. *Schindler's List*, p. 288.

11. Ibid., p. 397.

12. *Show Your Tongue* is cited according to the translation by John E. Woods (San Diego: Harcourt Brace Jovanovich, 1989). The first description of the statue of Bose is on p. 1 of this edition.

13. *Show Your Tongue*, p. 66.

14. Grass comments frequently on the Victorian public buildings and monuments in India, as well as the prevalence of Victorian furniture, e.g., the "Victorian reading room" in the National Library in Calcutta (p. 35).

15. The narrator embeds this remark in a discussion of German anti-Semitism since the Enlightenment (p. 26).

16. *Show Your Tongue*, p. 3.

17. *The Lover* (New York: Pantheon Books, 1986), pp. 11–12.

18. I am thinking here of the study by Philippe Lejeune, *On Autobiography* (Paris: 1975; English translation 1989). Lejeune's thesis that, in autobiography, the "self" becomes "another" is too reductive to do justice to the structure of a novel like *The Lover*.

19. Though informed and enriched by Edward Said's *Culture and Imperialism* (1993), this paper goes beyond his argument that "the history of imperialism and its culture can now be studied as neither monolithic nor reductively compartmentalized, separate, distinct" (p. xx). While Said argues for the "diversity and complexity of experience that works beneath [...] totalizing discourses" (p. xxiv) and declares: "Gone are the binary oppositions dear to the nationalist and imperialist enterprise" (ibid.), he sees his study as an "exilic" book written by a critic "belonging, as it were, to both sides of the imperial divide" (p. xxvii). What I have tried to show in this paper is the way in which some recent authors put us all, as readers, into a position that brings with it a more complex dialectic than one that merely oscillates between two "sides," however diverse within themselves each of these sides may be.

13

National Literatures in a Global World?— Sometimes—Maybe

Stephen Owen

After many years in this profession, a literary scholar develops habits that can approach self-parody. When given a rubric like this—"National Literatures in a Global World?"—my first instinct is to question the question. Is it really a question about literature? What indeed is the future of writing national literatures in a global world? Or is it secretly a question about the academy? Does it still make sense to study and teach national literatures as such, and—imagining the question as it is posed by university administrations—should we continue to support these expensive national-literature departments?

The next question I have about the question is the degree to which it really is a question. I notice the way it invites a particular answer. We obviously remain free to resist the invitation, but the "right" answer is implicit in the formulation. On the one side is the "global world," redundantly becoming itself at last by a modifier that restates the term modified. This is a recent phenomenon, the wave of the future, achieved through the collapse of many of the old divisions of nation states. On the other side of the question are "national literatures," the old, received categories that are tied to the moribund nation-state. In the particular form of the question, the "global world" is the given; it is the "national literatures" whose value and contined existence as a category are in question. It would seem conservative, perhaps downright reactionary, to continue to support national literatures in face of such a question.

When presented a question like this, my instincts are perverse. I begin to think of possible answers that are excluded. For example, I might say that I am strongly committed to the continued study of national literature except in the case of the French. Or perhaps: I favor a global literature except for the Slavic literatures, where it is well known that modest phonological changes generate irreducible national essences and untranslatable languages. There are many comic variations.

Eager to discover something serious behind my perverse impulses, I note that the comic variations that come unbidden to mind play on the universalizing claims of both the "global world" and "national literatures." That is, the question assumes that either all boundaries cease to exist or that all boundaries, however small we willfully draw them, are to be respected. The perverse responses keep the terms of the question, while denying those terms their universal claims, their "either/or." They point to the possibility of a historical answer rather than a theoretical answer; that is, in those places and times where literary production and reception occur in a strong transnational context, studying national literatures in isolation makes no sense at all.

Thinking primarily of the modern context (implicit in "global world"), I prefer the term "transnational" rather than sweeter words such as "global" or "international." Those latter words lead one to believe that everyone is equal in sharing this thing called "literature" or "culture." Such sweet talk is closely related to the notion of a universal discipline of "literary studies" or "cultural studies" that applies seamlessly to different locales and times. I use the term "transnational" here specifically to evoke a corporate model, with historically local links across particular national boundaries, with clear centers of power, hierarchies of subordination, and routes of circulation that pass through those centers of power. This is very clear in contemporary literature. For the work of a contemporary Greek poet to get to Romania, it probably must go first to New York, Paris, or Berlin, where its value is weighed against other work coming in through particular lines of distribution. If the Greek poet's work is judged valuable for the world market in those centers, it may be translated and only then exported to Bucharest.

Well-known writers from "other" countries often are invited to universities in the United States to teach; indeed many take up permanent or partial residence here. The American university and the foreign writer each lends prestige to the other, and it is often through the university that the writer increases the contacts with American publishers that contribute to international distribution of the writer's work. Internationally known novelists writing in languages other than English often have contracts for translations of their work while they are writing, and I have even been told of novelists who keep in contact with their translators while they are in the process of writing. If a writer reaches the pinnacle of fame and political success, he or she may be awarded the most important prize usually given for literature in translation, the Nobel. In the contemporary literary world the very possibility of "national literature" is dissolving rapidly. The transnational literary community in Paris earlier in the century pales in comparison to the current situation. What we have now is not national literatures but local color in a fungible idiom. I don't believe that Europe ever had "national literatures," but they did exist elsewhere—and they don't anymore.

Insofar as the question initially posed concerns contemporary literature, the answer is obvious: national literatures are rapidly dying. If, however, the question concerns contemporary literary studies, with responsibility to represent the past as well as the contemporary situation, then the answer becomes more complicated.

Institutional structures can accept only the universal answers to the question of national literatures in a global world: yes, there should be national literary studies; no, there should be no more national literary studies; or there should be some elegant compromise. But if I go to the dean of the faculty at Harvard and say the school should offer national literary studies or area literary studies for these literatures in the following periods, but not for others, I won't get very far.

The context for my redeployment of the question is, of course, Chinese literature. So when I am asked the large question, "Should there be national literary studies?" I can reply with unwaffling decisiveness: sometimes yes, sometimes no.

Contemporary Chinese literature is a transnational literature as I have described. To treat it purely as a national literature is to misunderstand it and to make its national identity into a fetish. If it shows itself uniquely "Chinese," it is advertising that quality in a transnational context. It becomes local color, constructing an image of itself on an international map. You can see the same phenomenon quite clearly in international contemporary film culture and restaurants. For the study of a contemporary literature one must understand the language; one must understand the historical specificity of context; but it is provincialism to take such a literature in isolation.

Premodern Chinese literature is a very different situation. It has its own history apart from the European literary tradition. Here the claim of internationalism and the coherence of a universal discipline called "literary studies" shows its more dangerous colonial side. It is instructive and pleasurable to read premodern Chinese literature in relation to works of European literature, but it does not fit. If you try to make it just one more literary "case" in a general discipline called "literary studies," you simply won't read it well. The bad fit between the questions of the discipline and such literatures reminds us of the degree to which the discipline is itself constituted from a particular historical experience. Premodern Chinese literature was itself a transnational literature, a one-way exporter of values to Korea, Vietnam, and, in a more complex way, to Japan. And I think you know the other transnational families, all dead now, that worked much the same way. You can transfer skills learned in reading seventeenth-century English poetry to French or German poetry of the same period; you will see differences, but the skills are unchanged. But if you try to transfer those skills to seventeenth-century Turkish poetry or Chinese poetry, or Bengali, or Japanese, those same skills will largely fail. The skills in reading Chinese poetry are more directly transferable to the study of Chinese painting or to the structure of seventeenth-century merchant elites in Yangzhou than to English poetry.

If I stress these things, which generally matter so little in large reflection on literary and cultural studies, it is to leave some holes in our confidence in the possibility of a discipline and to remind the practitioners of the discipline that they are unwittingly practicing European area studies.

But if, for the sake of honesty, one sets aside reservations for former cultures that played by their own rules, there is no reason not to have a department of English, European, and American literary studies; I might throw contemporary in there as well, but that might be best left as a different department. Within that large space literary works have *always* moved across national boundaries with dazzling speed. Maintaining language competence is essential, and historically specific cultural contexts must be understood, but those do not pose serious intellectual problems.

We should not hide the financial forces at work behind what seems to be a purely intellectual question. We are in an age of downsizing and streamlining institutions. National literature departments are expensive to maintain, and a tidy sum could be saved by consolidation. This is not to say we should not defend existing turf, but I think we should be aware of this component of the intellectual issue.

In this volume's claim to discuss "literary and cultural studies," the "and" is a compromise that conceals an "either/or." On one side is the internal coherence of disciplines such as literary studies—the conclusion encouraged by the question of "national literatures in a global world?"—accompanied by the idea of the "interdisciplinary," the "literature and X" model, which celebrates disciplinary boundaries in crossing them. On the other side is cultural studies and the real dissolution of disciplinary boundaries within what was once the humanities. The debate remains an interesting one.

The corollary to the question "National Cultures in a Global World?" is: are the boundaries between the disciplines in any way more substantial than the boundaries between national entities or languages? If we allow that technical skills—languages—must be mastered in literary studies, but that those do not in themselves contain or draw boundaries in the enterprise, then is that in any way different from mastering a technical skill such as musicology? I understand the institutional inertia and vested interests that make institutional change unlikely, but should this not be part of the question—the reconfiguration of the humanities in general and the dissolution of the current structure of disciplines?

PART FOUR

One Poem, Three Readers

Robert Lowell's "For the Union Dead"

FOR THE UNION DEAD

"Relinquunt Omnia Servare Rem Publicam."

The old South Boston Aquarium stands
in a Sahara of snow now. Its broken windows are boarded.
The bronze weathervane cod has lost half its scales.
The airy tanks are dry.

Once my nose crawled like a snail on the glass;
my hand tingled
to burst the bubbles
drifting from the noses of the cowed, compliant fish.

My hand draws back. I often sigh still
for the dark downward and vegetating kingdom
of the fish and reptile. One morning last March,
I pressed against the new barbed and galvanized

fence on the Boston Common. Behind their cage,
yellow dinosaur steamshovels were grunting
as they cropped up tons of mush and grass
to gouge their underworld garage.

Parking spaces luxuriate like civic
sandpiles in the heart of Boston.
A girdle of orange, Puritan-pumpkin colored girders
braces the tingling Statehouse,

shaking over the excavations, as it faces Colonel Shaw
and his bell-cheeked Negro infantry
on St. Gaudens' shaking Civil War relief,
propped by a plank splint against the garage's earthquake.

Two months after marching through Boston,
half the regiment was dead;
at the dedication,
William James could almost hear the bronze Negroes breathe.

Their monument sticks like a fishbone
in the city's throat.
Its Colonel is as lean
as a compass-needle.

He has an angry wrenlike vigilance,
a greyhound's gentle tautness;
he seems to wince at pleasure,
and suffocate for privacy.

He is out of bounds now. He rejoices in man's lovely,
peculiar power to choose life and die—
when he leads his black soldiers to death,
he cannot bend his back.

On a thousand small town New England greens,
the old white churches hold their air
of sparse, sincere rebellion; frayed flags
quilt the graveyards of the Grand Army of the Republic.

The stone statues of the abstract Union Soldier
grow slimmer and younger each year—
wasp-waisted, they doze over muskets
and muse through their sideburns…

Shaw's father wanted no monument
except the ditch,
where his son's body was thrown
and lost with his "niggers."

The ditch is nearer.
There are no statues for the last war here;
on Boylston Street, a commercial photograph
shows Hiroshima boiling

over a Mosler Safe, the "Rock of Ages"
that survived the blast. Space is nearer.
When I crouch to my television set,
the drained faces of Negro school-children rise like balloons.

Colonel Shaw
is riding on his bubble,
he waits
for the blessèd break.

The Aquarium is gone. Everywhere,
giant finned cars nose forward like fish;
a savage servility
slides by on grease.

Figure 1

Thematics	Poetics	Dynamics
The Republic	Group elegy	1) Temporality (then-now)
Civil War	Single elegy	2) Narrative planes (factual, fanciful, imaginative)
Moral heroism	Self-elegy	3) Syntactic variation (sentence length)
Theory of manliness	Ekphrastic poem	4) Reference (I/Other)
Decline of culture	Ubi sunt poem	5) Spatiality (here/Hiroshima/South/space/etc.)
Race relations	Civic poem	
Ethnic relations	Historical poem	
Commercialization	Prophetic poem	
Technology	Satiric poem	
Regionality	New England poem	
Childhood	Hero poem	
Urban renewal	Race-relations poem	
Brahmin history	Ethnic-relations poem	
Civic virtue	Psychoanalytic poem	
The year 1960	Family poem	
	Allusive poem	
	State-of-the-nation poem	
	Roman poem	
	Stanzaic poem	
	First-person poem	
	Unhappy-ending poem	

For the Union Dead
The Hundred Years of the Poem

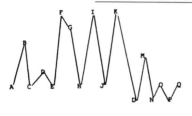

Civil War (1861)
Shaw's Death (1863)
Dedication of Monument (1897)
"Once" (c. 1927)
WW II (Hiroshima) (1945)
"Last March" (1959)
"Now" (1960)
Future (break/ditch/space)

Fact, Fancy, and the Imagination

Fact	Fancy	Imagination
Aquarium		
Common		
	dinosaurs	
	sandpiles	
	Puritan-pumpkin color	
Statehouse		
excavations		
Shaw relief		
March		
Death		
Dedication		
William James	hear…breathe	
	fishbone	
		Colonel is/has/seems/is/rejoices/leads/cannot bend
	sincere rebellion	
	flags/quilt	
	grow slimmer & younger	
	doze/muse	
Shaw's father		
"niggers"		the ditch
last war		
Hiroshima		
"Rock of Ages"		
space	crouch	
TV/Negro children	balloons	
		Colonel/bubble/break
Aquarium gone	fish	
		savage servility
grease		

14

Reading a Poem

Helen Vendler

I want to begin by scotching an old notion—that there was ever a school that said one should refer, in reading a poem, "only to the words on the page." The critics who asked that attention be paid to the words on the page were, most of them, poets, such as Allan Tate, Robert Penn Warren, Randall Jarrell, Robert Lowell, John Crowe Ransom, and I. A. Richards. They all assumed that a reader studying poetry would have had an excellent education in Latin, modern languages, philosophy, history, theology, and canonical works of literature. What they objected to were essays in literary history, literary theory, and the history of ideas that displayed only the skimpiest knowledge, if that, of what a poem was up to, what its author was up to. The New Critics asked not for a "close" reading, as it is nowadays referred to, but what I would call "a writer's reading"—the study that another writer would give to what had been attempted, and accomplished, on the page. The writer-reader would of course know the history of previous poetry and would be curious what interesting new aesthetic practice was being brought off by the writing writer.

To attempt to describe the reading protocol of a writer-reader when confronted by the poem of a writing writer, I've schematized in Figure 1 a few of the scanning devices, or lenses, a writer would have at hand to look at this poem with, or through. Everyone's first scan is probably thematic, and has to do with cultural information-retrieval. You might go to this poem as one of your examples if you were writing an essay on the imaginative treatment of the Civil War, or the year 1960, or the state of race relations, or urban literature, or a history of Yankee Brahmin attitudes. But this sort of scan would be equally appropriate to an essay or a newspaper editorial. It hasn't much to do with the arresting qualities of "For the Union Dead" as a poem.

The second scan, which looks at the large issues we subsume under poetics, comes closer to the question of poetic originality. There is a long history of the elegy, of the ekphrastic poem, of the New England poem, of the family poem, of the Roman poem, and so on. As soon as the poem is placed under one of these rubrics, clusters of other poems come (ideally) to mind, and the question of originality begins to arise. Has there ever been another ekphrastic poem about a bas-relief? Has there ever been a group elegy of a military regiment? Has there ever before been an ethnic-conflict poem pitting the Brahmins against the Irish? Has there ever been a previous poem about Negroes that was about Negro soldiers? What sort of family poem is it that conceals its own genre? (Lowell was related by marriage to Robert Gould Shaw, who married Josephine Lowell; and it was Charles Russell Lowell, her brother, also an officer in the Civil War, who said, in a letter to the family, that his brother-in-law wanted "to be buried with his niggers." Augustine Lowell, establisher of the Lowell textile mills, lived very near the bas-relief on Beacon Hill.) What sorts of American poems make reference to Rome, and why does this one do so? The writer-reader begins, I think, to envy the writer of this poem, thinking, "Good heavens, what a lot of good ideas just lying around waiting to be written about! Why didn't *I* think of writing about Negroes in the military, such a different slant on America's Negroes from the more familiar subject of Negroes in the cotton fields or Negroes in Harlem? Why didn't *I* think of doing a group elegy in black and white? Why don't any of *my* poems have a satiric edge when they're being nostalgic? Why have all the poems about New England been about the countryside or the shore: why didn't *I* think about doing a Boston poem?" And so on. It is the admiring envy of other writers, over time, that ultimately makes a poem canonical.

But even these large ideas for poetic subjects don't approach the heart of the poem, which is always the *treatment* of its poetic idea. As Stevens said, "Every poem is a poem within a poem: the poem of the idea within the poem of the words" ("Adagia," *Opus Posthumous*, p. 199). In Lowell's case, the poetry of the idea lies in the originality of some of those notions that our putative writer-reader has enviously admired, and of course there are more: "Why didn't *I* think of writing a poem redefining the manliness of the hero as composed of vigilance, gentle tautness, privacy, and uprightness, instead of belligerence, vengeance, valor, and cunning?" The redefining of the great subgenres of poetry is always going on; the 1960 hero is not the Homeric hero, any more than the 1960 ekphrastic poem could be the "Ode on a Grecian Urn." Modernity and originality have to do with reconceiving the old subgenres, as well as with expanding new subgenres such as the race-relations poem.

Treatment interests the writer-reader even more than generic redefinition or generic invention—though both of these, as implicit queryings of the past's commissions and omissions, are invigorating for poetry. But new treatment—the invention of original style—is the most envied quality of all, and the writer-reader wants to see what makes Lowell Lowell (in the same way that one sees what makes Milton Milton). Of course, a single poem won't define all of Lowell's individual moves, but one can make a beginning there. The writer-reader might admire the compression of time—most lyrics don't cover a hundred years (almost two hundred if one counts, as I have not in Figure 1, the reference to "rebellion" as a reminder of 1776). A "normal" version of Lowell's poem in linear time-evolution would look something like my pastiche in Figure 2; the first thing one notices about the poem, technically, is Lowell's departure from a linear time line.

The second thing one might notice is Lowell's freakish jumps from the factual to the fanciful to the imaginative, jumps that I've sketched briefly in Figure 1; most elegies have nothing comic in them such as dinosaurs, nothing shocking in them such as Lowell's use of the word "niggers," nothing blasphemous in them such as the Mosler safe described by "Rock of Ages," a hymnal epithet for the crucified Jesus. Imagining your elegiac hero riding on a bubble conjured up from the fish-bubbles in the vanished Aquarium is hardly the act of a classical elegist, and represents a characteristic piece of Lowell boldness.

The third thing one might notice, technically, is the strategic punctuation of the poem by six extraordinarily brief sentences, each less than a line long: "Its broken windows are boarded. My hand draws back. He is out of bounds now. The ditch is nearer. Space is nearer. The Aquarium is gone." These give the poem, first, its air of factuality and, second, its air of apodictic prophecy. There are many other such strategies of management to be noticed, from the unobtrusiveness of the "I" (usually so prominent in lyric) to the "psychoanalytic" creeping up on the main subject by a form of free association linking the recent nose-to-the-fence to the childhood nose-to-

Figure 2

FOR THE UNION DEAD (PASTICHE IN LINEARITY)

One morning last March,
I pressed against the new barbed and galvanized
fence of the Boston Common. Behind the cage,
yellow dinosaur steamshovels were grunting
as they cropped up tons of mulch and grass
to gouge their underworld garage.

Pressing against the fence, I remembered how
once, in the South Boston Aquarium,
my nose crawled like a snail on the glass;
my hand tingled to burst the bubbles
drifting from the noses of the cowed, compliant fish.

I often sigh still for the dark downward and vegetating kingdom
of the fish and reptile. But the old South Boston Aquarium stands
in a Sahara of snow now. Its broken windows are boarded.
The airy tanks are dry.

The Common is being excavated for a garage even though
parking spaces luxuriate like civic
sandpiles in the heart of Boston.
Everywhere, giant finned cars nose forward like fish;
a savage servility slides by on grease.

The new governors, with the Aquarium gone,
are now destroying the Common and its surroundings.

A girdle of orange, Puritan-pumpkin colored girders
braces the tingling Statehouse
shaking over the excavations, as it faces Colonel Shaw
and his bell-cheeked Negro infantry
on St. Gaudens' shaking Civil War relief,
propped by a plank splint against the garage's earthquake.

Colonel Shaw marched his regiment through Boston;
when he led his black soldiers to death,
he could not bend his back.
Two months after marching through Boston,
half the regiment was dead;
Shaw's father wanted no monument
except the ditch
where his son's body was thrown

and lost with his "niggers."
At the dedication of the monument,
William James could almost hear the bronze Negroes breathe.

Their monument sticks like a fishbone
in the city's throat.
Its Colonel is as lean
as a compass-needle.

He has an angry wrenlike vigilance,
a greyhound's gentle tautness;
he seems to wince at pleasure,
and suffocate for privacy.

He is out of bounds now. He rejoices in man's lovely,
peculiar power to choose life and die.
He is in a continuum with the leaders of the American revolution;
on a thousand small town New England greens,
the old, white churches hold their air
of sparse, sincere rebellion;

but the spirit of the Republic is waning; frayed flags
quilt the graveyards of the Grand Army of the Republic.
The stone statues of the abstract Union Soldier
grow slimmer and younger each year—
wasp-waisted, they doze over muskets
and muse through their sideburns.

There are no statues for the last war here;
on Boylston Street, a commercial photograph
shows Hiroshima boiling
over a Mosler Safe, a "Rock of Ages"
that survived the blast. Space is nearer.
When I crouch to my television set,
the drained faces of Negro school-children rise like balloons.

Colonel Shaw
is riding on his bubble,
he waits
for the blessèd break.

the-Aquarium-glass; thence to the abandonment of the Aquarium by the immigrant Irish who took political control of Boston, even though the Aquarium was in their own bailiwick, South Boston; thence to the days when fish were compliant, and no bubble would break; thence to the giant fishlike automobiles favored by the infantile Irish who build parking lots for them like playgrounds; thence to the vandalizing of Boston by the building of an underground garage under the Boston Common, a construction not only based on graft and corruption but also one literally endangering the nearby State House, morally and physically; thence to the endangered relief; and so on. This use by American poets of the "free association" of apparently insignificant details as poetic form is new since the encounter with Freud.

The writer-reader would be interested, too, in the halting progress of the poem. A line. Two lines. Two lines. A breath of several lines. Then a one-line halt. Then two lines. This, more or less, is the way the poem goes. Its syntactic form is notational, but what it notes is not internally coherent. It notes a temporal fact: the ditch is nearer. It notes a historical fact: William James was at the dedication. It notes a whimsical fancy: the statues grow slimmer and younger each year. It notes a visual fact: the colonel is as lean as a compass needle. The notations are, in the end, made to "add up"—but their expressive form remains that of a strained eye keeping notes on its culture, and trying to keep everything in its taxed focus.

Of course, there is no point noting a poet's treatment unless the mode of treatment stands for something, allegorizes something. I've just said what Lowell's terse half-line, one-line, or two-line notations mean about the modern historical and metaphysical consciousness—how nervous it is, how restless, how ranging and unhappy, how unsystematic, how subject to fits and starts. And, to return a moment to the temporality of the poem, we have seen how it continually veers nervously out of its now and toward something else—1776, the Civil War, the dedication, Charles Russell Lowell's quotation, the vanished Aquarium, the future. The time line of secure progress has vanished, and the modern mind circles restlessly over the history of the United States and its threatening present as it also peers into an unknown, but certainly dark, future. Yet what I have mentioned concerning satiric energy, prophetic denunciation, restlessness, and so on, entirely leaves out the childishness of the poem. In some ways, the poem is written by an outlaw child who won't grow up. He wants to see the earthmovers as dinosaurs, the orange girders as "Puritan-pumpkin colored," the "giant finned cars" as monster fish, even—in the most grave moment of the poem—the drained faces of Negro schoolchildren as—as what? Would anyone have guessed balloons? Or would anyone but an outlaw-Brahmin have perched Colonel Shaw on the bubble? These irruptions of the fanciful also need explaining; they

Augustus Saint-Gaudens, Shaw Memorial, detail.
Photo: Paul B. Franklin

Augustus Saint-Gaudens, Shaw Memorial,
detail. Photo: Paul B. Franklin

are, so to speak, a refusal to behave with the gravity expected of a proper
Brahmin when he sees his city being vandalized. There's a certain counter-
cultural glee in Lowell that will never let itself be quelled.

Finally, the writer-reader would, I think, speculate on why this anti-Irish
poem never mentions the Irish, this Lowell family poem never mentions the

Lowells. This strategic decision—to give enough detail to make the opposing civic parties visible without naming them—removes the poem from the explicit autobiographical occasion of its writing. Besides, I am sure that Lowell knew that Saint-Gaudens' mother was an Irish immigrant; Saint-Gaudens himself was born in Dublin. This adds a further irony to the poem; if the Irish are wrecking Boston by abandoning the Aquarium and excavating the Common for their cars, the Irish are also making memorials by which the Lowell family, in the person of Robert Gould Shaw, will be remembered, and, by the technical mastery of casting in bronze, ensuring the aesthetic survival of a civic virtue, white and black, that one can only call Roman. And it is not the Lowells alone who are defending the republic; the Latin inscription on the 1897 Saint-Gaudens relief says "Relinquit," "He leaves all things to serve the Republic," but Lowell altered it in his poem to "Relinquunt": the Brahmin Cincinnatus is joined to the Negro freemen who volunteered for service in the Union Army. The final layer of historical irony is conferred by the single most astonishing word in the poem, the word "crouch." The protagonist does not arrogate to himself the usual position of one who embodies the values he defends; he worships the new god of television, like the veriest savage; and the malevolence of segregation in the South is one sustained by white Protestants, the ethnic group to which Lowell himself belonged. There is a savagery of the WASPs, as well as a savagery of the Irish.

A poem that demands so many lenses, that redefines many subgenres at once, that finds new technical means, that eyes its author as satirically as it eyes its enemies, that allows whimsicality of observation even with respect to its objects of value (as the statues progress in slimness and youngness, they will approach the degree zero of both qualities and vanish), that ranges through all the tones possible to a cultivated and imaginative and original mind, that criticizes its own cultural group—such a poem is simply more interesting than a single-layered poem. And of course I've said nothing about many other things, such as the construction of stanzas, or the management of space, or the binding of words to each other. One can't simply abstract statements of ideas or themes from such a poem and represent it faithfully; that is why those writer-critics of the New Criticism wanted readers to notice tonality, and originality of strategy, and whimsicality, and mood, and syntactic punctuation, and the redefinition of genre, and the poetry of the idea, and a multitude of other triumphs. The New Critics—and everyone after them who has wanted subtlety and accuracy of response—never advocated ignorance. On the contrary. To do a close reading of Lowell's poem, you need to know Latin, and American history, and the political history of Boston, and the Roman ideals of the founding fathers, and who William James was, and what the last war was and why there are no statues for it on the Common, and what Hiroshima was, and how Latin elegy was managed, and the usual subjects of ekphrastic poems, and all the rest. But, knowing all that, you have not yet begun to read the poem. That was all the writer-critics and their followers meant to say. A poem, as Mallarmé said, becomes, when it is complete, a single complex word. To read it successfully is to know it as one indivisible word; or, to shift metaphors, as something like a multi-cellular organism with colors, and motions, and an inner metabolism, and cilia that it waves, and suckers attaching it to other objects, and a single, siren-like note that it sings. It is that note that the writer-reader wants to hear.

15

Ode on a Public Thing

Barbara Johnson

Both the title ("For the Union Dead") and the epigraph (*"Relinquunt Omnia Servare Rem Publicam"*) of Lowell's poem lead the reader to expect that the poem will be an elegy with political ramifications. Lowell's change in the Saint-Gaudens monument's inscription from the original *"Relinquit"* ("he leaves") of the motto of the Society of Cincinnati to the plural *"Relinquunt"* ("they leave") appears to make a simple but powerful point: that the black soldiers who enlisted in Colonel Robert Gould Shaw's 54th Massachusetts Regiment were as heroic and self-sacrificing as their leader. In keeping with the structure of loss one might expect from an elegy, the poem indeed begins with a contrast between "now" and "once." But that contrast is not about the Civil War or about American race relations. It is about fish. The first lost thing in the poem is the old South Boston Aquarium. What do fish have to do with the Union dead?

The poem lists an astonishingly disparate collection of things and moments while drawing everything together through the language in which they are described. Look at the way the word "nose" unites the poet, the fish, and the cars at the end of the poem: "Once my *nose* crawled like a snail on the glass…," "my hand tingled to burst the bubbles drifting from the *noses* of the cowed, compliant fish," and "Everywhere, giant finned cars *nose* forward like fish; a savage servility slides by on grease." "Cowed, compliant" also echoes "savage servility." And servility seems to mock the "servare" from the epigraph. A few more echoes: "parking *spaces* luxuriate" and "*space* is nearer." "Space is *nearer*" and "the ditch is *nearer*." The colonel "lean as a compass-needle" echoes the "bronze weathervane cod." A "girdle" of "girders." "One morning last *March*." "Two months after *marching* through Boston." Colonel Shaw is riding on a bubble. Negro schoolchildren's faces rise like balloons. Bubbles come from the noses of the fish. "My hand tingled to burst the bubbles." Colonel Shaw waits for the blessèd break. The poem quickly reveals itself to be a network of echoes. But what does it all mean?

The poem is seductive in its skill in seeing a dinosaur in a steamshovel, Colonel Shaw in a bubble like the fish. But the poem also suggests that metaphors taken out of context can be used for commercial purposes: Hiroshima and the hymn "Rock of Ages" combine to advertise a Mosler safe. Does the poem give us any means by which to distinguish between its own figurative promiscuity and that of the commercial? Its own fishy images and those of 1960 model cars? Is there any difference between poetry and advertising?

Here we might go back to Lowell's second modification of the motto on the monument. Like many modern Latin coinages, the motto of the Society of Cincinnati, "*Omnia relinquit servare rempublicam*," is of dubious grammatical exactitude. *Relinquo*, I am told, does not usually take the infinitive alone to express purpose.[1] *Servare* does not mean "to serve" but rather "to save." It is *servire* that means "to serve." What, then, does Lowell's revision of *rempublicam* to *rem publicam* mean? Given the echo in the poem between *servare* and "servility," and between the subjacent *servire* and the question of slavery, could it be legitimate to conflate *servare* and *servire* as the Norton Anthology's translation of the original motto ("He leaves all else to serve the republic") appears to do? This would give the somewhat fanciful translation of Lowell's epigraph as "They leave all else to serve (as) a public thing."

A monument is a public thing. The 54th Regiment has relinquished life to become a monument, a thing. The poem mentions other statues of Union soldiers, other graves. Yet, in contrast, Shaw's father wanted no monument except the ditch where his son's body was thrown and lost with his "niggers." There are no statues for the last war here. Does the poem think a monument is a good thing? Was Shaw's father wrong? Should there be a statue for the last war? What, exactly, is a monument?

In this poem a monument is very much a thing. It is vulnerable to the construction work going on around it. The abstract Union solder is growing slimmer each year. The boarded-up aquarium, too, stands like a monument, almost like Ozymandias in the desert—here, a Sahara of snow. The city is full of stuff. How can we tell a monument from a fishbone?

A monument may be a thing, but things have a curious capacity to become animate. William James could almost hear the bronze Negroes breathe. The Statehouse tingles. The dinosaur steamshovels grunt and crop. The colonel seems to wince and suffocate. The stone statues doze and muse. The statues and monuments seem more alive than anything else in the poem. Even the city becomes animate when the poem says "Their monument sticks like a fishbone in the city's throat." Yet the moment that Colonel Shaw comes alive most fully is when the poem says, "He rejoices in man's lovely, peculiar power to choose life and die." To choose life and die. Is this the same as to become a thing and live? The idealization the poem conveys if not endorses is an idealization that sees the highest of human capacities in choosing life and dying. This is what gets monumentalized. "They leave all else to serve as a public thing." Without that, what would a republic be? But there is perhaps something rigid about this structure—"When he leads his black soldiers to death, he cannot bend his back." This may be a simple description of Shaw's posture in the monument. Or it may have something to do with the absolute nature of what is monumentalized.

Here, parenthetically, I mention a Lowell family motto, quoted and mistranslated by Lowell in his prose memoir "91 Revere Street": *malo frangere quam flectere*, "I prefer to break rather than bend." Lowell writes: "On the joint Mason-Myers bookplate, there are two merry and naked mermaids—lovely marshmallowy, boneless, Rubensesque butterballs, all burlesque-show bosoms and Flemish smiles. Their motto, *malo frangere quam flectere*, reads 'I prefer to bend than to break.'"[2] What is the meaning of Lowell's mistaken association between bonelessness and his paternal heritage? Since Shaw cannot bend in the poem, does this help us interpret the enigmatic mention of the "blessèd break" Shaw is waiting for? Is it better to break than to bend? Is the "grease" in the last line of the poem like the "bending" that Shaw cannot or will not perform? If the poem's use of "savage servility" seems to cast "sliding by on grease" in a negative light, does the poem then prefer the breakage that comes with the absolute? Is Shaw a father or an antifather? Is the poem a monument or an antimonument? How can we know, since the question itself may be based on an error of translation?

The poem seems to admire Shaw's stance of choosing life and dying, but to see it as unavailable in the present. "He is out of bounds now." When the poem says, "the ditch is nearer," it refers at least in part to the excavation next to the monument, the encroachment of urban modernization not only on the monument of the past but on the values of the past. But is it possible to choose life and live? Has New England culture gone from a heroism of and for the slaves to a savage, servile present? Has there been no compensating progress? Perhaps white New Englanders have learned not to say "niggers," but technological progress, which has brought space nearer (a literal translation of the word "television"), nevertheless places the white New England poet in front of his television screen merely watching the faces of Negro schoolchildren in the early Civil Rights period as if they were a mere spectacle, separated by a wall of glass, in a bubble, like the fish in the old aquarium. William James may have been able to hear the bronze Negroes breathe at the dedication ceremony, but Negroes remain trapped in the plane of representation in this poem. The television screen, which brings the vision nearer, also places it in a domain of unreachability because the people on the screen are in the plane of representation, under glass.

The poem therefore ultimately asks about its own participation in this structure of representation. The poem itself is one of the series of objects it interrogates. Each has its rigid but fragile outline—the Saint-Gaudens relief, the statue of the Union soldier, the fish tanks, the television. Only the Mosler safe seems invulnerable. Does this mean that the poem is lamenting the fact that commercial values are driving out heroic values? That the only thing safe is what can be put in a safe? That technological progress, which gives us televisions, space exploration, and the atom bomb, does not yield any corresponding moral progress? Yes, in part, but that doesn't quite explain the role of the aquarium. While the lament for the lost capacity to choose life and die seems to express mourning for the loss of the heroic, what exactly is being mourned in the loss of the aquarium? Let us look at what the poem says:

> Once my nose crawled like a snail on the glass;
> my hand tingled
> to burst the bubbles
> drifting from the noses of the cowed, compliant fish.
>
> My hand draws back. I often sigh still
> for the dark downward and vegetating kingdom
> of the fish and reptile.

The scene is one of desiring to burst the plane of representation, to break through the glass separating the spectator from the spectacle. If the fish are cowed and compliant, the boy's desired gesture of violence is both transgressive and a protest designed to provoke them out of their compliance, perhaps even to liberate them. The gesture prefigures and parodies one the poet may be tempted to repeat as he crouches before his television or looks at Shaw in his bubble. Between the second stanza and the third, the tense of the poem goes from past to present. "My hand draws back" is in the present. If the poet's hand draws back in the present, it has a pen in it. The piercing of the plane of representation through to the thing itself has been enacted in reverse. The hand that was in the memory draws back into the writing present. "I often sigh still for the dark downward and vegetating kingdom of the fish and reptile." If the poem mourns for the heroic, it also sighs over the prehuman, the premoral universe. But in the last stanza, "Everywhere, giant finned cars nose forward like fish." It is as though we are presently *in* the aquarium. The small boy has his wish. But at the same time *things* have taken the place of everything, fulfilling the mandate of the monumentalizing process.

The poem laments, then, two things—access to the premoral universe and access to the monumental universe—which it recognizes as having been nightmarishly combined and brought back in the form of an entirely commercial, urban, modernized universe. This unidealizable fulfillment is not only a decline from past to present; it puts in question the clarity of the values of the past. While everything in the poem is organized as though there is a clear *then vs. now* division, its own creation of networks of similarities among all its elements erases the possibility of maintaining the clarity of that structure. It is as though you cannot have seductive metaphors *and* moral clarity. The structure of loss still functions, but the difference between heroic and commercial, natural and technological, aesthetic and moral, monument and urban debris, is no longer clear. Perhaps what the poem is really lamenting is the possibility of writing a then/now elegy that would not become drowned in its own self-irony. But since that irony is created by the poem's aesthetic success, by the tightness of its system of transferred properties, even *that* lament is double-faced. Which is why, I think, this poem has become so canonical. There is nothing like a good thick description of ambivalence toward monumentality to promote a poem to the status of monument in the literary canon.

NOTES

1. My thanks to Jan Ziolkowski, for whose philological wisdom I am greatly indebted throughout these remarks.

2. Robert Lowell, "91 Revere Street," in *Life Studies* (New York: Farrar, Straus and Giroux, 1956), p. 12.

MEMORIÆ POSITUM
R. G. S.
1863

I.

Beneath the trees,
My life-long friends in this dear spot,
Sad now for eyes that see them not,
I hear the autumnal breeze
Wake the sear leaves to sigh for gladness gone,
Whispering hoarse presage of oblivion,—
Hear, restless as the seas,
Time's grim feet rustling through the withered grace
Of many a spreading realm and strong-stemmed race,
Even as my own through these.

Why make we moan
For loss that doth enrich us yet
With upward yearnings of regret?
Bleaker than unmossed stone
Our lives were but for this immortal gain
Of unstilled longing and inspiring pain!
As thrills of long-hushed tone
Live in the viol, so our souls grow fine
With keen vibrations from the touch divine
Of noble natures gone.

'T were indiscreet
To vex the shy and sacred grief
With harsh obtrusions of relief;
Yet, Verse, with noiseless feet,
Go whisper, "*This* death hath far choicer ends
Than slowly to impearl in hearts of friends;
These obsequies 't is meet
Not to seclude in closets of the heart,
But, church-like, with wide door-ways, to impart
Even to the heedless street."

II.

Brave, good, and true,
I see him stand before me now,
And read again on that clear brow,
Where victory's signal flew,
How sweet were life! Yet, by the mouth firm-set,
And look made up for Duty's utmost debt,
I could divine he knew
That death within the sulphurous hostile lines,
In the mere wreck of nobly-pitched designs,
Plucks heart's-ease, and not rue.

Happy their end
Who vanish down life's evening stream
Placid as swans that drift in dream
Round the next river-bend!

Happy long life, with honor at the close,
Friends' painless tears, the softened thought of foes!
     And yet, like him, to spend
All at a gush, keeping our first faith sure
From mid-life's doubt and eld's contentment poor,—
     What more could Fortune send?

          Right in the van,
     On the red rampart's slippery swell,
     With heart that beat a charge, he fell
          Foeward, as fits a man:
But the high soul burns on to light men's feet
Where death for noble ends makes dying sweet;
     His life her crescent's span
Orbs full with share in their undarkening days
Who ever climbed the battailous steeps of praise
     Since valor's praise began.

                    III.
          His life's expense
     Hath won for him coeval youth
     With the immaculate prime of Truth;
          While we, who make pretence
At living on, and wake and eat and sleep,
And life's stale trick by repetition keep,
     Our fickle permanence
(A poor leaf-shadow on a brook, whose play
Of busy idlesse ceases with our day)
     Is the mere cheat of sense.

          We bide our chance,
     Unhappy, and make terms with Fate
     A little more to let us wait:
          He leads for aye the advance,
Hope's forlorn-hopes that plant the desperate good
For nobler Earths and days of manlier mood;
     Our wall of circumstance
Cleared at a bound, he flashes o'er the fight,
A saintly shape of fame, to cheer the right
     And steel each wavering glance.

          I write of one,
     While with dim eyes I think of three:
     Who weeps not others fair and brave as he?
          Ah, when the fight is won,
Dear Land, whom triflers now make bold to scorn,
(Thee! from whose forehead Earth awaits her morn!)
     How nobler shall the sun
Flame in thy sky, how braver breathe thy air,
That thou bred'st children who for thee could dare
     And die as thine have done!

16

Enlistment and Refusal
The Task of Public Poetry

Meredith L. McGill

It is difficult to come third in this series, and particularly difficult to follow someone who has theorized the position of third-in-a-series as both that of maximum insight, and that in which the observer is most likely to blunder, mistaking her particular outlook for an objective viewpoint. Imagine my relief, then, at discovering that what we had in front of us was not the forbidding ratio "One Poem, Three Readers," but at least three and possibly four poems (depending on how you count them). The poem we have been examining, "For the Union Dead," was titled "Colonel Shaw and the Massachusetts 54th" in its first incarnation—an occasional poem delivered to thunderous applause at the Boston Fine Arts Festival in June 1960. The poem was then tipped into the paperback edition of *Life Studies* as the last poem in that series, and published on its own under its current title in *The Atlantic* Magazine, before it took its more familiar place as the final poem in the eponymous volume *For the Union Dead*.[1]

What interests me about the publishing history of this poem is the way in which "For the Union Dead" becomes representative of Lowell's poetic practice while at the same time representing a terminal point or stalling of that practice. Lowell himself described the period in which he wrote the poem as marked by a kind of suspension. In accepting the National Book Award for *Life Studies* in March 1960 he declared, "When I finished *Life Studies* I was left hanging on a question mark. I am still hanging there. I don't know whether it is a death-rope or a life-line."[2] Without confining ourselves to Lowell's alternatives, I think it is important to ask what kind of answer this poem provides to the question of the direction of Lowell's poetry and of American poetry in general. For the public performance of "For the Union Dead" was very much framed as an answer to this question. According to Ian Hamilton, these lines from Lowell's acceptance speech were printed in the Boston Fine Arts Festival program,[3] making the suspension between paralysis and recovery that had characterized the moment of composition a matter of public concern.

Ultimately, however, I am as interested in *our* investment in this poem as I am in Lowell's. For despite the stutter whereby the same poem returns to conclude successive volumes, Lowell went on to write many poems that took up the question of the function of poetry in different ways. What does it mean, then, that for decades, readers and anthologists have let *this poem* stand in for Lowell's poetic practice? Which is, finally, to ask a question not simply about the horizons of the poetic as Lowell imagined them in 1960, but about the ways in which critics, publishers, and readers ratify and perpetuate these limits.

To give you some sort of lifeline to hang on to through my condensed and hurried reading, let me say that what most interests me is the way in which this poem's trenchant social critique gets attached to what seems to be a major concession—a ceding of the public, memorializing function of poetry. The quickest way for me to make this argument is to examine how the poem's obsession with the inability to breathe functions as an image for the failed relation between public and private, the self and the social world—a relation that poetry no longer seems capable of mediating.

Although I risk giving an account of the overall structure of this poem that has been better described by those before me (see Vendler and Johnson in this volume), let me make the general claim that a dislocation between public and private space links the poem's three major sites: the dilapidated aquarium, which had been a self-contained but publicly accessible natural environment; the Boston Common, which—through a scam in which taxpayers as well as "mush and grass" were "gouged"—had begun to stand for the privatization of public space; and the Shaw monument itself, which tells a tale of private sacrifice that the public refuses to hear. Lowell frequently turns to images of confinement and unboundedness to convey the consequences of this dislocation. For example, the windows of the old aquarium are both "broken" and "boarded," simultaneously suggesting rupture and blockage—opposing versions of a failed relation between public and private spheres. The small New England towns, which have been more successful in maintaining their identity through time, are nevertheless marked by "old white churches" that "hold their air." This equation of New England composure with holding one's breath might seem ludicrous in another poem, but not so, I think, in the wake of Lowell's description of the dedication ceremony, where William James "could almost hear the bronze Negroes breathe," and of St. Gaudens's Colonel Shaw, who "suffocates for privacy," his asphyxiation compounded by the syntactic ambiguity of the line: does he suffocate for lack of privacy, on behalf of privacy, or because of privacy? Does he represent the loss of self—the disinterestedness that is the hallmark of civic virtue? Or, does his suffocation constitute a warning *against* such dedication to the public good? Does he suffocate in order to preserve his privacy, or to remind us—as we learn later—that the monument itself is a kind of affront to privacy: "Shaw's father wanted no monument / except the ditch." We can't really know the answer, however, because Shaw is "out of bounds," a figure of speech that suggests both liberty and violation.

James Russell Lowell's little-known elegy for Shaw, "Memoriae Positum," can help us take the measure of this dislocation between public and private space and weigh its consequences for poetry. James Russell Lowell faced a different poetic challenge than that of his great-grandnephew Robert. Writing during the Civil War at a time of great uncertainty about its outcome and debate over its principles, James Russell Lowell ran the risk of offending Robert Gould Shaw's recent memory. As he suggests in the second stanza, elegy seems unnecessary if the community is still faithful to the cause for which Shaw died: "Why make we moan / For loss that doth enrich us yet / With upward yearnings of regret?" The very need for elegy betrays a "doubt" or "wavering" that threatens to make a mockery of Shaw's sacrifice. Shaw came to represent for Lowell an escape from the problem of doubt that his death had so powerfully raised for those who survived him: "And yet, like him, to spend / All at a gush, keeping our first faith sure / From midlife's doubt and eld's contentment poor, / What more could Fortune send?"

Despite the twin risks of doubt and contentment, James Russell Lowell insists on the ability of poetry to mediate between private grief and public need:

> Yet, Verse, with noiseless feet,
> Go whisper: "This death hath far choicer ends
> Than slowly to impearl in hearts of friends;

> These obsequies 't is meet
> Not to seclude in closets of the heart,
> But, church-like, with wide doorways, to impart
> Even to the heedless street."

Shaw's death can be redeemed from the problem of doubt by being made public—"Our wall of circumstance / Cleared at a bound, he flashes o'er the fight / A saintly shape of fame, to cheer the right / And steel each wavering glance"—and the vehicle of that publicity is poetry itself. Lowell explains how Shaw is able to transcend and redeem in a single bound in the final stanza of his elegy: "I write of one, / While with dim eyes I think of three; / Who weeps not others fair and brave as he?" Here Lowell recalls his own losses (three of Lowell's nephews died in the war), then confirms the representative status of Shaw's death, positing the poem as the vehicle for a collective act of mourning.

I make this comparison not to claim that James Russell Lowell's poem is a better poem than Robert Lowell's, but to underscore the failure of the Shaw monument to perform a parallel function in the later poem. St. Gaudens's monument cannot link public and private mourning because its very existence is a reminder of the discrepancy between the private act of mourning, which refuses display ("Shaw's father wanted no monument / except the ditch"), and the problem of the public conscience, which requires it. This disjunction is written on the face of the monument itself, which includes a stanza from "Memoriae Positum" describing Shaw's valiant death—"Foeward, as befits a man"—on the bloody ramparts of Fort Wagner, a constant reminder of the geographical dislocation and supererogatory nature of the Boston monument. I'd like to suggest that it is the self-divided and self-cancelling aspect of this monument that most powerfully draws Robert Lowell, and that it is Shaw's father and the iconoclasm he represents that proves the most attractive model for the poet.

It is not surprising that Robert Lowell, whose most courageous and consequential civic actions were his refusal to enlist when drafted in 1943 and his refusal to attend a Festival of the Arts held at Lyndon Johnson's White House, should identify strongly with a public act of moral refusal. Indeed, William James's dedication speech would have provided Lowell with a highly problematic set of reflections on the relation between publicity and morality, heroism, and memorialization. In his speech, James performs a powerful act of rhetorical relocation, redefining Shaw's heroism as civic courage, not martial courage. For James, Shaw's civic courage was proven at the moment of his enlistment in the 54th and tested in the march through Boston, not on the ramparts of Fort Wagner.[4] It is easy to see how the figure of Shaw would

have raised for Lowell with particular intensity the opposition between heroic enlistment and heroic refusal.

The problem with Lowell's identification with the elder Shaw's leveling
iconoclasm can be seen in a line that is both extraordinarily pathetic and
strangely affectless, flatly descriptive: "There are no statues for the last war
here." This line sounds a double note of relief and regret: suggesting the
appropriateness of this state of things ("the ditch is nearer"); a nostalgia for a
time when loss could adequately be monumentalized; and, most importantly, I think, Lowell's disturbing awareness that a refusal to commemorate cannot ultimately be distinguished from forgetfulness.

I want to point, if only briefly, to a number of other places in the poem
where Lowell's oscillation between enlistment in, and refusal of, the task of
public poetry causes disruptions on the surface of the verse. Perhaps the most
jarring is the verbal excess of the lines "on Boylston Street, a commercial
photograph / shows Hiroshima boiling." Here Lowell calls attention to the
participation of the poem itself in the trivialization of death it criticizes. A
similar reluctance to engage in the social critique that this poem also pursues
is evident in the lines recalling the child's desire for demystification: "my
hand tingled / to burst the bubbles / drifting from the noses of the cowed,
compliant fish. / My hand draws back." What in another poem might be a
figure for the satirist's trade is here legible only—or chiefly—as recoil. Most
significant, however, is the poem's inability to find a figure for its own workings. It is striking that the center of the poem's moral indictment—its most
memorable image—is also an image of failed or impossible speech: "The
monument sticks like a fishbone / in the city's throat." This is not the "full-
throated ease" of Keats's nightingale or the speaker in Whitman's "Song of
Myself" who delights in "the smoke of my own breath /...my respiration
and inspiration, the beating of my heart, the passing of blood and air through
my lungs." The closest I can come to a correlative in the poem of the ideal
workings of a public poetry is the arresting detail of the "bell-cheeked Negro
infantry," a figure that bears a trace of a public monument that both alerts
and sings. But Shaw's infantrymen also "hold their air."

I want to conclude by reflecting briefly on my style of reading—or at least,
what I understand to be at stake in reading the way that I do. I can hardly
be alone in feeling exasperated by historicist approaches to poetry which
often seem driven by paraphrase—a desire to extract the portable content of
the poem—rather than a substantive engagement with the complex relation to
order and arbitrariness that is scripted by the poem, usually in forbiddingly
nonlinear fashion. Tied to a rhetoric of demystification, historicists can
become caught up in what Jerome Christensen has described as "the endless adjustment of the literary text to the social real."[5] A fuller historicism

would, in my mind, take into account the history of how the aesthetic under-stands its relation to the social world, the strongest evidence of which is writ-ten into the poems themselves. Which is to argue that poetic self-reflexivity is not simply an indrawing of the already asocial lyric into contemplation of itself, but can be understood as an ongoing dialogue among poets, and between poetry and other discourses, about the function of poetry in the world.

NOTES

1. "Colonel Shaw and the Massachusetts' 54th" appeared as the final poem in the Vintage Books edition of *Life Studies*. "For the Union Dead" was first printed in *The Atlantic* (November 1960), 54–55, along with a photographic reproduc-tion of St. Gaudens's bas-relief.

2. Quoted in Ian Hamilton, *Robert Lowell: A Biography* (New York: Random House) 1982, 277.

3. Ibid., 277.

4. "Oration by Professor William James," *The Monument to Robert Gould Shaw: Its Inception, Completion, and Unveiling 1865–1897* (Boston: Houghton, Mifflin, and Co.) 1897, 73–87.

5. Jerome Christensen, *Lord Byron's Strength: Romantic Writing and Commercial Society* (Baltimore: The Johns Hopkins University Press) 1993, xiv.

PART FIVE

Textual Editing

The Most Conservative Practice,
or the Most Radical?

17

Textual Deviance

Ganymede's Hand in *As You Like It*

Jeffrey Masten

[Shaw] might have been churlish about the knowing giggles of an audience all too ready to read more into the cross-dressing than Shakespeare ever imagined. [T]he night I saw the production, a lot of the laughs seemed to have less to do with the text than with the double-entendres sought out by the audience.

—Vincent Canby in *The New York Times*, reviewing the October 1994, all-male Cheek-By-Jowl production of *As You Like It*[1]

The habits of Compositor D with respect to [the spelling of] other words than "do," "go," and "here"—both his preferences and his *tolerances*—are yet to be thoroughly studied. So too are such non-spelling peculiarities as may be discovered in his work.

—Charlton Hinman on the typsetting of the 1623 First Folio collection of Shakespeare's plays[2]

Taking my cue from the binary question that heads this section of the volume,[3] I want to assert that it's time for "the most conservative practice" in the editing of early modern texts. If you're not in the field of Renaissance literature, and possibly even if you are, you have, I'm guessing, no sense of how radical our editions of Shakespeare and others from this period have become. Editors and publishers, intent on undermining our shared cultural heritage, the very foundations of Western Culture, have changed (or, as they euphemistically say, "emended") whole words and lines of the very texts that are most important to us; even when purporting to represent to us the texts as written, they have given us what are essentially *translations* from the early modern English, simplifying and reinterpreting (or again, as they would have it, "modernizing") the complexities of a language spoken and written before the advent of standardization. They have, furthermore, given us editions of Shakespeare that, in their very monumentality, or in their paperback slickness, bear no resemblance either to the original staged productions at the Globe and the Blackfriars, or to the editions of his texts printed during his lifetime. As surely as judicial activism subverts the intent of the Framers of the Constitution, current editorial practice is subversion, and editors are outside agitators imposing their own agendas on the relics of Western Culture. The only possible response is an avowed conservatism. *We must reclaim what Shakespeare wrote.*

You don't think I'm going to let that stand, do you? Take that as an example, at least, of one direction in which a conservative practice might proceed. I do mean to disavow this rhetoric, and I've attached it to Shakespeare in order to raise the pitch and the stakes, though many of the same points could be made of early modern texts in general; at the same time, I nevertheless want to argue, for reasons I have at least hinted at above, for a conservative editorial practice. By *conservative* I mean a practice that will, to the greatest extent possible, conserve the documents, and the texts inscribed in those documents, in the forms in which they initially were written, and/or performed, and/or read, and/or circulated, in early modern England. I will argue this from what I take to be a historicist perspective, though I do so while remarking that many of the practitioners of new historicism, whatever the historical attentiveness of their arguments in general, have continued to quote Shakespeare and others from modern, emended, reformatted, modernized, repunctuated editions.

There isn't space in this brief essay to discuss all of this, particularly the questions of modernization as translation I've raised above.[4] I'll restrict my task here to finding an example of editing so inflammatory in its radicalness that you will be convinced that you should care about editorial matters— matters we've been taught institutionally to devalue as pedantic and largely inconsequential, the tedious work that happens prior to the real business of literary and cultural studies today. With the caveat that I know I'm participating in a certain canonical hegemony, I'll examine *As You Like It*, or rather, one page of *As You Like It*, since the play may (for whatever reasons, including the *New York Times* coverage of the controversial 1994 production) retain some interest and accessibility for those outside the field. My intention, however, is to make an argument that speaks about early modern English texts and culture more generally.

In the final moments of *As You Like It*, with a number of weddings seemingly both imminent and impossible, and with Rosalind (disguised as the young man Ganymede) having promised to return, sort out the marriage plots, and "make all this matter euen" (TLN 2594),[5] the following text appears in the 1623 First Folio edition, the only early printed text of this play:

Enter Hymen, Rosalind, and Celia.
Still Musicke.
Hymen. *Then is there mirth in heauen,*
When earthly things made eauen
attone together.
Good Duke receiue thy daughter,
Hymen from Heauen brought her,
Yea brought her hether.
That thou mightst ioyne his hand with his,
Whose heart within his bosome is.

(TLN 2681-90)[6]

The radicalism of the editorial tradition is clear and virtually univocal; to my knowledge there is no recent edition that conserves the Folio text joining "his hand with his,"[7] and as the 1977 Shakespeare Variorum edition notes in its survey of previous editions:

2689–90 *his hand...his bosome*] The editors are almost unanimous in finding *his hand* an error for *her hand*...—COLLIER (ed. 1842) notes that *his* is an easy misreading of *hir*—but are deeply divided over whose bosom is the repository of whose heart.[8]

The note proceeds to quote a number of the "deeply divided" editors, but notice that they are deeply divided on this second issue only once one has decided that the first (men holding hands in the last scene of a Shakespearean comedy) is simply "an error" or "an easy misreading"—deeply divided, that is, within a heterosexualizing paradigm. (We can call this "the radical heterosexual agenda.") By the time the note gets around to quoting an editor who conservatively retains the Folio reading "his hand with his," that reading is already on the defensive, already a defendant: the Folio's reading "is defended by CALDECOTT (ed. 1820) on the ground that *his* in both places refers to Rosalind as Ganymede, whose costume he thinks she still wears."

But if you were reading the Variorum carefully, you might have seen this coming in the much earlier note on Rosalind's chosen male name, Ganymede:

Ganimed] SMITH (ed. 1894) "A beautiful boy, beloved by Jupiter, who (in the form of the eagle) carried him off and made him his cup-bearer. (Ovid, *Met[amorphoses]* x.155–161.)" WALTER (ed. 1965, p. 7): "[In the Renaissance,] Ganymede was thought to represent intelligence, or rational thought, more elaborately his name was thought to derive from two Greek words meaning to joy or rejoice, and advice or counsel, and this was extended to suggest that he led people to love of divine truth. So greatly is Rosalind composed of these qualities of intelligence, joy, wisdom, and truth that it is difficult not to believe that Shakespeare deliberately clad her in the myth of Ganymede."[9]

Perhaps he did, and I'll have more to say about Shakespeare's deliberations in a moment, but, to say the absolute minimum, the Variorum's note suggests that the editorial tradition has privileged abstraction and allegory over the erotic meanings of this myth, meanings that were widely available in Renaissance culture and not necessarily separate from those celebrated in the note.[10]

There remains, of course, the possibility that the interpretation I am about to suggest is, in the words of the Variorum editor's handbook, "mere nonsense of course to be excluded."[11] Critics skeptical of the Folio's reading will remark that Rosalind and Celia have returned to the stage dressed "as themselves,"[12] and Rosalind has been referred to as "her" in the lines that directly precede "his hand with his." Of course, those critics are probably reading out of the radical editorial tradition that has routinely inserted a stage direction indicating for Rosalind a return to women's dress, and, if Rosalind in this speech is referenced as both female and male, it is neither the first nor the last time in the play that this occurs, as those familiar with the play's epilogue will already have anticipated. In any event—and here I'm relying on recent work on Renaissance homoeroticism by social and cultural historians, theorists, and literary critics[13]—I wouldn't want to exclude too quickly the possibility of two male hands joined in the last scene of a play that repeatedly directs attention to the boy actor playing the part of Rosalind, has emphasized the choice of the name "Ganymede," and has earlier, in Act 4, Scene 1, staged the rehearsal of this same marriage between two men: "Come sister," Rosalind-as-Ganymede says, "you shall be the Priest, and marrie vs: giue me your hand *Orlando*" (TLN 2033-34).[14]

The radical tradition of editing would settle this question by asking whose hand is responsible for these joined hands; if the hand is Shakespeare's, or a hand near Shakespeare's—and the Folio text of *As You Like It* is often said to derive from a copy of Shakespeare's manuscript—then the reading "ioyne his hand with his" should stand. If not—if the hand is said to be that of a transcriber, or the Folio collectors, or the publisher, or the compositor who set the type—then the reading is said to be a corruption (an "error" or "easy misreading") and should be changed.[15] Editors have avoided this first possibility (that Shakespeare wrote "his" and the compositor then set this word), either because they have thought the line nonsensical, and therefore non-Shakespearean, or (and?) because the line as printed may raise uncomfortable questions about Shakespeare's "preferences," "habits," "tolerances," or views on the subject of early modern boys' relations with men—what we might call, appropriating Hinman, Shakespeare's "non-spelling peculiarities."[16]

I don't mean to save Shakespeare from the perceived threat of homoeroticism by suggesting some other possible agencies for this reading; I think it's more than possible that "his with his" was initially written into the play by Shakespeare. But I also think that, lacking a manuscript in Shakespeare's hand, this is an unanswerable question, and even were we to possess such a manuscript, we would not know whether Shakespeare made an "error," or performed an "easy misreading" of his own intention, in writing "his for his." What we *do* possess is a text that was produced through the collaborative efforts and mediations of, yes, a playwright (and probably a later revising playwright who could be Shakespeare or someone else),[17] several songwriters, probably the actors of the King's company, the book holder of the company, who supervised the use of the script in performance, the publishers of the Folio volume produced in part from that script or a copy of it, the compositor or compositors who typeset the text, and the proofreaders who either failed to correct this "error" or didn't see it as such.[18] Each of these persons or groups of persons might have, to quote Hinman's terms again, "preferences and tolerances" that might lead him to retain or change the reading of this line. By these terms, Hinman means that a compositor has certain spellings he prefers and that he also "tolerates" certain spellings that go against those habits when they're present in the documents from which he's setting type. I want, in the space remaining, to speculate briefly about the hands and habits of the compositors.

Hinman says, on the basis of particular spellings and types that appear in the text, that the page on which "his with his" appears was set by Compositor B from typecase y (II: 448). I would argue that the idea of fixed spelling habits and preferences among compositors needs to be retheorized in the context of a language system without standardized spelling,[19] and, as Randall McLeod has shown, printed spellings seem to have been dependent as much on the local exigencies of printing as on ostensible, individually produced differences.[20] But even Hinman, who's deeply invested in the separability of compositors, admits that Compositor B's spellings are sometimes variable and that B's work is sometimes difficult to distinguish from that of Compositor E elsewhere in the folio (II: 512, I: 226).[21] Though he argues that "it is now quite plain that sins committed by E have been laid to the charge of B" (II: 512), Hinman further notes that the habits and preferences of E (who he thinks is an *inexperienced* compositor) actually change over the course of the pages of the Folio he works on—that early on he "follows copy" closely but quickly develops "strong spelling preferences" of his own (I: 213n2).[22] Such evidence might be said to undermine the separability of B and E, or the separation of E's work from that of the other compositors who helped in the composing of Shakespeare. In other words, by Hinman's own logic, there is the possibility that the reading that "ioyne[s] his hand with his" on page 206 of the Folio Comedies was produced by B, an experienced compositor, working with the younger, inexperienced E. Two hands joined, one of whom Hinman calls "The Prentice Hand" (I: 214).[23]

As I've been hinting, I think much of this evidence is highly tenuous, and I've emphasized the language of "preferences" and "tolerances" in order to suggest that it may be based on a notion of essential individuality that is more at home in the mid-twentieth century than in the seventeenth.[24] But this evidence may at least serve to remind us of knowledges available in other forms and sources: first, that the texts we now associate with the name Shakespeare were collaborative creations at a number of points in their production;[25] second, that the system that produced these texts in the printing house was organized around adult/apprentice relations in a way that closely resembles the organization of the acting company that produced these plays and in which Shakespeare himself participated as actor and writer on a daily basis; and third, that such relations are themselves (in a way I have only gestured toward here) legible within a discourse circulating in the play and elsewhere that used the name *Ganymede* in a homoerotically charged fashion—a fashion that often existed *alongside* the possibility of what we now call "heterosexual" marriage.[26] We might read, as an example of such relations, this entry from the will of Augustine Phillips, a sharer in the King's Men—a will in which Phillips' wife Anne is also named executrix:

> Item, I give to Samuel Gilborne, my late apprentice, the sum of forty shillings, and my mouse-colored velvet hose, and a white taffeta doublet, a black taffeta suit, my purple cloak, sword and dagger, and my bass viol.[27]

While I would not argue that an all-male collaborative process is always homoerotic or always produces a homoerotic text, I think we also can't ignore that the process by which this play was first performed *and* published is informed by discourses, rehearsals, and practices of homoeroticism prominent in early modern English culture. Many of these questions disappear—the cultural history that literally unfolds from the Folio pages disintegrates—when editions fail to conserve the words (and, in a way I haven't had space to argue for here, the actual material *form*) of the only text we have of this play.[28] Editing that attempts to "reclaim what Shakespeare meant" has often left us unable to determine what Renaissance culture meant, and means. Without necessarily knowing whose hand is whose, we need a conservative editorial practice that will keep open the possibility of "ioyn[ing] his hand with his, / Whose heart within his bosome is."

And, as you've no doubt guessed by now, I'm hoping that such a conservative practice will ultimately put into play meanings that are, in complicated ways, radical.

NOTES

Thanks to Jay Grossman, Jules Law, Meredith McGill, Stephen Orgel, and Paul Werstine for comments that have shaped this essay. An earlier version was presented at the 1993 Modern Language Association convention as part of the panel "Postmodern Shakespeare Variorum?" and benefited from discussion in that context. This essay relies on the work of Randall McLeod in a way these notes cannot fully record.

1. Vincent Canby, 'As You Like It,' "Sunday View," *New York Times*, October 16, 1994.

2. Charlton Hinman, *The Printing and Proofreading of the First Folio of Shakespeare*, 2 vols. (Oxford: Clarendon, 1963) 1: 199, Hinman's italics. Subsequent references to these volumes will appear parenthetically in the text.

3. "Textual Editing: The Most Conservative Practice, or the Most Radical?"

4. The commentary to my edition of *The Old Law*, a collaborative play-text included in *The Collected Works of Thomas Middleton*, general ed. Gary Taylor (Oxford: Oxford University Press, forthcoming) suggests some of the problematics of simultaneously modernizing a text and reading historically. See also the preface and commentary to Stephen Booth's edition of *Shakespeare's Sonnets* (New Haven: Yale University Press, 1977); Margreta de Grazia, "Homonyms Before and After Lexical Standardization," *Shakespeare Jahrbuch* (1990): 143–56. For a more quietistic view of historicism's relation to the "unchanging" "basic issues" of textual criticism, see G. Thomas Tanselle, "Historicism and Critical Editing," *Studies in Bibliography* 39 (1986): 1–46, especially 45–46.

5. Except in the photoquotation below, *As You Like It* is cited from *Mr. William Shakespeares Comedies, Histories & Tragedies* (London: by Isaac Iaggard, and Ed. Blount, 1623), as reproduced in *The Norton Facsimile: The First Folio of Shakespeare*, prepared by Charlton Hinman (New York: Norton, 1968). Parenthetical citations refer to that edition's through-line numbering (TLN).

6. *Mr. William Shakespeares Comedies, Histories & Tragedies* (London: by Isaac Iaggard, and Ed. Blount, 1623), page 206 of the Comedies; the photoquotation is from one of the Houghton Library copies, Harvard University. Photo courtesy of the Houghton Library.

7. The Folio reading has been advocated most recently by Maura Slattery Kuhn, "Much Virtue in *If*," *Shakespeare Quarterly* 28 (1977): 40–50. For Kuhn, the importance of the Folio reading lies in its raising of the theatrical question of whether Rosalind resumes women's clothes for her final entrance in 5.4; Kuhn is largely uninterested in the issues of homoeroticism that concern me in this essay.

8. Richard Knowles, ed., *As You Like It*, A New Variorum Edition of Shakespeare (New York: MLA, 1977), 293.

9. Knowles, Variorum *As You Like It* 64 (italics and brackets in the original).

10. There is widespread evidence for the erotic meanings of *Ganymede* in early modern England. Here for example is John's Minsheu's definition of the word: "*a* Ganimede *or* Ganymede, *a boy hired to be vsed contrary to nature, to commit the detestable sinne of Sodomie. Vi. Ingle*"; Iohn Minsheu, *Ductor in Linguas, The Guide into the tongue.* (London: Iohn Browne, 1617), 211. On the convergence of the idealizing and homoerotic meanings of this myth, see in particular Leonard Barkan, *Transuming Passion: Ganymede and the Erotics of Humanism* (Stanford: Stanford University Press, 1991). On Renaissance representations and contextualizations of Ganymede more generally, see: Gregory W. Bredbeck, *Sodomy and Interpretation* (Ithaca: Cornell University Press, 1991); James Saslow, *Ganymede in the Renaissance: Homosexuality in Art and Society* (New Haven: Yale University Press, 1986); Bruce Smith, *Homosexual Desire in Shakespeare's England: A Cultural Poetics* (Chicago: University of Chicago Press, 1991). Mario DiGangi observes an important class dynamic in the Ganymede myth and its early modern appropriations, including *As You Like It*; he remarks that the story "concerns the disruption by a male servant and lover of the family of Jupiter, Juno, and their daughter Hebe"; "Queer Outsiders Inside the Renaissance Family" (paper delivered at MLA 1993), 8.

11. *Shakespeare Variorum Handbook* (New York: MLA, 1971).

12. This is the stage direction of the new Oxford edition at 5.4.105; William Shakespeare, *The Complete Works*, Stanley Wells and Gary Taylor, gen. eds. (Oxford: Clarendon, 1986), 732.

13. Alan Bray, *Homosexuality in Renaissance England* (London: Gay Men's Press, 1982); Bray, "Homosexuality and the Signs of Male Friendship in Elizabethan England," in *Queering the Renaissance*, ed. Jonathan Goldberg, (Durham: Duke University Press, 1993), 40–61; Jonathan Goldberg, *Sodometries: Renaissance Texts, Modern Sexualities* (Stanford: Stanford University Press, 1992); Bredbeck; DiGangi; Smith. Discussions of gender and cross-dressing in the period and in this play have also been formative for this reading; see Catherine Belsey, "Disrupting Sexual Difference: Meaning and Gender in the Comedies," in John Drakakis, ed., *Alternative Shakespeares* (London: Methuen, 1985), 166–90; Marjorie Garber, *Vested Interests: Cross Dressing and Cultural Anxiety* (New York: HarperCollins, 1993); Goldberg, *Sodometries*; Jean E. Howard, "Crossdressing, the Theatre, and Gender Struggle in Early Modern England," *Shakespeare Quarterly* 39 (1988): 418–40; Laura Levine, "Men in Women's Clothing: Anti-theatricality and Effeminization from 1579–1642," *Criticism* 28 (1986): 121–43; Stephen Orgel, "Nobody's Perfect: Or, Why Did the English Stage Take Boys for Women," in *Displacing Homophobia*, ed. Ronald R. Butters, John M. Clum, and Michael Moon (Durham: Duke University Press, 1989), 7–29; Phyllis Rackin, "Androgyny, Mimesis, and the Marriage of the Boy Heroine on the English Renaissance Stage," *PMLA* 102

(1987): 29–41; Mary Beth Rose, "Sexual Disguise and Social Mobility in Jacobean City Comedy," chapter 2 of *The Expense of Spirit: Love and Sexuality in English Renaissance Drama* (Ithaca: Cornell University Press, 1988), 43–92.

14. Kuhn also quotes this line in support of her interpretation: "The final stage picture of these two boys holding hands should mirror the earlier scene" (43). But Kuhn's larger argument suggests, in fact, that the idea of male-male marriage that she too sees figured in the play is part of the larger "unreal condition of the play itself," figured and facilitated by "if."

15. In the context of another emendation of *his* to *hir/her*, Gary Taylor writes: "In an Elizabethan secretary hand, terminal *s* was often almost impossible to distinguish from *r*, and in contemporary orthography *her* could be spelled with a medial *i*; in such circumstances, a "hir" and a "his" are materially identical, and can only be differentiated by cultural context" (217); "Textual and Sexual Criticism: A Crux in *The Comedy of Errors*," *Renaissance Drama* 19 (1988): 195–225. Part of the argument of the present essay, of course, is that the cultural context does not easily settle the question in this instance. That this "exceptionally easy misreading, well attested elsewhere" seems to occur in other plays (223 n17) does not guarantee the correctness of this correction in the context of *As You Like It*; that Taylor cites this instance in *As You Like It* as a transparent case suggests that we need to return to the other instances of presumed his/her confusion.

16. I don't mean to imply that Hinman believes that sexual preferences or behaviors can be ascertained on the basis of spelling choices. On the other hand, I *do* mean to suggest that the language of twentieth-century compositorial study, in its search for stable essences/identities that can be read out from spelling behaviors, bears resemblance to, and is contemporaneous with, other twentieth-century attempts to discern identities—*sexual* identities—on the basis of visible physical signs and behaviors. On the detection of homosexuality in the 1950s and 1960s, see Lee Edelman, "Tearooms and Sympathy; or, The Epistemology of the Water Closet," in *Homographesis: Essays in Gay Literary and Cultural Theory* (New York: Routledge, 1994), 148–70.

17. I base this suggestion on G. E. Bentley's argument that "almost any play first printed more than ten years after composition and...kept in active repertory by the company that owned it is most likely to contain later revisions by the author or, in many cases, by another playwright"; *The Profession of Dramatist in Shakespeare's Time 1590–1642* (Princeton: Princeton University Press, 1971), 263.

18. There is the remote possibility that this line is the site of a press variant not yet observed/recorded. Hinman did not exhaustively collate all copies of the Folio for his study (or even all the Folger copies), and others have found further variants. For a discussion of additional variants and the utility of this pursuit, see

Paul Werstine, "More Unrecorded States in the Folger Shakespeare Library's Collection of First Folios," *The Library*, 6th ser., 11 (1989): 47–51. Hinman's *Norton Facsimile*, it is important to recall, is "an ideal representation of the Folio" (xxii) that reproduces no single extant book, but rather brings together the "best" pages of a number of copies of the Folio that reside at the Folger Shakespeare Library. On Hinman's principles of selection, see xxxiii.

19. The assumption of compositor-identification studies would seem to be that, even if the language as a whole did not operate according to principles of standardized spelling, each individual writer/speaker/typesetter operated according to a personal, largely self-standardized, glossary. My term "standardized" is shorthand: in this period, as Juliet Fleming argues, "English appears to have been not unruled, but ruled differently—perhaps in accordance with a rhetorical rather than grammatical, lexical, and orthographic order"; "Dictionary English and the Female Tongue," in *Enclosure Acts: Sexuality, Property, and Culture in Early Modern England*, ed. Richard Burt and John Michael Archer (Ithaca: Cornell University Press, 1994), 301–302.

20. McLeod shows, for example, that the name "Shakspeare" is typeset to take into account the fact that, in certain typefaces, certain letters of type (in this case, "k" and long "s") will collide with those around them, necessitating the medial *e* and/or hyphen to avoid type breakage; "Spellbound: Typography and the Concept of Old-Spelling Editions," *Renaissance and Reformation*, n.s., 3 (1979): 50–65.

21. Though *not* in the Comedies. Still, there has been a fair amount of work on this issue, and the evidence for B's ostensible consistency isn't nearly as stable as Hinman suggests. Hinman himself notes that "both A and B now and again used non-characteristic spellings, and sometimes without ascertainable reason" (I: 185). In a reconsideration of Hinman's and Alice Walker's work on Compositor B, Paul Werstine confronts this problem: "perhaps an editor must conclude that compositor variability is so high, as Compositor B's is between the comedies and *1H4*, that compositor identification is a useless tool"; "Compositor B of the Shakespeare First Folio," *Analytical and Enumerative Bibliography* 2.4 (1978): 260. See also Andrew S. Cairncross's disputing of Hinman's and Howard-Hill's attributions to Compositor B in "Compositors E and F of the Shakespeare First Folio," *Papers of the Bibliographical Society of America* 66 (1972): 369–406.

22. Commenting on and revising Hinman's work, T. H. Howard-Hill concludes: "We can see more clearly than before the closeness of E's working relationship with compositor B, and, throughout the Tragedies, we can observe E's gradual acquisition of typographical expertise. ...He was, as the Nurse in *Romeo* puts it, 'a man of wax'" (178); "New Light on Compositor E of the Shakespeare First Folio," *The Library*, 6th ser., 2.2 (1980): 156–78. Cf. Cairncross: "That

Compositor E was the type of man he was is a mixed blessing. His inefficiency is unfortunate; but his strong imitative tendency, which has so effectively concealed his presence and caused such confusion, may yield valuable results" ("Compositors E and F," 395–96). (On this discourse, see note 16 above.)

23. Since Hinman finds E only in the Tragedies, he would resist these statements. My point is that the very flexibility and malleability of E's spellings make it possible, by Hinman's own logic, to find the impressionable E almost *anywhere* (I: 213n2). While disputing some of Hinman's findings, Cairncross has, by Hinman's methods, found "uneqivocal" evidence of E's "presence" in the Comedies and in the page in question ("Compositors E and F," 378–80).

24. For a brilliant and highly detailed critique of printing-house study (and Hinman's findings) on evidentiary and logical grounds, see D. F. McKenzie, "Printers of the Mind: Some Notes on Bibliographical Theories and Printing-House Practices," *Studies in Bibliography* 22 (1969): 1–75. On the embeddedness of compositorial study in twentieth-century epistemology, see note 16 above.

25. On the collaborative theatre, see G. E. Bentley, *The Profession of Dramatist in Shakespeare's Time 1590–1642* (Princeton: Princeton University Press, 1971); Stephen Orgel, "What is a Text?" in *Staging the Renaissance: Reinterpretations of Elizabethan and Jacobean Drama*, ed. David Scott Kastan and Peter Stallybrass (New York: Routledge, 1991), 83–87; Jeffrey Masten, "Beaumont and/or Fletcher: Collaboration and the Interpretation of Renaissance Drama," *ELH* 59 (1992): 337–56.

26. Thus, to continue the argument in note 14 above: unlike Kuhn, I think that there is significant traffic between, on the one hand, the conditions of the play's production and printing as registered in contemporary discourses, and, on the other, the discourse of the play itself, however "unreal" it might seem.

27. Quoted in Bentley 19–20.

28. On this, see Margreta de Grazia and Peter Stallybrass, "The Materiality of the Shakespearen Text," *Shakespeare Quarterly* 44 (1993): 255–83; and D. F. McKenzie, *What's Past is Prologue: The Bibliographical Society and the History of the Book*, Bibliographical Society Centenary Lecture, July 14, 1992, (Hearthstone Publications, 1993). This is perhaps the place to point out the problematic class politics of my calling for a research and teaching practice based on early, rare editions, while doing research and teaching at Harvard University, where there is easy access to such materials. The emergence and proliferation of inexpensive facsimiles, the Short Title Catalogue collection in microfilm, and, eventually, electronic facsimiles, may at least begin to address this issue.

18

Medieval Irish Manuscript Culture

Patrick K. Ford

Scholars, teachers, and students of medieval literature rely heavily on printed editions of the texts they study. Access to the manuscripts of those texts is often difficult, and even when they or facsimile editions of them are available, they can be used efficiently only by the few who have been trained in paleography. Diplomatic editions of manuscripts obviate that problem, but one suspects that they are not consulted often because most scholars are interested in individual texts, not in the manuscripts in which those texts appear. Therefore, the process by which the individual, handwritten text is turned into a printed edition of that text is crucial: the printed edition will, for all practical purposes, take the place of the manuscript text. One question governing the process is, will the edition attempt to reproduce a single manuscript version of the text? Or will the edition use several manuscript versions in an attempt to reconstruct a supposed original text of which the individual manuscript versions are the flawed remains?

And we do often regard our texts as flawed. As John Dagenais says in his recent book, *The Ethics of Reading in Manuscript Culture*, "From the beginning academic medievalism has taken as its mission the restoration of coherence, sense, to these texts, which appear to us to lie just behond the horizon of modern European linguistic and cultural understanding."[1] But, he insists, the mission is a misguided one, for the coherence we seek reflects our modern tastes and sensibilities. Medieval texts must be taken on their own terms. The "restoration" process entails creating a text, an archetype, from a family of manuscripts, or choosing a "best" text as a base into which "better" readings from other texts may be introduced. For Dagenais, the restoration process presents interesting problems but it has "little or nothing to do with medieval literature as it was produced and received by medieval people...the end product, the critical edition, as it is currently constituted and used in scholarly work on medieval texts, is of absolutely no evidentiary value" (p. 112).

Dagenais insists that to understand medieval culture, medieval literature, we must get away from an author and text perspective, that is, from a focus on an individual text detached from its manuscript context, and adopt a reader perspective, for medieval manuscript culture was reader oriented. That there was an author who produced a text is without question. The question is to what use that text was put once it entered the manuscript. Scholars and scribes copied it, read aloud from it. It was glossed, added to, whole passages erased and replaced, and so on. For Dagenais the operative phrase is "indeterminacy," which, he says, "gave to the text an *aliquid minus*, a negative charge that allowed a gloss to spring up at any point" (p. 80).

Dagenais urges us "to move among medieval scripta and their margins rather than among editions of authorial texts," where "a new set of relations among our texts emerges." Put another way: the meaning of any text is not to be sought in the text in isolation but in the text as it occurs in the manuscript with all that surrounds it. Speaking of the problems editors wrangle about, such as where to place variants, musical scores, illustrations, emendations, and the like, Dagenais comments, "I would just point out again that these things will always be found in precisely the correct place in the manuscripts themselves" (p. 112).

Thus, the text (or scriptum, as Dagenais prefers to call it) includes its medieval readers and not just its author. "Margins were the place for dialogue with other readers of the text. Texts were shared, not private affairs." Dagenais gives an interesting example from Old English literature of how separating text and readership can lead to curious distortions. He cites Kevin Kiernan's recent article reopening the question of Caedmon's hymn, where Kiernan suggests that the "hymn" is, in fact, nothing more than a slightly amplified translation into Old English of Bede's Latin paraphrase. So originally, the hymn is a gloss on Bede, while in modern scholarship, Bede becomes a gloss on the hymn. We have a similar situation with a lovely and much anthologized early Irish poem of two quatrains that we might call "Wall of Woodland."[2]

But I'd like to turn now to a discussion of these issues, a case study as it were, as reflected in two recent editions of the Irish *Sex Aetatis Mundi*. The two editions were examined recently in a detailed and very erudite review article by Dr. Máire Herbert.[3] One edition, by Dr. Hildegard Tristram, is based on a single manuscript, Rawlinson B502, and is justified by a principle first articulated by Professor Edgar Slotkin about Irish scribes' attitudes toward fixed texts. Slotkin's argument focuses on vernacular texts and hinges on the tension between oral and literary. He urges us to consider that variant manuscript versions of a given text may represent scribal "performances" of those texts, in which case critical editions of such texts are out of the question. According to this principle, the authentic text is that of a single manuscript. The other edition, that of Dr. Dáibhí Ó Cróinín, is based on more general procedures of textual criticism.

Herbert criticizes Tristram's decision to present a single text, saying it lacks a convincing theoretical basis; Herbert takes Slotkin's arguments as not yet proved or as inapplicable to a text like *Sex Aetates Mundi*. She states:

> Overall, examination of the work in the light of its content and sources reinforces the conclusion reached on the basis of critical study of the text tradition, that the *original* Irish *Sex Aetates Mundi* is best represented by the shared witness of all manuscripts. (p. 106; my emphasis)

It may be true that the original Irish *Sex Aetates Mundi* can be recovered by the evidence of all the manuscript versions of it, but does reconstructing a hypothetical original *Sex Aetates Mundi* give us information about the use or function of *Sex Aetates Mundi* in medieval Ireland? What would the audience of such an original be? How might the text have functioned? What kind of *manuscript* would have been home to the hypothetical original?

The only value in constructing the archetype might be to provide a measure of the degree to which individual texts decline from it. Indeed, Herbert comments on the divergence of Rawlinson B502 from the original *Sex Aetates Mundi*, saying, "[it] may be seen to reflect zeal on the part of its compiler to improve and extend his text wherever possible, and with whatever type of material he considered relevant" (p. 106). The result is "an awkward mélange of history and exegesis," whereas "the *SAM* archetype established by critical methodology, however, is not such a conglomerate, but is, rather, a factual exposition of the main events of the world ages" (p. 108).

Dr. Hans Oskamp's work on the Rawlinson version of the text, to which Herbert refers, is, in my view, crucial to the question of the tension between reconstructed archetype and individual text. He comments:

> There is always the possibility that a scribe did not copy the entire text which
> he found in his exemplar, but picked out those paragraphs that for one reason
> or another attracted him.... There are many indications that the scribe added
> information to the transcript, even after he had finished it. Many glosses and
> notes *inter lineas* and *in margine* are evidence of the fact that this man was a
> scholar rather than a professional scribe. *Sex Aetates Mundi* in Rawl. MS B502
> is a text that "has been worked on"; the scribe was not satisfied with a mere
> transcript, but added everything he could find and think of.[4]

Oskamp seems to envisage a reader culture of the sort that Dagenais is positing, a culture in which, as we have seen, manuscripts were glossed, added to,
subtracted from, and so on—in a phrase, "worked on."

So the question is, again, is there value in establishing the archetype
through critical methodology, or should we be more interested in the text as
found in a particular manuscript, with all its "shortcomings" or *aliquid
minus*? Should the focus be on author/text or on reader/culture? For
Herbert, the establishment of the archetype is an important first step, after
which we may gauge the significance of individual texts:

> Examination of the Irish *Sex Aetates Mundi* text extends our knowledge of the
> historiography of the Middle Irish period. Moreover, following the present revised
> analysis, it is possible to gain a view both of the vernacular *SAM* itself, and of the
> manner in which it was glossed and expanded by subsequent redactors. By
> means of the copy of the text in [Rawlinson], in particular, one may observe
> the singular contribution of a twelfth-century scholar, whose mind—and
> library—provided him with a store of reference material with which to amplify
> his original. It may be, indeed, that [Rawlinson B502] embodies a version of
> *SAM* adapted for instructional purposes, since several of its interventions are
> framed in the catechetical manner, but further conclusions must await further
> study of the work. (pp. 108–109)

Clearly, individual manuscript versions of a text allow us to examine the
mind of the medieval scribe/scholar at work and, in the process, to aquaint
ourselves with medieval Irish readers and literary process. The restored original or archetype, however, is always in danger of being taken as the "true"
text, and thus of frustrating our attempts to know medieval literature. The
critical edition is, as Dagenais puts it, "of absolutely no evidentiary value"
for such a purpose.

NOTES

1. (Princeton: Princeton University Press 1994), p. 111.
2. This is one of a number of poems at the center of a recent debate over early Irish monastic or hermit poetry that rejoices in nature. The poem occurs in a single manuscript, a ninth-century manuscript of Priscian's Latin grammar, now at St. Gall in Switzerland. It is written in the lower margin in a section of the grammar that deals with the positions of personal pronouns in Latin; and though the poem's two quatrains tell of the monk's delight in nature as he scribes away in the out-of-doors, one of the most pronounced features of our Irish poem is the frequency of infixed personal pronouns in it. To my mind, this is a clear case of the scribe or reader entering into a dialogue with his text, and we should think not so much in terms of generic hermitic poetry or nature poetry but of "grammar" poetry. The poem was set down as part of a dialogue with other readers of the principal text, a discourse on Latin grammar. The fact is that we have no medieval manuscripts of hermitic or nature poetry even if people were moved to treat the subject of nature in a subjective way. Thus if we take the poem out of its manuscript and put walls around—edit it and put it along with others similar in tone or style far removed from its original context—then we create (authorially) a genre of hermitic or nature poetry and insist that it be understood as such. What passes for hermit/nature poetry in modern editions and anthologies is, in manuscript culture, prosody poetry (those found in metrical tracts), grammar poetry, and similar categories that reflect the original text and its reader(s).
3. "The Irish *Sex Aetates Mundi*: First Editions," *Cambridge Medieval Celtic Studies* 11 (Summer 1986): 97–112.
4. Oskamp, "On the Author of *Sex Aetates Mundi*," SC 3 (1968): 127–40.

19

Editing Homer, Rethinking the Bard

Gregory Nagy

Let us shift backward as far as we can in the European literary tradition, all the way to what some might think is the primordial period or, as the Greeks of the Classical period of the fifth century B.C.E. would have liked to put it, all the way back to their own original author, Homer. Here we find the prototypical Bard, separated by well over two millennia from that ultimate Bard of the English-speaking world, Shakespeare.

To edit the text of Homer—that is, the two monumental epics that we know as the *Iliad* and the *Odyssey*—is to reconstruct the history of a wide variety of different texts. Once we start viewing Homer from the historical perspective of the evolving Homeric texts, we may start to rethink even the identity of Homer.

Here I invoke the pathfinding Homeric research of two former professors at Harvard University, Milman Parry[1] and his successor, Albert Lord.[2] According to Parry and Lord, Homeric poetry is the product of an open-ended and evolving process of oral poetry, where composition and performance are aspects of the same process, and where each performance entails a potential recomposition. In my own research on the Homeric text, I have applied the findings of Parry and Lord by formulating an "evolutionary model" of this text.[3] Such a model cannot be pinned down to any single "Age of Homer." Instead, we may choose to think of several ages of Homer.

Here is an outline of what I see as five distinct consecutive periods of Homeric transmission, "five ages of Homer," with each period showing progressively less fluidity and more fixity:

1. a period of maximum fluidity, with no written texts, extending from the early second millennium B.C.E. into the late eighth century in the first millennium

2. a more formative or "pan-Hellenic" period, still with no written texts, from the late eighth century to the middle of the sixth

3. a definitive period, centralized in the city-state of Athens, with potential texts in the sense of "transcripts," at any or several points from the middle of the sixth century to the later fourth; this period starts with the reform of Homeric performance traditions in Athens during the régime of tyrants known as the Peisistratidai

4. a standardizing period, with texts in the sense of transcripts or even "scripts," from the later fourth century to the middle of the second; this period starts with the reform of Homeric performance traditions in Athens during the régime of Demetrius of Phaleron, which lasted from 317 to 307 B.C.E.

5. a period of maximum fixity, with texts as "scripture," from the middle of the second century onward; this period starts with the completion of Aristarchus's editorial work on the Homeric texts, not long after 150 B.C.E. or so, which is a date that also marks the general disappearance of the so-called eccentric papyri.[4]

By "transcript" I mean the broadest possible category of written text; a transcript can be a record of performance, even an aid for performance, but it is not a performance in and of itself. We need to distinguish a transcript from an inscription, which can traditionally refer to itself in the archaic period of Greece as just that, a performance.[5] As for "script," I mean a narrower category, where the written text is a prerequisite for performance. That is, the need for a "script" in any given performance implies that the performer depends on a written text in order to perform. By "scripture" I mean the narrowest category of them all, where the written text is independent of performance. That is, a "scripture" does not even need to be performed to maintain its status as the authoritative word.

The basic Homer text that we have is by and large what has come down to us through the medieval Byzantine textual tradition, derived from a textual tradition that the scholars of the city of Alexandria (in the period from the beginning of the third century till the middle of second B.C.E.) used to call the Koine, or "Standard Version."

The task that confronts the editor of the Homeric text is to develop objective editorial criteria that take into account the variation within a continuum of performances repeated over vast stretches of time, where the very process of performance entails different degrees of recomposition in different periods. To establish a multitext edition of Homer, the editor would need to take all authenticated variants into account. Such a multitext format would help establish which variant was more suitable at which time and place.

Keep in mind that the Alexandrian editors of Homer, who deserve credit for collecting most of the variants that have come down to us, had objectives that clearly differ from the one just proposed. They were bent on recovering the original text of the original author. Aristarchus, the last and most prominent Alexandrian editor, thought that Homer was an Athenian who lived around 1000 B.C.E.,[6] and that Homer wrote his poems.[7] Accordingly, his objective was to recover the original text of this original Homer.

Still, Aristarchus accepted and respected the reality of Homeric textual variants. He wanted to make sure that he had all available alternatives so that he could decide which was the one that Homer "wrote." In this respect he was more cautious in methodology than some contemporary editors of Homer who are quick to say which is the "right" reading and which are the "wrong" ones.

To return to my argument: the historical reality of multiformity in the Homeric text, as recognized and recorded by Aristarchus and the other Alexandrian editors, can be explained as a reflex of oral tradition. The variants of Homeric textual tradition reflect for the most part the multiforms of a living tradition in which each performance is in part a recomposition. Such an explanation may destabilize the concept of an original text produced by the original author, Homer, but it compensates by restabilizing a sense of continuity in a living performance tradition. Thus the idea of "right" and "wrong" variants is misleading, because it slights the historical aspects of variation. Let us rephrase, then, from a historical point of view: in the diachronic continuum of Homeric transmission, different variants are "right" or "wrong" in different periods.

To destabilize the original Homer, moreover, is to expose a myth. It was not only the Alexandrian editors of Homeric texts who posited an original author called Homer: so too did myth. All the narrative traditions about this figure amount to mythologized lore. The author's acts of composition are mythologized as well. The further back we go in time, the greater the repertoire of this Homer, including in the earlier times not only the *Iliad*, the *Odyssey*, the Homeric Hymns, but also all the so-called Cycle, all the Theban epics, and so on.[8]

From an evolutionary point of view, however, we have not really lost Homer. Granted, we may have lost a historical author, but we can recover from this same perspective a matter of even greater cultural importance. That is, we can reconstruct the historical evolution of the myth of the author, of a cultural hero credited by his own culture with the ultimate centerpieces of Hellenic literature, the *Iliad* and *Odyssey*.

NOTES

1. The writings of Milman Parry have been published by his son, Adam, as *The Making of Homeric Verse: The Collected Papers of Milman Parry* (London: Oxford University Press, 1971).

2. Lord's definitive work is *The Singer of Tales* (Cambridge: Harvard University Press, 1960).

3. Gregory Nagy, "An Evolutionary Model for the Making of Homeric Poetry: Comparative Perspectives," *The Ages of Homer: A Tribute to Emily Townsend Vermeule*, ed. J. B. Carter and S. P. Morris (Austin: University of Texas Press, 1995), 163–179.

4. The arguments for these "five ages of Homer" are presented in ch. 5 of my *Poetry as Performance: Homer and Beyond* (Cambridge: Cambridge University Press, 1996). The Festschrift for Emily Vermeule, mentioned in the previous note, is appropriately titled *The Ages of Homer* instead of the *The Age of Homer.*

5. Jesper Svenbro, *Phrasikleia: An Anthropology of Reading in Ancient Greece*, translation by Janet Lloyd (Ithaca: Cornell University Press, 1993).

6. Proclus F a 58–62 Severyns; cf. *Life of Homer*, p. 244.13, p. 247.8 Allen.

7. Scholia A to *Iliad* XVII 719.

8. See my *Pindar's Homer: The Lyric Possession of an Epic Past* (Baltimore: Johns Hopkins University Press, 1990), ch. 2.

PART SIX

Reading Visual Images

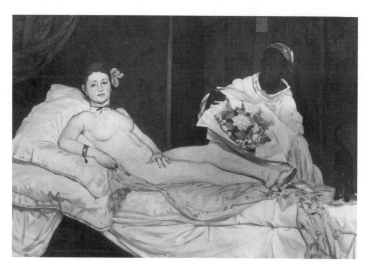

figure 1. Edouard Manet, *Olympia*. Louvre, Paris.

20

Morimura's *Olympia*

Norman Bryson

Art historians often take their brief to involve looking at works of art from the past through period eyes, not modern eyes; their task is, accordingly, to figure out what paintings meant, how they were viewed and discussed, in their own day. It's hard to argue with this historicist scruple. If we *dis*regard it, the pastness of the past disappears; it offers no resistance to our own interpretations of images, now. And yet some difficult cases, some limit cases, can force one to rethink this principle, however admirable in itself.

My remarks here concern one such difficult case, Manet's painting *Olympia*, first shown in Paris at the Salon of 1865 (figure 1). It's a painting that may well perplex us *now* because although it takes its place in the long tradition of European nude painting, it doesn't idealize in the same way as Titian's *Venus of Urbino*, say, or Ingres's *Grande Odalisque*. Olympia's face and body aren't abstracted from social circumstance and lifted up to an exalted aesthetic plane. On the contrary, the picture refers to a very worldly situation indeed.

Olympia's flowers are not an attribute of her beauty, exactly; they are a bouquet of the kind an admirer or patron might purchase from a shop and take with him or send on ahead. Who is that patron? Maybe "us," since visually we are in his place. Or, possibly, the bouquet may be a gift that Olympia has received from her *last* patron or customer, rather recently.

Our own perplexity with this nude, which is like and unlike Titian's *Venus of Urbino* or Ingres's *Grande Odalisque*, might well, if we are good art historians, send us back to the record to see how Manet's painting was received when it was first shown. Surely *that* will help clarify the case? But when we delve into the record, we find that *Olympia*'s original audiences were even more perplexed than we; they were bewildered and outraged. *Le Grand Journal*'s reviewer wrote:

> A sort of female gorilla, a grotesque in India rubber outlined in black, apes on a bed, in a state of complete nudity, the horizontal attitude of Titian's *Venus*: the right arm rests on the body in the same fashion, except for the hand, which is flexed in a sort of shameless contraction.[1]

And another reviewer, in *Le Monde Illustré*:

> The august *jeune fille* is a courtesan, with dirty hands and wrinkled feet...her body has the livid tint of a cadaver displayed in the morgue...her greenish, bloodshot eyes appear to be provoking the public, protected all the while by a hideous Negress.[2]

Such period reviews could be easily multiplied. In the face of this overheated reaction the modern art historian may well want to ask, *why* were the period viewers so distressed? And indeed this has been one of the central questions in discussions of the painting over the past decade.

The historian who has done the most to account for the scandal around *Olympia* is T. J. Clark, writing about it just ten years ago.[3] In his view, what Manet had exposed was class, the class difference of Olympia vis-à-vis her Salon viewers: the painting placed its bourgeois spectators face to face with a working-class prostitute, and at the same time connected that kind of class vision with allusions to high art. What was revealed was that the expectation of visual pleasure at the Salon came from the same provenance as other, more carnal expectations of pleasure, and practices of pleasure, in a real world.

A fundamental operation of art history over the past ten years has been to see how art exists not only as a domain of the beautiful, but as a domain caught up in a network of worldly relations, a field of power. Within a few years, T. J. Clark's interpretation was challenged by feminist art historians such as Griselda Pollock, who pointed out that the power relations being unmasked in works like the *Olympia* weren't only those of *class* difference, the view of a privileged and moneyed spectator looking *de haut en bas* on to the class beneath it, the provider of its nocturnal pleasures. They were also the power relations of *sexual* difference: a visual régime in which men were set up as possessors of a sexual gaze, its insiders, its subjects, while the female body was placed before that gaze as its outside, its object, the image for that looking.[4] *Olympia* displayed the powers over vision that were exclusive to the men of the bourgeoisie, since it was they who had the keys to the city, its diversions and pleasures, at the café-concerts, the race-track, the boulevards. Only they could wander as flâneurs through the city and contemplate and paint the prospects it offered to men. No woman of that class had these privileges, and to walk the streets alone at night was socially unthinkable: to do so would invite being confused with a prostitute, with Olympia.

I now move to the image I really want to talk about, the appropriation of Manet's *Olympia* by the Japanese artist Yasumasa Morimura in 1988 (figure 2). My first suggestion is that although it is an image, not an essay by an art historian, the statements it makes about Manet's painting are as forceful and historically astute as the interpretations put forward by T. J. Clark and Griselda Pollock. What neither of those accounts really dealt with was the dimension of race in *Olympia*. The focus had been on Olympia as the victim of a predatory bourgeois and masculinist gaze. Somehow *Olympia*'s second, black figure remained unseen in those analyses, had entered a blind spot in the readings. Morimura's image made the dimension of race undeniable by inserting a non-European body into both of *Olympia*'s figures, black and

figure 2. Yasumasa Morimura, *Portrait* (Futago), 1988.

white. By so doing, his work brought to the surface another set of exclusions and power relations within Manet's image: one in which Olympia, though from the lower end of the market of pleasure, and an object served up to the gaze as though on a plate, was still placed *higher* than her black attendant. Morimura's gesture outlined in *Olympia*'s gaze a power ratio in addition to those of male over female, bourgeoisie over working class: white vision and white art over nonwhite vision and art.[5]

A further aspect that I'd like to touch on is the way in which the insertion of an Asian body into *Olympia* makes a connection between certain Western constructions of femininity and certain Western constructions of Asia. Morimura's Olympia lies on a bridal kimono, and the cat in the original Manet has become the cat figurine that in Japan is found in places of business where the customer hands over money; it is the equivalent of "bye bye, come again"—a sign of commerce. The two together, kimono and commerce, in this context touch on one of the great Western stereotypes of Japan, the "geisha": the figuration of Japan as a woman, and as the preordained victim of the West's depradations.

Bear in mind two things. In 1865, when the Salon displayed Olympia, the Western powers were at last on the brink of "opening" Japan to the West, a forcible entry at gunpoint, followed by the humiliating Unequal Trade Treaties. Equally relevant is the emergent myth—in France through Pierre Loti's writings about Japan, in America through David Belasco's play *Madam Butterfly,* and finally through Puccini's opera—of the Asian woman as the predestined victim of the West's military, commercial, and sexual aggression combined. What especially interests me, though, is the way in which Morimura's image puts his own, male body into the Butterfly role, and what that might mean.

A good gloss on what it might mean comes from David Henry Hwang's play *M. Butterfly,* from 1988, exactly contemporary with Morimura's picture. The play deals with a rather amazing story—one that has been brilliantly explored by Marjorie Garber in her essay "The Occidental Tourist"[6]:

> A former French diplomat and a Chinese opera singer have been sentenced to six years in jail for spying for China after a two-day trial that traced a story of clandestine love and mistaken sexual identity. M. Boursicot was accused of passing information to China after he fell in love with Mr. Shi, whom he believed for twenty years to be a woman.[7]

Boursicot, the French diplomat, had believed his male Chinese lover to be a woman for twenty years. How? How could a male body seem female to a lover of twenty years? Hwang gives the following explanation:

> The "impossible" story of a Frenchman duped by a Chinese man masquerading as a woman always seemed perfectly explicable; given the degree of misunderstanding between men and women and also between East and West, it

seemed inevitable that a mistake of this magnitude would one day take place.[8]

As the diplomat's Chinese lover puts it in Hwang's play:

The West thinks of itself as masculine—big guns, big industry, big money—so the East is feminine—weak, delicate, poor—but good at art, and full of inscrutable wisdom—the feminine mystique....

Her mouth says no, but her eyes say yes. The West believes the East, deep down, *wants* to be dominated.... You expect Oriental countries to submit to your guns, and you expect Oriental women to be submissive to your men. That's why you say they make the best wives.[9]

Morimura's cross-dressing allows to emerge into vision two different Eurocentric constructions of Asia: as feminine, as Butterfly, as the natural victim of the aggression that Commodore Perry or Lieutenant Pinkerton directed at Japan. It also, I think, discloses another construction at the intersection between gender and nationalism, the feminization of the Asian male. Morimura's body rhymes closely with Olympia's. One body type, male, Asian, and another, Olympia's, are merged together. Morimura can take Olympia's place so convincingly because both he and she occupy a similar place of powerlessness before the visual régime that seeks to represent them.

What encourages me in this reading of Morimura's *Olympia* is another series of Manet appropriations by Morimura, also in 1988, that centered on Manet's painting *The Fife Player* (figures 3, 4, 5). The Manet is an image that is unlikely to suggest to a Western viewer any particular implication concerning the non-West. But what Morimura's image of this young soldier in the attire of the French army of the nineteenth century might well remind one of is what those French and European armies of the nineteenth century were up to: the colonial empires in Africa, the race to absorb the last stretches of the African continent into those empires, and also the same race in Asia, in China and Indo-China, and, very nearly, in Japan.

Morimura's *Fife Player* fills the body of the colonizer with the bodies of the colonized: African and Asian, both, in a double return of the repressed. Why, in the third image, does the hand of a white woman appear, coming through the black figure's legs? And why that kind of *grab*?

In these works Morimura seems to be exploring the placement of Asian and African bodies in the Eurocentric cultural imaginary: the Asian male as the place of imagined phallic lack or deficit, the black male body as the place of imaginary phallic excess. A fantasy of the body outside of Europe as organized in terms of pluses and minuses: a feminization of the Asian male, as in Morimura's *Olympia*, and the fantasmatic equation between the black male body and phallic surplus.

179

figure 3. Yasumasa Morimura, *Portrait (Shounen 1)*, 1988.

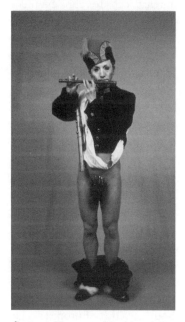

figure 4. Yasumasa Morimura, *Portrait (Shounen 2)*, 1988.

figure 5. Yasumasa Morimura, *Portrait* (*Shounen 3*), 1988.

Art historians, we know, are supposed to view the art of the past through period eyes, in this case the eyes of the nineteenth century. But this approach may not work easily with paintings where the *original* audience was baffled and outraged and unable to analyze its feelings, and was reduced to venting its spleen at the cadaver of Venus, the gorilla in the boudoir. With such a limit case the late-coming audience, no longer seeing the work across the same historical organization of the gaze, may grasp more clearly what remained unamenable to its original audience, and inexpressible except as scandal and outrage. In such a case, Morimura's appropriations raise this question: to what extent are they distortions imposed upon Manet's original paintings, subsequent interpretations that have no real relation to Manet's project? Or are they, in some sense, true to Manet's project, and to *Olympia*, a prolongation of the painting's challenge to what we think we see when we see, and to what we also cannot see, then and now?

NOTES

This paper grew from conversations with Yasumasa Morimura, Paul B. Franklin, and Kaori Chino; my sincere thanks to all three.

1. Cit. T. J. Clark, *The Painting of Modern Life: Paris in the Art of Manet and His Followers* (London: Thames and Hudson, 1985), 94, 287–88.
2. Cit. T. J. Clark, *The Painting of Modern Life*, 96, 288.

3. See *The Painting of Modern Life*, chapter 2 ("Olympia's Choice").

4. See, for example, Griselda Pollock's essay "Modernity and the Spaces of Femininity," in *Vision and Difference: Femininity, Feminism, and the Histories of Art* (London and New York: Routledge, 1988), 50–90.

5. On the question of race in relation to *Olympia*, see Sander Gilman, "Black Bodies, White Bodies: Toward an Iconography of Female Sexuality in Late Nineteenth-Century Art, Medicine and Literature," *Critical Inquiry* 12, 204–242; as well as Mieke Bal's essay: "His Master's Eye," in *Modernity and the Hegemony of Vision*, ed. David Michael Levin (Berkeley and London: University of California Press, 1993), 379–404.

6. Marjorie Garber, "The Occidental Tourist: *M. Butterfly* and the Scandal of Transvestism," in *Nationalism and Sexualities*, ed. A. Parker, M. Russo, D. Sommer and P. Yaeger (New York and London: Routledge, 1992), 121–46.

7. *New York Times*, May 11, 1986.

8. David Henry Hwang, *M. Butterfly, with an Afterword by the Playwright* (New York: New American Library, 1989), 98.

9. *M. Butterfly*, Act 3, Scene 1.

21

Reading Invisibility

Jann Matlock

In the year 1800, the *Journal des Dames et des Modes* touted the advice of a new conduct book by an Englishman called Dr. Gregory, published for the first time in France. Though the *Journal's* success depended on fashion illustrations and commentary that encouraged women to draw attention not only to their garments but to the bodies they quite spectacularly revealed, the editors nevertheless applauded Gregory's advice to his daughters to make themselves—and their gaze—as invisible as possible: "One of the great charms of women's character is that modest reserve and that delicacy, friend of secrecy, that avoids the eyes of the public, disconcerted even by admiring the gaze of admiration."[1] Gregory's advice, seconded by other conduct books throughout the first half of the nineteenth century, might seem to provide further evidence for scholarship of the last two decades on the differences in men's and women's ways of seeing. For critics like Laura Mulvey, Stephen Heath, and Kaja Silverman, women's gaze is always "partial, flawed, unreliable, self-entrapping," at best caught up in economies that co-opt it at every turn.[2] "Men look at women. Women watch themselves being looked at,"[3]

figure 1.

announces art critic John Berger in a much-cited essay that could be said to sum up a filmic and art historical discourse about the gaze that has been transformed, literally, into the story of the impossibility of representing women's looking as an autonomous act, what critics have even referred to as the "law of the male gaze,"[4] as if it existed in a timeless ahistorical warp untouched by class, racial, or national distinctions. This has always seemed to me wrongheaded, because formulations such as Berger's tend to obfuscate the nuances in the material conditions of vision. Advice such as Dr. Gregory's testifies to a complex network of exchanges that served to bolster a fantasy of a "mastering gaze"[5] but never entirely consolidated a mastery of any kind. Indeed, such advice points to an enormous anxiety about what might happen if women *met* the eyes of those who looked at them. The story I have to tell about looking would require attention to the way the material conditions of vision are historically constructed. My own search for this supposedly invisible gaze has required a kind of detective work of tracking representations of those conditions in accounts, both visual and written, of the period associated with the invention of modern techniques of observation.[6] The story of that search began with my discovery of a text and an image of an "invisible woman."

Some four years ago, while poking through nineteenth-century materials in the Bibliothèque Nationale, I came upon a remarkable engraving (figure 1) in a pamphlet titled "La Femme Invisible et Son Secret Dévoilés."[7] At first glance, the image was bewildering. An elaborate acoustic device seems to have been set up between two levels of the same building. On the upper level, a young woman, poised on something like a piano stool or a confessional bench, appeared to be talking through a thin tube to a man on the lower level as two women looked on in amazement. The caption offered a bit of assistance: "Le curieux" was supposedly asking, "Françoise, what am I holding in my hand?" The girl, whose name I now took to be Françoise, was described as having looked through her "petit judas"—an opening that would allow someone to see without being seen. According to the engraving's caption, she had then announced, correctly, "un baton crochu," "a crooked stick." And the whole group supposedly gasped, "It's incomprehensible." What was so incomprehensible here, I wondered, and what made it significant enough for a pamphleteer and an engraver to have conspired to create this brochure that claimed to unveil a woman's secrets?

The pamphlet itself was little help. Decrying the "Invisible Woman" as "a puerility," the pamphlet proclaimed it had no scruples about dissipating "the marvel that fascinates the eyes of the blind multitude."[8] It directed readers to build an acoustic contraption in a room connected to the room above it by only a slit in the floor, and to hang a glass box above the hole in the ceiling of the lower room to distract the public. "Place in the above room on cushions, so her movements make no noise, a girl who puts her eye to this oblongue opening in the floor of her room so she can see the objects presented to her...and then name them by applying her lips to the opening in the hidden tube." From her hidden room, the girl would regale observers with what she saw in a room where she was supposed to be invisibly residing. "You will thus have all the magic," declared the pamphlet, "of the Invisible Woman."[9]

But what was this "Invisible Woman," and why was she sufficiently fascinating to justify such demystification? I was intrigued, especially by the way the image staged the gazes of the three women and men. Although Françoise was not shown looking, the image staged her gaze as part of an elaborate machine for looking up the tubes from which her voice apparently came. Did the female observers know the trick or were they truly amazed? And why did no one see the hole in the ceiling that permitted this omnipotent gaze?

The undated pamphlet was printed in Paris, with only the bizarre author's name of Ingannato. The costumes placed the figures between 1795 and 1810, but there was nothing to prove the pamphlet dated from the same period. I supposed that the entire thing was an in-joke, perhaps part of a discussion of ways to marry off one's daughter without her being seen by her courtiers, or maybe even a subtle mockery of what Joan Landes has called the fall of public women after the Terror.[10] Even without knowing what it referred to, I was taken by the image, its rigging of the female gaze a kind of fantasmic evidence of a fascination with women's ways of seeing, its silence on the sources of the intrigue a provocation to wonder why anyone would want to stage a woman's invisibility in the first place. I used the picture when I talked about theories of voyeurism, in particular to demonstrate that, despite twentieth-century assertions that women do not engage in the perverse pleasures of seeing without being seen,[11] at least once in the nineteenth century an elaborate fantasy was spun around exactly that kind of female gaze.[12] This was not evidence of female voyeurism, I always explained, but a representation of the nineteenth century's obsession with the powers—and display—of a female gaze.

The story of the "Invisible Woman" did not stop there, fortunately, for I had been reading her invisibility far too metaphorically. Last year I unraveled her mysteries at last, and although the image leaves me with unanswered questions, I learned that it referred, remarkably, to three real spectacles that began in February 1800 and crossed Europe for decades afterward, baffling crowds just as the image had once baffled me.[13] The Invisible Woman Show was so popular that two vaudeville plays were produced about it, and one commentator remarked that the news of its marvels even reached London, where "to be stylish, one must speak in society of nothing [else]."[14]

Newspapers of all genres and political persuasions set out to discover the secrets of the "Invisible Woman." An editor of one paper claimed to have initially believed that the source of the voice was a ventriloquist. When he tested his theory by whispering so softly into the phonographic tube that "it was absolutely impossible that anyone besides her hear what we said," he finally conceded that "a *really invisible girl*" was in the box above the crowd—or at the very least a dwarf like that in the court of Stanislas of Poland.[15]

Press discussions about the "Invisible Women" of 1800 were similarly pre-occupied with the relation of their invisibility to their gender. "The Invisible Woman does not make her fortune," announced one paper, which added, despite all appearances to the contrary: "The way to succeed in France is not to announce the discovery of an art that will steal women from sight."[16] One writer imagined that most fathers would give their fortunes to make their daughters so invisible.[17] Another worried that the continually growing number of invisible women might make "le beau sexe en entier" want to follow their fashion.[18] The *Journal des Dames et des Modes* denounced the invisible woman by comparing her to prostitutes: "This is not the only woman at whose house one pays to enter; but this one, though a *femme publique*, nevertheless has the modesty not to appear before the eyes of the curious who buy her."[19] Another newspaper warned, "This example should serve as a lesson to many women who are not invisible, and who are dropped as soon as they are known. Curiosity is the principle of love; it disappears as soon as it is satisfied."[20] Two vaudeville plays offered clever songs on how useful the secret of invisibility might be to "women who cheat on their husbands."[21] One man lamented that he, too, had known an invisible woman—"I was taken one beautiful morning with the folly of marrying her: from that unhappy day, she was always at the Opera, at the Bagatelle, at Tivoli, at fashion merchants, at friends of her friends: she was *visible* for everyone else; but for her husband, she was the *invisible woman*."[22]

A most remarkable letter came to the newspaper from a woman who signed herself Thérèse M***. It asked the press to call on women to join together to "unveil this madness and force her to appear for what she is, so that visible beauty no longer be humiliated by hidden ugliness." It seems that Thérèse's husband was so taken by this "spectacle held up as the triumph of [the female] sex" that he demanded that she make herself invisible and have no further communication with him except through acoustic horns out of a globe of glass. "You can easily imagine that a woman of 23, not badly treated by nature, would not accommodate herself with facility to such a condition," wrote the disconcerted wife. Nevertheless, she explained, she would give anything in the world to know this woman's secret, for, she realized, "it is enough to be invisible, however ugly one is, to receive the most flattering compliments."[23] Reading such letters, one begins to ask what the relationship might be between the spectacular girl's invisibility and what historians have described as a forced absence of women from the public sphere in the early Consulate and Empire.[24] The Invisible Woman Shows burst into the popular imagination at precisely the moment when, indeed, women's public visibility was most fervently debated. "Girls' convents have changed into spice stores and rustic balls," remarked Mercier in 1799; "twenty years ago, girls would not have set foot out the paternal house without their mothers, walking under their wings with eyes religiously lowered; the man whom they dared to look at was the one they were permitted to hope for or choose as a husband. The Revolution changed that subordination; they run around morning and night with complete liberty."[25]

The fantasies of such a liberty, though, are hardly an indication that Étienne-Gaspard Robertson, the most likely author of this pamphlet and master of the most famous magic and fantasmagoria show of the era, wanted to put women under cover.[26] Rather, in fact, shows like Robertson's were part of an obsession, in the year 1800, with the invisible and the possibilities of making it *visible*. "We are in an unknown world full of invisible ghosts," announced Mercier just before the French Revolution.[27] By the time of the Directory and Consulate, that unknown world had become haunted by ghosts of the all-too-visible Terror. Around the time of the "Invisible Woman's" appearance, historians have argued, came a spectacular preoccupation with invisibility in a number of new, secular domains. A burgeoning artistic discourse grew around what Barbara Stafford has called an "aesthetics of the invisible."[28] Robert Fulton's panorama was imported to Paris in 1799, purporting to "trick the eye to such an extent that it hesitated between nature and art."[29] Charlatan magic shows and the new science instructor "manipulated gadgetry to visibilize an invisible realm."[30] Optical instruments—the microscope,[31] the telescope,[32] its personalized smaller version, the *lorgnette*,[33] and magic lanterns[34]—came into broader use among a bourgeoisie excited about the possibilities of seeing what remained invisible to the naked eye.

Such obsessions with making visible the invisible seem related to the paradigm shift described by Foucault from a society of spectacle to a society of surveillance.[35] It is not surprising, then, that this singular spectacle of invisibility replicates, in a peculiar way, the workings of the imaginary panopticon. Hidden in her watchtower, the invisible woman holds her captives in thrall. Seeing but unseen, she manages to put a roomful of people under surveillance—at their expense. If viewers of 1800 were bewildered about whether they were being watched by a dwarf or a fraud hidden in the attic above them, the spectacle of 1815 had become, for painter Léopold Robert, a "machine"[36] that described what was to be seen.

As a secular panoptic machine, the invisible woman show produced the miracle of a woman's vision. It guaranteed an obsession with what she saw as well as an interrogation of her position as viewer. What really pleased the public about this invisibility show? Was it the guessing game of figuring out how the show worked? Was it the amazement that so many others had been duped into believing there was something to see here? Was it the flirtation of the girl? Was it the pleasure of complaining that women ought to be seen and not hidden? Press accounts suggest that it was above all this voice coming out of nowhere, commandeering a space of tubes and onlookers: "what astonishes and seems to derive from the marvelous, is that nothing escapes the Invisible One. She sees and hears everything."[37] Crowds were above all amazed at the way the voice of the disembodied girl reminded them that she held them under the power of her gaze.

I don't have the space here to track the debates about the "Invisible Woman" further, or to unveil what I think are her secrets, but rather only to discuss briefly what questions I asked and give some clues to why they are significant.[38] Confronted with these accounts of the Invisible Woman Show, I wanted to know three things: (1) what made invisibility so intriguing—why were the biggest theater stars in the year 1800 people without bodies? (2) what was the relationship between discussions of the "Invisible Woman's" gender and other discussions about female display and exposure in the year 1800—from debates over revealing fashions to an elaborate visual discourse that showed women looking through new optical instruments? and (3) how did this show relate to other discourses about women's visibility and invisibility from public life?

The key to the significance of this representation of female vision is perhaps not just that of the woman looking through the hole in the floor but that of the other two women looking on, referred to regularly by contemporary accounts of women's passion for shows of this genre.[39] The women portrayed looking at the "Invisible Woman" spectacle do not seem to understand what is at stake in this disembodied voice any more than the man does, but they are depicted as having the good sense to stand back and let him make a fool of himself by looking up the acoustic tubes. And they are, furthermore, shown bucking social criticism not only by wearing the very kinds of gowns moralists raved against[40] but by venturing into shows like this. There, one commentator suggested, they might lose themselves in the crowd, escaping the critical gazes that would tell them where to appear and how to behave.[41] They might find a control over their own bodies and their own vision that only Invisible Women, in 1800, seem to have been able to retain.

But operating in these new spaces for subjectivity, the gaze of such Invisible Women nevertheless announced the permeability of old barriers and the fragility of such categories as public and private. They had learned new secrets that no spectacles could unveil.

The century that followed would engineer machines for looking that were far more elaborate and deceptive than that of the Invisible Woman Show. In order to tell the story of the relationship between the voyeurism at stake in those later machines and this early account of vision at risk, one would need to imagine that nineteenth-century technologies of vision are not just machines of torture but mechanisms making possible the pleasures of visibility and the telling of those pleasures. From the contraptions that surrounded the Invisible Woman to the bachelor machines of Duchamp,[42] these technologies of vision account for a subjectivity through bodies. But even invisible bodies send forth signs that never fail to point back to the subjects incorporated there.[43] Knowable through their gestures of vision, empowered through their own knowing gazes, these unseen bodies procure spaces in which their voices can be heard to control the signs of their own visibility.

NOTES

I am indebted to Frédéric Cousinié, Jim Livessey, Peggy Waller, and Antoine de Baecque for provocative discussions of the perils of invisibility, voyeurism, and Directory politics. I am also grateful to my research assistants, Marina Harss and Lynn Ramey, for their help in tracking references. Research support for this project was provided by a J. Paul Getty Postdoctoral Fellowship in the History of Art & the Humanities and by a Clark Fund Grant from Harvard University.

1. Review of Gregory, *Legs d'un père à ses filles, Journal des Dames et des Modes,* Year VIII, p. 514.

2. The citation here is from Kaja Silverman, *The Acoustic Mirror* (Bloomington: Indiana University Press, 1988), 31. For other influential accounts of the defective or occluded female gaze, see Laura Mulvey, "Visual Pleasure and Narrative Cinema" (1975), reprinted in *Visual and Other Pleasures* (Bloomington: Indiana University Press, 1989), 14–28; Stephen Heath, "Difference," *Screen,* 19, No. 3 (Autumn 1978), 51–112; E. Ann Kaplan, "Is the Gaze Male?" in *Women and Film: Both Sides of the Camera* (New York: Methuen, 1983); Linda Williams, "When the Woman Looks," in *Re-Vision,* ed. Mary Ann Doane, et al. (Frederick, MD: University Publications of America, 1984), 83–99; Mary Ann Doane, "Film and the Masquerade: Theorizing the Female Spectator," and "Masquerade Reconsidered: Further Thoughts on the Female Spectator," in *Femmes Fatales: Feminism, Film Theory, Psychoanalysis* (New York: Routledge, 1991); Teresa de Lauretis, *Alice Doesn't: Feminism, Semiotics,*

Cinema (Bloomington: Indiana Universitiy Press, 1984), and *Technologies of Gender: Essays on Theory, Film, and Fiction* (Bloomington: Indiana University Press, 1987); Tania Modleski, *The Women Who Knew Too Much: Hitchcock and Feminist Theory* (New York: Methuen, 1988); Janet Bergstrom and Mary Ann Doane, "The Female Spector: Contexts and Directions," and other contributions to the special issue "The Spectatrix," *Camera Obscura* 20–21 (May–September 1989), 5–27. One interesting critique of work on a hegemonic male gaze is Edward Snow, "Theorizing the Male Gaze: Some Problems," *Representations*, 25 (1989), 30–41.

3. John Berger, *Ways of Seeing* (London: Penguin, 1972), 47.

4. Nancy K. Miller, "Performances of the Gaze: Staël's *Corinne, or Italy*," in *Subject to Change* (New York: Columbia University Press, 1989), 186.

5. See Griselda Pollock, *Vision and Difference: Femininity, Feminism, and the Histories of Art* (London: Routledge, 1988), 87.

6. For different accounts of the dating of the vision of modernity—which vary from the late eighteenth century (Stafford) to the July Monarchy (Crary) to the Second Empire (Clark), see Jonathan Crary, *Techniques of the Observer* (Cambridge: MIT Press, 1990); Barbara Maria Stafford, *Body Criticism: Imagining the Unseen in Enlightenment Art and Medicine* (Cambridge: MIT Press, 1991); T. J. Clark, *The Painting of Modern Life* (New York: Knopf, 1984); and Martin Jay, *Downcast Eyes: The Denigration of Vision in Twentieth-Century French Thought* (Berkeley: University of California Press, 1993).

7. Frontispiece to E. J. Ingannato, *La Femme Invisible et ses secrets dévoilés* (Paris: Gueffier, n.d. [1800]).

8. "Nous croirons au contraire devoir nous faire un mérite et un gloire de lui donner la recette suivante pour opérer le faux miracle qui l'émerveille tous les jours, et qui, s'il abusoit plus long-temps sa crédulité, la reporteroit aux siècles des apparitions et des enchantemens" (Ingannato, 1).

9. Ingannato, 8.

10. See Joan Landes, *Women and the Public Sphere* (Ithaca: Cornell University Press, 1989).

11. See, for example, Michael Fain, "Contribution à l'étude du voyeurisme," in *Revue francaise de psychanalyse*, 18 (1954), 185; Irvin D. Yalom, "Aggression and Forbiddenness in Voyeurism," *Archives of General Psychiatry*, 3 (1960), 306. Freud's brief account of voyeurism in "Psychogenic Visual Disturbance according to Psycho-Analytic Conceptions" (1910) (reprinted *Standard Editon*, 11: 104–12), does not explicitly broach the question but accounts only for male scopophilia.

12. See my "Exhibiting and Exposing: Historicizing the Gaze in Nineteenth-Century France," paper delivered at the College of Art Association Conference, Chicago, February 1992, a version of which will appear as the introduction to

the book I am completing, *Desires to Censor: Spectacles of the Body, Vision, and Aesthetics in Nineteenth-Century France*. Other chapters of this book related to this argument may be found in "Censoring the Realist Gaze," in *Spectacles of Realism: Gender, Body. Genre*, ed. Margaret Cohen and Christopher Prendergast (Minneapolis: Minnesota University Press, 1995), pp. 28–65; "Blagues lithographiques et les spectacles des femmes: Gavarni, le rire, et la modernité de Juillet," forthcoming in *Les Annales, E.S.C.*, 1996; and "Seeing Women: Rhetorics of Visibility, The Women's Periodical Press, and the July Monarchy Salon," (forthcoming, *Art Journal*, 1996).

13. In an article of 22 prairial Year VIII, a contributor to the *Courrier des spectacles* (pp. 3–4) claimed there had been *five* Invisible Woman Shows in Paris in the previous six months. I have found records of only three—Laurent's at Saint-Germain l'Auxerrois, Étienne-Gaspard Robertson's in the former Couvent des Capucines, and Rouy Charles's on the rue de Longueville—though one might add two theatrical works of Year VIII (Jardinet's *La Dame Invisible* of the Théâtre Montansier, and Alexis Daudet and Randon's *La Femme Invisible* of the Théâtre des Troubadours) to the three magic shows to make five in all. Robertson's version of the Invisible Woman Show, though the second to appear in Paris, was by far the most long-lasting. Testimony and press advertisements show that Robertson continued to include the Invisible Woman until he took the show abroad in 1802, and exhibited her between 1814 and 1818 in his Paris cabinet. Painter Léopold Robert desribed the show in a letter from 1815, cited in Jean Clair, "Les Machines célibataires: quelques répères," in *L'Ame au corps* (Paris: Réunion des musées nationaux, 1993), 441. A handbill from Robertson's last Madrid show in the 1830s suggests he was still performing this "experiment" 30 years after its beginnings (Brochure titled, *Noticias curiosas, sobre el espectaculo*, reproduced in Françoise Levie, *Étienne-Gaspard Robertson: la vie d'un fantasmagore* [Longueil, Quebec: Préambule, 1990], 257). The *Magasin Pittoresque* of 1833 provided a detailed article explaining the secrets of this show. Richard Altick details various versions of this show in England and the U.S. into the mid-19th century (*The Shows of London* [Cambridge: Harvard University Press, 1978], 36, 249. 353, 360, 430). Wordsworth makes reference to her in the *Prelude*, VII, 683, encountered in 1802 at Bartholomew Fair in England (Altick, 353).

14. *Ami des Lois*, 5 germinal, Year VIII, p. 4.

15. *Gazette de France*, 5 ventôse, Year VIII, p. 619.

16. *Journal des Arts*, 10 ventôse, Year VIII.

17. *Almanack de l'Année théâtrale pour l'an IX* (Paris: Dupont, 1801), p. 281.

18. *Courrier des spectacles*, 8 messidor, Year VIII, p. 4.

19. "L'Invisible," *Journal des Dames et des Modes*, Year VIII, p. 290.

20. *Le Journal des Défenseurs de la Patrie*, cited in *Le Journal des Dames et des*

Modes, Year VIII, p. 297.

21. See the excerpts from *La Femme Invisible*, in the review of the play, *Le Journal des Dames et des Modes*, Year VIII, pp. 399–400.

22. *Journal des Dames et des Modes*, Year VIII, p. 297.

23. *Courrier des spectacles*, 29 messidor, Year VIII, p. 4.

24. See especially Landes, *Women and the Public Sphere*; Madelyn Gutwirth, "Postface," *The Twilight of the Goddesses: Women and Representation in the French Revolutionary Era* (New Brunswick, NJ: Rutgers University Press, 1992); the articles in *Rebel Women: Women and the French Revolution*, ed. Sarah Melzer and Leslie Rabine (New York: Oxford University Press, 1992); Geneviève Fraisse, *Muse de la Raison: La Démocratie exclusive et la différence des sexes* (Aix-en-Provence: Alinéa, 1989); and Lynn Hunt, *The Family Romance of the French Revolution* (Berkeley: University of California Press, 1992).

25. Louis-Sébastien Mercier, *Nouveau Paris* (Paris: Year VII), 2: 297; second citation from Mercier in *Journal des Dames et des Modes*, 15 brumaire Year VII, pp. 66–68.

26. On Robertson, see Levie's biography as well as Terry Castle, "Phantasmagoria: Spectral Technology and the Metaphorics of Modern Reverie," *Critical Inquiry* 15 (Autumn 1988), 26–61; and Max Milner, *La Fantasmagorie: essai sur l'optique fantastique* (Paris: Presses Universitaires de France, 1982). I am grateful to Levie for meeting with me to share insights into the popularity of the Robertson shows.

27. Louis-Sébastien Mercier, *Tableau de Paris*, XII, 352–55, cited in Robert Darnton, *Mesmerism and the End of the Enlightment in France* (Cambridge: Harvard University Press, 1968), 38. Mesmerism, writes Darnton, "seemed to offer a new scientific explanation of the invisible forces of nature" (83). Perhaps not surprisingly, newspapers heralded the return of Mesmer to Paris in the Year VIII (*Gazette de France*, 16 ventôse; *Clef du Cabinet des souverains*, 10 germinal), around the same time as the Invisible Woman attracted large crowds. Darnton characterizes the years of the 1780s as those marked by popular enthusiasm for science (29). Similar arguments may be found in Barbara Maria Stafford, *Artful Science: Enlightenment Entertainment and the Eclipse of Visual Education* (Cambridge: MIT Press, 1994).

28. Stafford, "Beauty of the Invisible: Winckelmann and the Aesthetics of Imperceptibility," *Zeitschrift für Kunstgeschichte*, 43 (1980), 74. For fascinations with the invisible in artistic works, see especially the works of Louis Boilly reproduced and discussed in Harisse, *H. L. L. Boilly, peintre, …sa vie et son oeuvre, 1761–1845* (Paris 1898); *Boilly: 1761–1845, Un Grand Peintre francais de la Révolution à la Restauration* (Musée des Beaux-Arts de Lille, 23 Oct. 1988–9 Janvier 1989); and *Louis Boilly* (Paris: Musée Marmottan, 1984), as well

as Stafford's discussion of Girodet's *Endymion*, "Endymion's Moonbath: Art and Science in Girodet's Early Masterpiece," *Leonard*, 15, No. 3 (1982), 193–98. Stafford has elsewhere argued that Goya's fantastic art likewise sought to make "the invisibile visible" as part of a program of banishing delusion from the world. See Stafford, "Fantastic Images: From Unenlightening to Enlightening 'Appearances' Meant to be Seen in The Dark," in *Aesthetic Illusion*, ed. Frederick Burwick (Berlin: De Gruyter, 1990), 178–79; and "From 'Brilliant Ideas' to 'Fitful Thoughts': Conjecturing the Unseen in Late Eighteenth-Century Art," 329–63. Goya is thought to have visited the Robertson Fantasmagoria show in Madrid in the 1820s (Stafford, *Artful Science*, 16; Priscilla Muller, *Goya's "Black" Paintings: Truth and Reason in Light and Liberty* [New York: Hispanic Society of America, 1984], 213–38).

29. Institut National des Sciences et des Arts, extract of the registers of the class of literature and the arts, séance of 28 fructidor year VIII, reported in *Moniteur Universel*, 8 vendémaire Year IX, cited in Francois Robichon, "Le Panorama, Spectacle de l'histoire," *Mouvement social*, 131 (April-June 1985), p. 65. On the history of panoramas see also Stephan Oettermann, *Das Panorama: die Geschichte eines Massenmediums* (Frankfurt-am-Main: Syndikat, 1980).

30. Stafford, *Artful Science*, 73. These shows of the postrevolutionary period represented the reemergence of a kind of magic show extremely popular in the decade or so before the Revolution. See Altick, Stafford, *Artful Science*, and Robert M. Isherwood, *Farce and Fantasy: Popular Entertainment in Eighteenth-Century Paris* (New York: Oxford University Press, 1986).

31. On the history of microscopy, see Stafford, *Body Criticism*, 211ff; and James Elkins, "On Visual Desperation and the Bodies of Protozoa," *Representations*, 40 (Fall 1992), pp. 33–56.

32. News of the English astronomer Herschel's success with a 25-foot long telescope was reported in the French press about the same time the Invisible Woman Show made its appearance (*Clef du Cabinet des souverains*, 1 prairial Year VIII, p. 6).

33. On *lunettes* and *lorgnettes* in the year VIII, see "Sur les Lunettes," editorial, *Journal des Dames et des Modes*, 30 Frimaire an VIII, pp. 137–38. I have discussed the popularity of the *lorgnette* in "Exhibiting and Exposing: Historicizing the Gaze in Nineteenth-Century France" and "Censoring the Realist Gaze."

34. On changing understandings of the *camera obscura* in late eighteenth-century France, see Crary, *Techniques of the Observer*, 25–66; and Stafford, *Artful Science*, 45. On the popular success of the magic lantern in late 18th- and 19th-century France, see *Lanternes magiques, tableaux transparents*, ed. Ségolène Le Men with Nelly Kuntzmann, Jann Matlock, et al., Exhibition Catalogue, Musée d'Orsay, September 1995–January 1996 (Paris: Réunion des Musées

Nationaux, 1995). Jean-Jacques Tatin-Gourier examines the obsession with magic lanterns in revolutionary discourse in "L'effet d'images projetées dans les lanterns magiques révolutionnaires," in *La Licorne*, 23 (1992), 121–30.

35. Michel Foucault, *Surveiller et punir* (Paris: Gallimard, 1975).

36. Cf. Robert cited in Clair, "Les Machines célibataires," 441.

37. *Courrier des spectacles*, 24 ventôse, Year VII.

38. A detailed discussion of these issues will appear as "The Invisible Woman and Her Secrets Unveiled," in my *Desires to Censor*. An analysis of this show's relationship to the fantasmagoria show of 1798 appears in my "Voir aux limites du corps: Fantasmagories et femmes invisibles dans les spectacles de Robertson," in *Lanternes magiques, tableaux transparents*, 82–99.

39. Though women were warned of the potential danger of nervous fits brought on by seeing the ghosts of the fantasmagoria show, Robertson's rival Laurent was adamant that "les amateurs des deux sexes" could enjoy the Invisible Woman spectacle. Women were not only admitted but avidly encouraged to join "physicians and other men of knowledge" in speculating upon the secrets displayed there (pamphlet reproduced in Étienne-Gaspard Robertson, *Mémoires: récréatifs, scientifiques, et anecdotiques d'un physicien-aéronaute* [1831; reprinted Langres: Cafe Clima, 1985], 221).

40. On women's public exposures of their bodies, see Margaret Waller, "Taking Liberties: (Re)Dressing Body Politics in Postrevolutionary France," paper delivered at the Nineteenth-Century French Studies Annual Colloquium, Lawrence, Kansas, October 1993, unpublished manuscript given to me by the author; as well as Aileen Ribeiro, *Fashion and the French Revolution* (New York: Holmes and Meier, 1988). Lynn Hunt delivered a provocative paper on this subject at the Clark Library conference at UCLA in April 1993.

41. Mercier, *Nouveau Paris*, 2: 191.

42. See the associations of the "Invisible Woman" with Duchamp's machines in Clair, "Les Machines Célibataires."

43. Cf. Norman Bryson's remarks on invisible bodies in *Vision and Painting* (Cambridge: Cambridge University Press, 1983), 163–71.

22

"Agency"

An Alternative to Subjectivity

Irene J. Winter

The utility of including a non–Euro-American cultural tradition in a discussion of the relationship between imagery and understanding is that it perforce raises the issue of "cross-cultural validity," a topic often debated in anthropology but too often taken for granted in cultural studies. Among other things, it requires that one consider how important the "original language" is for setting the terms of analysis. Underlying this question lurks the tension between history and criticism as presently construed, and no less the question of how one may still practice history in a postmodern scholarly universe.

The very fact of addressing the possibility of transcending, or at least traversing, cultural boundaries further encourages inquiry into normative explanatory models. It challenges proponents of such models to actually *demonstrate* that they (the models) can be useful across cultural boundaries—particularly when cultural boundaries happen to coincide with significant linguistic divides.

Of considerable interest in the current theoretical literature has been first, how the viewer/"subject" is to be distinguished from the viewed/"object," thereby rendering the content of paintings in particular, in the words of a distinguished art historian, more "object-matter" than "subject-matter"; and second, how the active role of viewing interacts with the nature and construction of "subjecthood" on the part of the viewing subject.[1] For me, working on ancient Mesopotamia, where one of the principal languages—Sumerian—does not *have* grammatical categories of subject or object, the challenge is clear.

I began with an interest in how Mesopotamians used visual narrative as a rhetorical device on political monuments; and with concern for how useful the Aristotelian (hence Indo-Europeanist) model, which explained Mesopotamian representations in terms of a "culminating moment,"[2] really was for works like the Victory Stele of Eannatum of Lagash of circa 2500 BC, better known as the Stele of the Vultures (fig. 1).[3] I wondered how the stele's representational strategies might reflect *Sumerian* narrative structures,

figure 1. Victory Monument of Eannatum of Lagash ("STELE OF THE VULTURES"), ca. 2450 BC, Telloh, obverse. Photo courtesy of the Département des antiquités orientales, Musée du Louvre, Paris.

197

and so I kept a file on the accompanying text and on the ergative grammatical construction peculiar to Sumerian and a number of Australo-Polynesian and other languages. This ergative construction marks an absence of distinction between transitive and intransitive as we know it, thereby eschewing subject-object shifts.[4] If *our* categories do not apply, how *does* one see, much less "read," scenes on the obverse of the Eannatum Stele, in which the god Ningirsu smites the enemy of Lagash at the same time as he has gathered them in his net?

Actually, two issues come into consideration here: first, the nature of the *agent* (or the agentive) and of the *patient* as alternatives to the subject and object in ergative grammatical construction;[5] and second, the nature of the *aspect*, as distinct from the tense, of the Sumerian verb.[6] In translating both text and experience, it is not difficult to replace the classification "subject" with that of the "agent," giving agency to Ningirsu—as the author of the monument does in the accompanying inscription. The ruler of Lagash may have physically effected the defeat of the neighboring state of Umma, the victory occasioning the monument in the first place (the ruler is actually seen in battle on the reverse); but by virtue of his having been elevated *by* the god Ningirsu to his position as ruler, and through his own declaration that he has brought about the return of appropriated lands *for* Ningirsu, the deity of Lagash is in effect credited with the victory in both text and image. What is more, the act has already been accomplished; the verb is translated into our "past" tense, but in Sumerian it is rendered in the aspective as an act *completed*, distinct from the only other tense, which indicates something *ongoing*. The battle is over; the enemy are in the net; and Ningirsu is declared as the agent of Umma's defeat.[7]

In the simplest of grammatical examples, our typical transitive sentence, "the god (subject) defeats the enemy (object)," or "the king (subject) builds the temple (object)," permits us to shift subject-object relationships in the intransitive, such that "the temple (now subject) is built by the king." In an ergative construction, by contrast, the agent producing the action, "the god" or "the king," remains constant no matter where the word is placed in the sentence, as does the product of his act, the patient—in this case, "the enemy," or "the temple." The agent is identified by a grammatical marker, while the verb shifts aspect to indicate the action as either durative or punctative, ongoing or completed.[8]

Building scenes, which form a major portion of the Sumerian iconographic repertoire, work much like battle scenes: for example, on the plaque of Ur-Nanshe, founder of Eannatum's dynasty at Lagash (fig. 2).[9] In English, Ur-Nanshe either carries (present tense) or is carrying (present progressive) the basket that contains the building materials on his head, thereby identi-

figure 2. Plaque of Ur-Nanshe of Lagash, ca. 2500 BC, Telloh. Photo courtesy of the Département des antiquités orientales, Musée du Louvre, Paris.

fying him as a pious worker in the fields of his lord. In the Sumerian text inscribed on the plaque, however, he is clearly identified as the man who *built* the temple—past tense, more preterit than past perfect: that is, the verb tells us this is an already accomplished act. What I would suggest here, then, is that we must avoid reading (and describing) the verb behind the image as "carrying"—an ongoing action, logical in English—and rather, see the imagery as focusing on the completed act effected by the agent in the action: "Ur-Nanshe, king of Lagash,... *built* the temple of Ningirsu."[10] Just as Ningirsu on the obverse of the Stele of the Vultures is the *agent* of Umma's defeat, so Ur-Nanshe is the agent of the building of the temple of Ningirsu in Lagash. Depicting him with basket on head is in effect using the *topos* as an icon for the class of act commemorated.[11]

Seen in this way, we come closer, I think, to sorting early Sumerian images into categories that may have been meaningful to Sumerians. First, we can begin to distinguish visual imagery—motifs—in terms of classes of action or events. And second, we are better able to see that in Sumerian art, however fleshed out the narrative, focus is on the *agent* who has performed the action indicated by the particular iconographic *topos*.

With that structure in mind, I turn to a later ruler of Lagash, one Gudea, whose images and accounts of temple building in circa 2110 BC are well known. In particular, the seated statue known as Gudea B preserves for us the tablet on which the plan of the temple has been inscribed, along with a lengthy account of the building project (fig. 3).[12] In a more complete account of the building project, known as the Gudea Cylinder A, the temple is presented as the product of the ruler's dream, a direct mandate from the deity.[13]

figure 3. Gudea of Lagash, Statue "B," ca. 2110 BC, Telloh.
Photo courtesy of the Département des antiquités orientales, Musée du Louvre, Paris.

The temple itself is not preserved to us; however, we know it to have been
set on a height, rising over the rest of the surrounding town. In the text, the
finished temple is said to be awesome and praiseworthy; it shines like the
sun and the moon; it sends forth positive qualities; and is, in turn, highly
acclaimed. We are told that not only the people, but even the lower-level
gods, made their way to view and admire it. The minor gods and the people
are therefore literal *spectators*; and it is *as such* that they are impressed.

Underlying the summary statements of value, then, is a positive response to the very act of viewing.

An additional clue to Sumerian meaning is preserved in the grammatical structure deployed in the text, however. It will be remembered that the agentive in a Sumerian ergative construction is indicated by a linguistic marker; the patient remains unmarked. In Gudea's account, once the temple is completed, not only do the verbs used suggest outward movement of the temple's properties (shining forth, cast over the land, etc.); the text further shifts the agentive marker from Gudea who built the temple to the temple itself as the agent in its own transmission of its qualities to a viewing public, thereby laying the foundations for our understanding of the *active* way in which the finished work was perceived to be affective.[14]

I stress that such agency is possible *only* once the work has been completed and fully endowed. But this brings us directly back to the distinction between agent and patient, rather than subject and object, that is crucial here. By noting the play in the use of agentive markers in ergative construction, I think it is possible to catch something of the active role, as well as the intended impact, of the art/work within Sumerian cultural experience; just as, by insisting that durative and punctative in verbal construction is not the same thing as present and past, we see better how roles and responses were represented both verbally and visually; and by noting the significant difference between *agent* and mere subject, we are better able to grasp the powerful visual rhetoric underlying Sumerian art. The king, as agent, has effected the building of the temple; the temple, as agent, actively affects all viewers.

In short, if we hope to describe Sumerian art on any but our own contemporary terms, we *need* to look at it through the lens of Sumerian grammar—that is, through the lens of the ergative—even as we maintain our "outsider" status as analysts and historians at a distance.

I realize that the once highly popular explanatory model of the Sapir-Whorf hypothesis, which suggested that linguistic categories determine the way an individual thinks, has been found to be overly deterministic;[15] but salvageable is the premise that language—and particularly grammar—provides both structures for and constraints upon the ways the individual member of a linguistic population is able to *articulate* experience. This emphatically does not mean that a speaker cannot work creatively around linguistic categories in order to suggest meanings that elude capture by existing categories; thus, the concept of agency, clearly, is not restricted to so-called "ergative" languages with agentive markers. However, to the extent that semantic strategies must be rendered in language, grammar (syntax) is the vehicle for the conveyance of meaning, just as thinking is thought *in language*. And if agency in general represents a culturally determined empowerment, in Sumerian the grammatical voice available for such public statements as the impact of the temple upon the viewer does significantly vest power in the building, rather than in the viewing individual.

This, in turn, raises questions of the nature of "the act of viewing" as it relates to subjectivity. It is so often treated in literary and visual studies as an active, instrumental, even aggressive role of identification, identity-formation and/or appropriation, and as if applicable in all times, places, and situations. What happens when, grammatically and culturally, the viewer is turned into the more passive patient by the active role of the affective "object-become-agent"?

In other words, once one stresses the relation between syntax and culturally specific meaning, cultural and linguistic difference may not be trivial for questions of hermeneutics; nor have psychosocial development patterns of identity-formation been demonstrated to be universal. Does Lacan then need a Sumerian corrective?

NOTES

1. J. Lacan, "The mirror stage as formative of the function of the I as revealed in psychoanalytic experience," in *Ecrits: A Selection*, trans. A. Sheridan (New York and London: W. W. Norton & Co., 1977), pp. 1–7. See also Kaja Silverman, *Male Subjectivity at the Margins* (New York and London: Routledge, 1992), esp. pp. 23–29 and 125–156.

2. See, for example, Ann Perkins, "Narration in Babylonian Art," *American Journal of Archaeology 61* (1957) 55 ; and H. A. Groenewegen-Frankfort, *Arrest and Movement: An Essay on Space and Time in the Representational Art of the Ancient Near East* (London: Faber & Faber Ltd., 1951), passim.

3. Published in A. Moortgat, *The Art of Ancient Mesopotamia*, (New York and London: Phaidon, 1969), figs. 118–121; See also the study in I. J. Winter, "After the Battle is Over: The 'Stele of the Vultures' and the Beginning of Historical Narrative in the Art of the Ancient Near East," in H. L. Kessler and M. S. Simpson, eds., *Pictorial Narrative in Antiquity and the Middle Ages*, Studies in the History of Art 16 (Washington D.C.: National Gallery of Art, 1985), pp. 11–32.

4. See Michael Silverstein, "Hierarchy of features and ergativity," in R. M .W. Dixon, ed., *Grammatical Categories in Australian Languages*, AIAS Linguistic Series 22 (Canberra: Australian Institute of Aboriginal Studies, 1976), pp. 112–171; and Bernard Comrie, "Ergativity," in W. P. Lehmann, ed., *Syntactic Typology: Studies in the Phenomenology of Language* (Austin and London: University of Texas Press, 1978), pp. 329–394.

5. See fn. 4, above; and for Sumerian specifically, D. Foxvog, "The Sumerian Ergative Construct," *Orientalia* 44 (1975), 395–425; and P. Michalowski, "Sumerian as an Ergative Language," *Journal of Cuneiform Studies* 32 (1980), 86–103.

6. Thorkild Jacobsen, "The Sumerian Verbal Core," *Zeitschrift für Archäologie* 78 (1988), 161–220, and "Sumerian Grammar Today," *Journal of the American Oriental Society* 108 (1988), 123–133, esp. 129.

7. Published in H. Steible, *Die altsumerischen Bau- und Weihinschriften*, Freiburger altorientalische Studien, Bd. 5 (Wiesbaden: Steiner Verlag, 1982), pp. 120–145, esp. pp. 128–129, and commented upon in J. S. Cooper, *Reconstructing History from Ancient Inscriptions: The Lagash-Umma Border Conflict* (Malibu: Undena Publications, 1983).

8. Jacobsen, "The Sumerian Verbal Core, p. 215; and idem., "Sumerian Grammar Today," p. 129. Note that Sumerian is often identified as a "split-ergative" language, in that nominative-accusative construction gives way to the ergative in the case of the perfective rather than the imperfective verbal aspect—on which, see M. L. Thomsen, *The Sumerian Language* [Mesopotamia 10] (Copenhagen: Akademisk Forlag, 1984), pp. 49–51.

9. Published in Moortgat, *Art of Ancient Mesopotamia*, fig. 109.

10. Steible, *Altsumerischen Bau- und Weihinschriften*, pp. 82–84.

11. A typical act associated with Mesopotamian rulers for some 2,000 years. See S. Lackenbacher, *Le roi bâtisseur: les récits de construction assyriens des origines à Teglat-phalasar III*. Etudes assyriologiques, Cahier 11 (Paris: Editions Recherche sur les civilisations, 1982).

12. For the image, see Moortgat, *Art of Ancient Mesopotamia*, fig. 167; for the Gudea Statue B text, see H. Steible, *Die Neusumerischen Bau- und Weihinschriften*, Freiburger altorientalische Studien, Bd. 9 (Stuttgart: Steiner Verlag, 1991), Text SB, pp. 157–179.

13. There is no easily accessible edition of the Gudea Cylinders in translation, except for the highly poetic rendition by Thorkild Jacobsen, in *The Harps that Once...: Sumerian Poetry in Translation* (New Haven and London: Yale University Press, 1987), pp. 388–425. A more scholarly version was presented in the dissertation of Richard Averbeck, *A Preliminary Study of Ritual and Structure in the Cylinders of Gudea*, Dropsie College, 1987.

14. See text, Cylinder B, 16: 3–4, Jacobsen, *The Harps that Once...*, p. 439.

15. For a history of this debate, see R. A. Hudson, *Sociolinguistics* (Cambridge: Cambridge University Press, 1980), especially chap. 3: Language, culture and thought, pp. 73–105, and within that, the section on The Sapir-Whorf hypothesis, pp. 103–105.

PART SEVEN

Law and Literature

Where Do We Go from Here?

23

Law's Literature

David Kennedy

Literature makes lawyers wise—while law makes literature uneasy, fact to its fiction, power to its pleasure. Disciplines separate and unequal. Or perhaps it's law that marks literary critics as wise, savvy about power, just as literature marks jurists weak, even effete.

But are these the only views? Law read as literature might well unravel—and literature might find in law a narrative of desire, returning to literature a consciousness of its power.

Let's just take Shakespeare in the Supreme Court; a convention, a cliché. Read aloud, the court's Shakespearian excursions can't help provoke a smile, even as the justices turn to Shakespeare for authority, for wisdom, for reassurance. Finding it "invidious to discriminate against [illegitimate children] when no action, conduct, or demeanor of theirs is possibly relevant," for example, the court affirms, "We can say with Shakespeare: 'Why bastard,wherefore base?' King Lear, Act 1 Scene 2."[1] We find Shakespeare figured as common-law judge, sketching a norm[2] or providing historical detail.[3] Of course, Shakespeare is not always an authority. As one witty justice put it:

> As to the…dissent's reliance on the Bard, we can only observe:
> Though Shakespeare, of course,
> knew the Law of his time,
> He was foremost a poet,
> in search of a rhyme.[4]

He nevertheless often finds himself in a string cite. In Caldwell v. Mississippi, finding a prosecutor's response to defense counsel's plea for mercy inappropriate, the court writes,

> This is true whether the plea for mercy discusses Christian, Judean or Buddhist philosophies, quotes Shakespeare or refers to the heartache suffered by the accused's mother.[5]

In Boutilier v. the Immigration and Naturalization Service, Shakespeare finds himself in surprising company:

> To label [homosexuals] "excludable aliens" would be tantamount to saying that Sappho, Leonardo da Vinci, Michelangelo, Andre Gide, and perhaps even Shakespeare, were they to come to life again, would be deemed unfit to visit our shores.[6]

Occasionally old Bill brings a refreshing relativism;[7] even irony.[8] Still, sometimes it's a stretch. Take Walters v. National Assoc. of Radiation Survivors, 1985:

> [The] statement ("The first thing we do, let's kill all the lawyers") was spoken by a rebel, not a friend of liberty. See W. Shakespeare, King Henry VI, pt. II Act IV, scene 2, line 72. As a careful reading of that text will reveal, Shakespeare insightfully realized that disposing of lawyers is a step in the direction of a totalitarian form of government.[9]

As this case suggests, there is a politics, as well as a history to the court's interest in Shakespeare, an interest that has peaked in recent years with concern about interpretation and reading. Over the last three decades, lawyers and courts have been occupied with precisely the questions studied at the Center for Literary and Cultural Studies in its first ten years—strategies of reading and narration, patterns of culture, limits and channels of power, the imponderables of interpretive conflict, the politics of reason.

We might read Shakespeare as a symptom, law leaning on literature in anxiety, and these are anxious times in law.

Some factoids, as they say on CNN: the Supremes have referred to Shakespeare a scant thirty times since 1790, the overwhelming majority in the last twenty years. And not, I feel sure, simply because opinions are increasingly written by clerks eager to display their undergraduate erudition. (Which plays, you wonder? Lear 1, Macbeth 1, Hamlet some 9 times—rarely before 1950. [Iago alone 6]) Lawyers are much fonder of Shakespeare, mentioning him in their briefs more than 75 times just since 1979.

If we look at all the cases of all the courts, state and federal, now accessible by computer search, we find Shakespeare more than a thousand times since 1789. But we note a changing citation rate—from .27 times per year in the last century to 44.6 times per year today. Even corrected for an astoundingly larger caseload (177,765 cases in 1994 compared to 7,077 in 1900, and only 110,109 from 1754–1900), the citation rate has doubled in this century, from .01171 percent of all cases in 1913 to .0244 percent in 1992.

Period	# of References	# Per Year
1754–1900	39	0.27
1900–1925	42	1.62
1925–1945	56	2.67
1945–1949	27	5.40
1950–1954	38	7.60
1955–1959	28	5.60
1960–1964	50	10.0
1965–1969	63	12.6
1970–1974	79	15.8
1975–1979	124	24.8
1980–1984	145	29.0
1985–1989	224	44.8
1990–1994	223	44.6

Year	Total Cases	Average # Shakespeare Cases	Percentage
1992	182,804	44.6	.02440
1987	141,718	44.8	.03161
1982	105,784	29.0	.02741
1977	75,749	24.8	.03272
1972	51,383	15.8	.03074
1967	38,453	12.6	.03273
1962	35,687	10.0	.02801
1957	28,497	5.60	.01965
1952	26,632	7.60	.02857
1947	22,557	5.40	.02389
1935	19,049	2.67	.01405
1913	13,840	1.62	.01171

Well, so much for empiricism.

The interesting point is that Shakespeare appears ever more frequently in disputes about interpretation—although he seems to support the widest variety of reading strategies. Shakespeare comes not to bury meaning but to praise it.

To praise the full meaning of statutes:

> Suffice it to say that we focus on the [complete] language of 22 U.S.C. @1732, not any shorthand description of it. See W. Shakespeare, *Romeo and Juliet*, Act II, scene 2, line 43 ("What's in a name?").[10]

To praise the historical meaning of terms. In holding that the right to "confront" witnesses guarantees a "face to face" meeting, the court notes:

> Shakespeare was thus describing the root meaning of confrontation when he had Richard the Second say: "Then call them to our presence—face to face, and frowning brow to brow, ourselves will hear the accuser and the accused freely speak" ...Perception as well as the reality of fairness prevails.[11]

Or, on the other hand, to praise historically contingent readings:

> To apply the rule blindly today, however, makes as much sense as attempting to interpret Hamlet's admonition to Ophelia, "Get thee to a nunnery, go" without understanding the meaning of Hamlet's words in the context of their age. (A footnote here helpfully explains that "Nunnery was Elizabethan slang for house of prostitution.")[12]

In 1990, Shakespeare weighs in against indeterminacy:

> To say that Polonius, Claudius, and Gertrude express differing views about Hamlet's "antic disposition" is not to say that Hamlet has no meaning.[13]

In 1993, for plain meaning:

> Of course it vastly understates the matter to say that the provision is "written in a fashion that contemplates actual delivery," as one might say Hamlet was written in a fashion that contemplates 16th-century dress. Causation of delivery is the very condition of this provision's operation—and the dissent says it does not matter whether delivery is caused.[14]

Shakespeare stands strong against obfuscation and ambivalence, for common sense. A frustrated dissent:

> If, as the Court holds, these employees are engaged in production of agricultural crops for commerce, I do not see how it can hold that they are not engaged in agriculture. If the Court could say "To be or not to be: that is the question," it

might reasonably answer in support of either side. But here the Court tells us that the real solution of this dilemma is "to be" and "not to be" at the same time. While this is a unique contribution to the literature of statutory construction, I can only regret the great loss to the literature of the drama that this possibility was overlooked by the Bard of Avon.[15]

Well, enough.

Enough to taste the politics of this encounter, a politics often paralleled in the encounter between legal academics and cultural or literary studies. Lawyers have largely studied literature, borrowed from literature, in a project of rebuilding, supporting, stabilizing law. If we can read Shakespeare, we can certainly read the Constitution. Subliminal message: the Constitution is every bit as cultured, as literary.

Cultural study enriches the judge, softens judgment, leavens the law. It reminds us of the people, the purpose, the power of decision. And it is good for our moral health.

For many current legal scholars, literature provides an exit from the anxieties and self-doubts of the sixties and seventies, release from indeterminacy, response to nihilism. It was the interpretive community, in the parlor, with the presumption.

And I sense a parallel on the other side, although I don't know it as well—law, in the eyes of literary critics, seems strangely stable, where the rubber meets the road, a place for real politics. To study old law cases instead of old novels—here also an anxiety to quiet, an anxiety about the irrelevance, the discontinuity, the deconstruction of literature. Subliminal message: literary study is no backwater, it could be about power, could read the law, engage the issues of the day.

Nevertheless, most surprising in my encounters with cultural studies has been the literary mavens' image of law: reason, authority, clarity, force…narratives that move from fiction to action; an image of law legal scholars can frankly only sustain by reference to literature…or sociology, or economics, or anthropology. Literature the promise of culture, of ground; law the promise of power, of figure. A match made in heaven…or at least on the Supreme Court.

But I advocate a different encounter, a different politics—in interdisciplinarity, less the end of anxiety than the beginning of critique. For lawyers, a look to literature not for reassurance, but for risks, for techniques of reading rather than revering.

I admit I am nostalgic for the last generation of literature students come to study law, armed with deconstruction and skepticism and the fire of critique, rather than the balm of reconstruction. And I revel in the energy, envy the sophistication, the savvy, the zealous uncertainty of today's cultural studies—engaged with ethnicity and identity, with culture in its broadest, perhaps its anthropological sense, a sense increasingly dismayed even to be termed "culture."

Indeed it seems only here, between law and literature, that cultural studies seems now to host an asymmetric encounter: from literature comes reconstruction, from law, critique. And I wonder if there isn't another side here as well. Might not law, its doubts, gaps, and ambiguities, its narratives, its realism about power—about the fragmentation, the readerliness, the dispersion, the porousness of power—reveal literature's own unconscious clout?

For the match made in heaven to work, for each discipline to reinforce the other, each must project the other as difference. The most important work of cultural studies might rather be encouragement to see two disciplines as one, law as culture, literature as the law.

It is here that we might have hope, the disruptive edge of each vibrating excitedly with the other.

NOTES

1. Levy v. Louisiana *ex rel.* Charity Hospital, 391 U.S. 68, 72 n.6 (1968). Or take Milkovich v. Lorain Journal, 1990; Finding a "cause of action for damage to a person's reputation by the publication fo false and defamatory statements," the court notes: "In Shakespeare's Othello, Iago says to Othello: 'Good name in man and woman, dear my lord, is the immediate jewel of their souls. Who steals my purse steals trash...'." Milkovich v. Lorain Journal Co., 497 U.S. 1, 11 (1990).

2. U.S. v Apfelbaum (1980):

   Shakespeare's lines here express sound legal doctrine: "His acts did not o'ertake his bad intent; and must be buried but as an intent that perish'd by the way: thoughts are no subjects, intents but merely thoughts."

   U.S. v Apfelbaum, 445 U.S. 115, 131 N.13 (1980) (citing Measure for Measure).

3. In 1948, Goesaert v. Liquor Control, commentary on discrimination against female tavern owners, the court opined: "We meet the alewife, sprightly and ribald, in Shakespeare." Goesaert v. Cleary, 335 U.S. 464, 465 (1948).

4. Browning-Ferris Industries Inc. v. Kelco Disposal Inc./ 492 U.S. 257, 265 (1989).

5. Caldwell v. Mississippi, 472 U.S. 320, 337 (1985) (quoting Caldwell v. Mississippi, 443 So. 2d 806, 817 (1984);)r in Tison v. Arizona, (1987):

   An intuition that sons and daughters must sometimes be punished for the sins of the father may be deeply rooted in our consciousness.... See, e.g., Horace, *Odes* III, 6:1 (C. Bennett trans. 1939) W. Shakespeare, *The Merchant of Venice*, Act III, scene 5; H. Ibsen, *Ghosts* (1881).

Tison v. Arizona, 481 U.S. 137, 184 & n. 20 (1987).

6. Boutilier v. I.N.S. 387 U.S. 118, 130 (1967).

7. See for example: "The dissent finds Dean Wigmore more persuasive than President Eisenhower or even William Shakespeare. Surely that must depend upon the proposition that they are cited for." Coy v. Iowa, 487 U.S. 1012, 1018 n.2 (1988) (citation omitted).

8. In an affirmative action case, the dissent:

> The majority emphasizes, as though it is meaningful, that "No persons are automatically excluded from consideration; all are able to have their qualifications weighed against those of other applicants." One is reminded of the exchange from Shakespeare's King Henry the Fourth, Part I: "GLENDOWER: I can call Spirits from the vasty Deep. HOTSPUR: Why, so can I, or so can any man. But will they come when you do call for them?"

Johnson v. Transp. Agency, 480 U.S. 616, 674 (1987).

9. Walters v. Nat'l Assoc. of Radiation Survivors, 473 U.S. 305, 317 n.24 (1985).

10. Dames & Moore v. Regan, 543 U.S. 654, 675 n.7 (1981).

11. *Coy*, Coy v. Iowa 487 U.S. at 1016 (1988).

12. U.S. v. Watson, 423 U.S. 411, 438 & n.3 (1976).

13. Bd. of Educ. v. Mergens, 496 U.S. 226, 282 (1990).

14. Fex v. Michigan, 113 S.Ct. 1085, 1088 n.2 (1993).

15. Farmers Reservoir & Irrigation Co. v. McComb, 337 U.S. 755, 772 (1949).

24

The Made-Up and
the Made-Real

Elaine Scarry

In the last several decades, the attempt to understand the nature of creation
and created things has become a central and collective intellectual project.
The energy that in an earlier age was directed toward the investigation of
"truth" has been redirected toward understanding the nature of inventing,
making, creating (or, as it has often been referred to lately, "constructing,"
especially in the sense of "the social construction of x"). This project is
young enough, and the outlines of its possibilities are rich enough, that it
could go in many directions; but certainly, at a minimum, both the phe-
nomenological attributes of creation and the ethical entailments of creation
are centrally at issue.

So far, the major accomplishment of this collective work has simply been to
designate what objects, events, or institutions should henceforth be taken as
"instances" of creation. An array of objects, events, or institutions has been
conspicuously relabeled, so that their createdness stands revealed and so that
whenever one of them enters our visual field, we at once recognize that it
bears in its form the record of creation. In other words, the major work of

the collective project[1] has so far been the gathering of samples, and the major outcome has been the production of an "inventory." The category of created objects (the category of objects that can be immediately recognized as created) has been vastly extended so that "art works" are no longer its solitary representative. They stand accompanied by countless other cultural artifacts: nation-states are fictions (in the sense of created things), the law is a created thing, a scientific fact (many argue) is a constructed thing, the wilderness is a made thing, a quark is a made thing, fire is a created thing, sexuality is a created thing, romantic passion is a created thing, the body (some say) is a created thing, gender (some say) is a made thing, childhood (Philippe Aries says) is a created thing, and so on. Much less widely preoccupying, but equally crucial, has been the fact that doors, cups, chairs, coal companies, vaccines, baseball mitts, and bandages are thought and spoken about as created things. There has been, then, a proliferation of the sites of creation. It is not that these phenomena were not previously recognizable as invented (the fact that they were invented was no doubt, in most cases, recoverable[2]). But they were not, in effect, framed by their fictionality or artifactuality; our apprehension of them did not require the active moment-by-moment perception of their inventedness; our earlier discussion of them did not require that any entry into their vicinity be preceded by a self-conscious acknowledgment of their artifactual nature and the explicit denial that they were "natural" or inevitable.

In the past, a solitary philosopher may have now and then emerged to work on the nature of creation, but there never emerged a large assembly of people working in concert; though the "fictionality" of a single, exceptional phenomenon such as Christianity may have been debated by a wide population, in no previous period did the fictionality of nearly every phenomenon simultaneously come under review. I want to postpone the question of whether the present collective undertaking is a good or a bad thing;[3] and postpone as well my own speculations about why this collective project should have emerged at this particular historical moment,[4] and instead simply proceed with the fact that it *is* our project, both for now and for the future.

Given that we aspire to understand the nature of creation, it is key that the representative instances should have been expanded from the extraordinarily narrow ground of art works (however beloved and remarkable) to a more expansive ground that includes art works and all other cultural artifacts. This is crucial because art works have some anomalous features that if contemplated in isolation distort, wholly misrepresent, the overall phenomenology of creating. As the first stage of work was devoted to the generation of an inventory, it is fair to hope that the second stage—hence "the future of the humanities"—will be devoted to the generation of accurate descriptions. The accuracy of these descriptions will turn on our ability to hold, within a single field of vision, the two categories of created objects[5] while simultaneously *not* allowing those two categories of created objects to become erroneously conflated.

The descriptive work has of course, even in the stage of making the inventory, already begun. But this description has had the peculiar outcome of producing a double negative. The recognition of the kinship between the once solitary realm of art and the capacious realm of artifacts has not worked to the advantage of either. This is startling: while it might have been too much to hope that the annexation of the two would lead to an enhancement of *both*, it seems entirely reasonable to anticipate that it might at least have led to an enhancement of *one*. Instead, the placing of the two side-by-side sometimes seems to have brought about a *two-directional demotion*. Now art seems less authoritative because its "exclusivity" has been unmasked. It aspires to be, or presents itself as being, a solitary exceptional phenomenon; but "now we see" it was not so exceptional after all. Conversely, the authority of the realm of cultural artifacts (constitutions, quarks, medical cures) has diminished, because they now stand revealed as "merely fictive," "merely made." Each aspires to be, or presents itself as being real, but "now we see" that each is actually "constructed," which deauthenticates it by several internally incompatible paths: either the object's loss of reality is perceived to entail a loss of authority or instead the object is seen as retaining its authority but doing so falsely (that is, its "constructedness" is attributed to sinister plots and "hegemonic" enactments[6]). The vivacity of the large realm of cultural artifacts—now composed of authorityless objects and authoritarian objects—is greatly diminished, as is, by the strange workings of the double demotion, the vivacity of art objects.

Nothing is inevitable about either of these two demotions. Even if the inventedness of cultural objects *did* entail the loss of realness (itself an error), one might anticipate a wholly optimistic response. Seeing that a phenomenon is constructed, our own access to the artifact increases, as does the chance to reshape it, if it is in need of reshaping: if, for example, it endangers or imperils other people. Further, the adjacency of the two realms ought to contain the possibility of reciprocal vivification.[7] Authority can be based on intervention in everyday practice or instead on abstention from everyday practice; but the sudden adjacency of the two has worked to efface both. This double demotion may seem merely attitudinal and therefore harmless; but it inhibits and deforms the ability to think clearly about artifacts, both in their primary outlines and in their secondary and tertiary attributes.

Moreover, and more important, each of the two demotions entails a conclusion that is phenomenologically false. What was formerly perceived as the cultural artifact's "realness" was not an illusion; nor was what was formerly perceived as art's "exceptionalness" an illusion. On a particular morning when the artifactuality of law (or any artifact) becomes suddenly and insistently visible, what should be striking is not the fact that the law is not real, or the sense that its reality was a fraud, or that there is no difference between the real and the artifactual, but rather that x (the particular law) *is* artifice and that the artifice of x entailed at its center, up until last night, the appearance and force and responsibilities of "the real." In other words, having been made up, as a poem is, the created thing then must have gone on to a second stage of creation, where the initial work of invention was compounded by an additional process through which reality was conferred on or discovered in it; and the essence of this second stage lay in the making invisible of the traces of its having been created in the first place.[8] At the moment when x is looked at as an artifact, it is being temporarily divested of the second stage of creation—which may be beneficial, so long as that act of divestiture is itself acknowledged to be taking place. But what is instead ordinarily the case is that this second stage of "realness" is retroactively treated as a "guise" or a "mistake" that has been "unmasked," as though x is now being made "to remember" what it *really* is. But what it *is* at this moment (a half-made thing, a half-unmade thing) is *not* what it *really* is, but is exactly what, until this morning, it really was not. The difference between art objects and other objects can therefore be understood as follows: both undergo creation, but almost all artifacts other than art undergo a second stage of creation to which art is never subject. Because art has only the first stage, one can see it as an incomplete artifact, as a truncated or abbreviated artifact, or as an adolescent artifact. But either way of naming single-stage and double-stage creations— either "the pure (art) and the complex (other objects)" or instead "the abbreviated (art) and the complete (other objects)"—clarifies why holding the two steadily side-by-side is key. As Richard Rhodes has recently written, "Works of art remain only partly realized, arrested in passage between the imaginary and the material world, like the figures caught in mid passage traversing the place of the great bronze doors of Renaissance churches."[9] Together the two genres of objects—one still in midair and the other landed in (and thickly entangled with) the material world—reveal secrets about the action of creating that could never be seen if that action were looked at in only one of the two places. The conclusions we draw if only one of them is looked at will be erroneous.

This brings us to the second of the two losses to which I referred: divesting art of its exceptionality is also a costly error. The imagination's ordinary attribute of self-effacement (in most artifacts other than art) raises a question about the idiosyncratic logic of her appearance in the realm of art, where, far from making any attempt to disguise her own activity, she is self-announcing. While an art work exists in the presence of endless other forms of made things, these others are not ordinarily accompanied by the announcement, "This is a made thing." But a poem or painting exists within the frame of this announcement. This overt fictitiousness or createdness or madeness is both the ground on which art has been extravagantly honored and, with equal frequency, the ground on which it has been despised or dismissed. Of relevance to the present discussion is not the interesting divergence between the responses of honoring and dismissing, but the fact that both responses are alike in identifying art as exceptional, nonnormative, or marginal. They are also correct in this identification, for in the *overtness of its fictionality*[10] (rather than in its fictionality), art *is* exceptional.

We see that poems, paintings, and songs—along with light bulbs, chairs, and coats; vaccines, courtrooms, and constitutions; economic structures, computers, and altars—are potent sources of revelation about the invisible activity of creating. But when the art work is taken as the *sole* source of revelation, the resulting portrait of the imagination will be systematically distorted by the faulty first premise that this is the single arena of her activity. One might conclude, for example, that the imagination's activity is rare, unusual, or narrow; but when we extend the ground of examples we quickly see that the imagination's territory is vast, extending to, because continually extending, the boundaries of the known world. One might conclude that the imagination is playful, irreverent, and the darling of the leisure class; but once we contemplate the expanded ground, we see that she is indefatigably at work, that she forfeits her own immunity, and that she is associated with leisure only because it, among endless other things, is one of her products. One might even conclude that she is amoral, tending to ignore, to divert attention away from, the vagaries and sadness of historical reality, or even rehearsing violence as though these things nowhere bring actual hurt; but we see that her gigantic enterprise is undertaken on behalf of live, historically real sentience, and that she is on this subject ethically strict. To these examples might be added a long list of similar distortions; but what is at the moment most important to see is that the imagination itself is partially to blame for this faulty portrait, that her habit of being self-effacing ninety-nine percent of the time, and self-announcing (some would say "strutting") one percent of the time, does not simply allow but actively invites a faulty portrait.

It may be that it just "happens to have happened" that civilization has both a vast realm in which things, after having been made up, are made real (and the traces of making are forgotten), and a narrow realm where things stand completed in the contracted state of made-upness. There may be no special logic to this, no special design. But we have seen that the human imagination, both in its individual and collective forms, seldom works without a plan; and so, supposing for a moment that the imagination here again has a strategy, I want to contemplate two alternative hypotheses. Although the two suppositions are quite different, they are not mutually exclusive or even antagonistic; for it may be that one holds precedence in one kind of era, while in another era the second comes into play. I want to describe each of the two briefly, to make clear what is being supposed, even if there is not room to make those suppositions fully plausible.

The First Alternative. One might argue that although the imagination is ordinarily self-effacing (quietly performing her work through the hands of nurses, automakers, scientists, and legislators), she cannot resist occasionally taking a bow, absorbing our attention, even our applause, and that in doing this, she singles out particular, peculiarly gifted women and men through whom she can make an appearance. If ninety-nine percent of the time she disguises herself, we can allow her this one percent where she captivates us, even brings us to our feet, and requires us to luxuriate in the pure fact of creating unconnected to any obvious use. But it quickly becomes apparent that this moment of self-celebration is not a lapse from her overall enterprise, but is instead of great assistance to it. If it is central to her project precisely that she remain disguised—if the benefits of her work are ordinarily greatly amplified by not being assignable to her—then by having a piece of ground where she is immediately recognizable, proudly self-announcing, she will obscure her activity on all other ground, deflect attention from her responsibility for the "real world's" realness. Finding her so easily *here* (in poetry), why should we labor to seek her *elsewhere*? Precisely by allowing us so easily to locate her here she prevents us from looking for her anywhere else; for who, *under ordinary conditions*, would suspect that one so self-delighting on one terrain would obscure and efface herself on another? The totality of her work must, on a day-to-day basis, be regarded as just this (Mozart), just here (Shakespeare), for better (as in moments of being excessively honored), or for worse (as in moments when art works are dismissed as merely fictions). Either of these two responses contents her; for when she hears herself applauded as "rare" she counts herself successful, and when she hears herself dismissed and undervalued because irrelevant to the world, she counts that, too, as a triumph.[11] Her aspiration is to be omnipresent and unrecognized—to be not the legislator of the world but, as Shelley saw, the *unacknowledged* legislator of the world.

The Second Alternative. The imagination's aura of restricted occurrence in art can alternatively be understood as amplifying her overall generosity in a second way, for here within the boundaries of uncountable lyrics, comedies, epics, poems, paintings, her endlessly reiterated and stunningly visible central act of invention (its motives, goals, and strategies) is rehearsed, practiced, experimented with, and, above all, held steadily visible. This means that if a population ever suddenly needs to find out the nature of creating, the place to begin the search will be immediately available, as will much of the vocabulary of description and analysis. Art, as though getting ready for an emergency, holds in steady readiness the intellectual equipment of creation in case (as seems now to be the case) the need arises to look for and make recognizable the act of creating in the many other previously unacknowledged sites. The imagination's aura of restricted occurrence may at first appear self-defeating, for if art appears exclusive, whatever attributes of creating it reveals will seem to be only its own. In fact, it is this very separation between art and all else that ordinarily blocks us from seeing the full picture of the process of creation waiting to be found there. But this is very smart, even brilliant, for if we need "to unmask" the imagination—if we need to relearn her responsibilities, reacquaint ourselves with the imagination's motives and full range of activities—it will only be because the imagination is in some way failing or is in need of self-conscious repair and reassessment. And when that happens, one of the first signs will be the fact that thing after thing stands revealed as a "fiction," divested of or unable to sustain or reattain its reality. When wilderness and fire and quarks and gods and legal transcripts and medical research and sexuality and childhood appear as instances of artifice, then art will no longer stand alone, irrelevant and incommensurable, but will (as is now the case) begin to give rise to endless comparisons between art and money, art and history, art and science, art and law, art and philosophic truths, art and dying cities as well as newborn ones, and the rigorous collective account of art's differences from and similarities to these once-real artifacts will make recoverable the full majesty and power of creation as well as the ethical requirements attending it. Art is our starting place. It would have been impossible to perform the recent inventory of relabeling if the imagination were not abiding somewhere already and eternally labeled. Art provides the perpetual ground for the self-conscious practice of artifice and for the development of at least an initial elemental vocabulary for describing that practice.

Institutional Recapitulation. If instead of *objects* (art works, cultural artifacts, constructed things) or the actions that produce those objects (imagining, creating, making, constructing), we talked about the *institutional location* of these same events, then the categories would not be the "made-up" and the "made-real" or "aesthetic objects" and "nonaesthetic artifacts," but the humanities on the one hand, and on the other, the sciences, as well as the medical school, the law school, and other centers of research. The major statements in the foregoing paper can therefore be restated in terms of these institutional locations, though the phenomena are of course much wider, more diffuse, and more powerful than the institutions.

(1) In recent decades, "creation" and "created objects" have been contemplated not only in departments of art, literature, and music but in a wide array of disciplines such as law, history, and physics where an aesthetic vocabulary, not formerly present, has become audible. (2) The outcome of this collective undertaking has been a proliferation of the sites of creation and hence the establishing of an inventory of made objects. (3) It is reasonable to expect that the next period of work will move beyond inventory and bring forth a series of revelations about the nature of creation that both draw on and account for the way aesthetic and nonaesthetic artifacts coinhabit the world. (4) So far, this descriptive labor has been inhibited by a double demotion whereby art objects are divested of their exceptionalness, and nonaesthetic artifacts are divested of their realness; both genres of objects, now unexceptional and unreal, are divested of their authority, which is held to be either nonexistent, or existent but fraudulent. The institutional signs of this peculiar outcome are visible in the fact that practitioners of disciplines such as law, physics, and history sometimes see the application of literary questions to their discipline's subject matter as the prelude to an attack on that subject matter. Conversely, the migration of literary vocabularies, theories, or practices to these other departments is seen by some friends of literature not as a validation of literary practice (a demonstration of its general usefulness) but as a repudiation of its own beautiful and great subject matter.

(5) This two-directional demotion, beyond the unhappiness it causes, impairs our ability to think clearly about the nature of invention because it depends on conclusions that are false. (6) Nonaesthetic artifacts (hence the subject matters of the sciences as well as of schools of engineering, medicine, law), far from being unreal, are precisely and essentially objects that, having been made up, then undergo a second stage where they are made real. A reality-conferring process—such as "ratification" in the law or "verification" in science—radically alters the "invention," "proposal," or "hypothesis" that was its starting place. It is not by retracting and ignoring that second transformative stage but by unfolding its powerful operations that the full picture of creation will become legible. (7) Art objects (hence the subject matter of literature, art, music departments), though not exceptional in their fictiveness, *are* exceptional in the *overtness* of their fictiveness: unlike most nonaesthetic artifacts, they never undergo a process of reality-conferring that obscures their made-upness. It is by attending to, not by denying or missing, this remarkable feature that we make the deeper strategies of the imagination enterable.

(8) The imagination's aspiration to be omnipresent yet unrecognizable, acknowledged only in the overt fiction of art, leads to an aura of restricted occurrence that superficially deforms our picture of the imagination while greatly magnifying her accomplishment. The logic of this, sketched earlier in terms of the imagination's own motives, can be resummarized in terms of its more familiar institutional analogues. (9) The humanities (like the imagination in the portrait given earlier) have always been seen to occupy exceptional ground in relation to the sciences as well as in relation to the professional and research schools. They are in some periods by some people excessively honored; they are in some periods by some people summarily dismissed as unserious, irrelevant, and unreal. (10) This discrepancy between being honored and being dishonored, however interesting, is much less crucial than what binds them, the fact that each is a way of cordoning off the humanities from the sciences, the research and professional schools. (11) In ordinary times—by which I mean times other than our own—this allows the work in those other areas to go on without self-conscious attention to the degree of invention entailed there. The humanities, by absorbing all our curiosity about creation, prevent that curiosity from straying to other sites. The humanities, in other words, at the very moment of being charged (whether admiringly or scornfully) with unreality, actively contribute to the reality-conferring stage undergone and enjoyed by those others. (12) This also means that in an emergency, when it becomes necessary to retract the making-real stage from these other phenomena in order to scrutinize the process of invention, the vocabulary of creating, constructing, or making, as well as manifest instances of created things, can be immediately located as examples. Hence the literary or artistic models can be, and are being, imported into history, into the history of science, into the study of law, into the study of medicine, into engineering, as, conversely, the project of "reality conferring" can be transported from these other realms into the humanities in the form of the preoccupation with "reference" and the attempt to reanchor language in the material world. The humanities are, in relation to the other spheres of knowledge, an ongoing laboratory, where creating in its most overt, most concentrated form, can be practiced, and where the vocabulary for describing that practice can be unfolded, displayed, and held in steady readiness.

NOTES

1. I stress here the collective project, since any individual analysis may of course expose scores of attributes belonging to a given fictive object and thus accomplish something additional to the act of registering the given object in the Directory of Artifacts.

2. The ease of "recoverability" differs among artifacts and may be a useful basis

for sorting created objects into three distinct genres. See E. Scarry, "The Structure of the Artifact," chapter 5, in *The Body in Pain: the Making and Unmaking of the World* (New York: Oxford University Press, 1985), especially pp. 311-14.

3. It is not necessarily the case that we should expose and unfold the nature of creation, because much of the work performed by created objects—whether verbal or material—occurs only when they are not self-consciously recognizable as creations. They have undergone a second state of creation that can be called reality-conferring, the outcome of which is to make less accessible that fact of inventiveness. This is ordinarily motivated not by political suppression but by artifactual enablement—by the fact, for example, that generating a sentence is much easier if one is not simultaneously thinking, "I am now inventing a sentence, I must move my tongue forward," and so forth. If one imagines scanning centuries, then randomly setting down in any one of them, and then asking the question, "Ought these people to be engaged in a self-conscious exposition of all their fictions? Not just one particular fiction such as the divine right of monarchs, but all of them?", it is not at all self-evident that we would answer, "Yes: in all times and in all ages, this would be a good project."

4. The most likely explanation centers on the unprecedented magnitude and rapidity of invention in the twentieth century coupled with the expanse in the radius of hurt that can be caused by any bad or deformed invention.

5. Although the two are here usually designated "art objects" and "other objects," many other vocabularies are useful. Contemporary arguments about narrative, for example, distinguish between overt narratives (novels, poems) and narratives embedded in history, science, medicine, and the law.

6. Some things *are*, of course, constructed precisely by these means, but during the first stage of work on artifacts this thesis has sometimes been applied globally, thereby disempowering us from remedying those instances where something actually *is* severely wrong. If no model of a benign and generous construction exists (or no instances of it), then the ground on which one might stand to critique damaging artifacts disappears.

7. It is easy to imagine a person who has a deep and longstanding regard for the poems of Keats or Shakespeare and, simultaneously, a longstanding disregard for, or simply indifference to, the law. It is easy to imagine further that on the day this person is confronted with the fact that a particular law is produced by a labor of the imagination kindred to that which produced the poem, it would suddenly take on some of the vividness or vivacity of the poem. Conversely, it is easy to picture a person who has a longstanding regard for the way concrete laws reshape the everyday world but who is quite unmindful of Keats or Shakespeare. Once the poem is shown in the depth of its complicity with concrete legal outcomes, the person might see the poem as a vivid linguistic instrument. Together,

then, the two persons might complete the project for the *Lyrical Ballads* envisaged by Wordsworth and Coleridge, with Wordsworth lifting the "film of familiarity" on prosaic diurnal events and Coleridge endowing the mystical and magical with the plausibility and potency of the diurnal and familiar.

8. For an extended account of the two actions of making up and making real, see Part II of *The Body in Pain*. On benign forms of reality-conferring, see 146-48, 171-72, 212-15, 220, 222, 235-40, 280; for a comparison with false forms of substantiation that ape the second stage of artifacts by hurting the body, see the discussion of analogical verification in torture and war, 13-14, 21, 27-59, 119-21, 125-33, 139, 146-47, 201-204, 350 n.138, 354 n.176, 361 n.39.

9. Richard Rhodes, "The Flesh Made Word," in *Writing in an Era of Conflict: National Book Week Lectures* (Washington, D.C.: Library of Congress, 1990), 12. He is also the author of *The Making of the Atomic Bomb* (New York: Simon and Schuster, 1986).

10. Again, the art object is "overt in its fictionality" because of the extraordinary fact that, unlike other objects, it never undergoes the reality-conferring (or fictiveness-erasing) level of making.

11. Plato understood this project perfectly and served her greatly. Let the poets be despised (as in some of the dialogues), or let the poets be extravagantly honored (as in other of the dialogues), but at all costs, let poetic work be perceived as distinct from the realm of real things: from real things like the numbers one through ten; from real things like the concept of justice; from real things like the laws that one must enter into with such conviction that one agrees not only to live, but to die by them; from real things like *caritas*; from real things like philosophic dialogues and conversation and a portrait of a man named Socrates. When Plato said that art was like reality, only three times removed, he shouted the final words—"three times removed"—so that the opening words—"art is like reality"—could be safely whispered aloud. Art *is* like reality…except that it is abbreviated, truncated, several times removed because it does not (unlike other key constructions) undergo the making-real stage. A major part of Plato's work is devoted to this second stage of making. In front of our eyes he performs the labor of reality-conferring on constructions such as justice, law, love, philosophy; the vivacity of each appears to be freestanding and to predate the very descriptions through which it is brought into being.

25

Narrative Battles in the Courtroom

Laura Hanft Korobkin

The most attention-getting episodic dramas in America today are not the weekly segments of *N.Y.P.D. Blue* but the actual criminal cases on which their scripts are often based. How will the O.J. trial "turn out"? What was in von Bulow's black bag? Are the Menendez brothers sympathetic victims or greedy and ruthless murderers? Americans follow these unfolding stories with the same—often far greater—interest than we give to best-selling novels. Indeed, the two are dynamically connected. The *way* we "read" actual trials is critically shaped by our experience as readers and viewers of courtroom dramas, movies, and TV shows. We cheer for familiar heroes, recoil from recognizable villains, and predict the trial's outcome based as much on the logic of the genre of courtroom drama as on the admissible testimony in a particular case. To an armchair juror wielding a television remote control, there is little distinction between the nightly news coverage of a case, the fictional episode loosely based on its facts, and the television docudrama rushed into production before the jury has even been seated in the same case.

Is the difficulty of drawing the line between fact and fiction merely a function of presentational similarity produced by television's competitive need to provide compressed, continuous dramatic entertainment? While "expert" legal advisors give law dramas a sheen of accuracy (references to legal precedents, use of hearsay and other procedural rules, etc.), the structural similarity between "factual" and "fictional" trial coverage seems to stem largely from shared formatting constraints. Real trials are astonishingly tedious, repetitious, and rarely dramatic. On *Law and Order*, however, as on the evening news, cross-examinations last two minutes, get right to the point, and hone in on the witness's moment of emotional breakdown.[1] Yet there is a much deeper—and, I think, more interesting—connection between the lawyer defending a real murdering antiabortionist and the actor playing a similar character on TV. That connection is rooted in the inherent narrativity of trial process, which often transforms adversarial litigation into a combat between two familiar, culturally powerful narratives.

As recent scholars have shown, opening statements and final arguments in real cases frequently borrow their language and their framing "stories" from popular movies and novels.[2] When prosecutors in the O.J. Simpson trial structured their opening statement around the thematic refrain that O.J. was a man so obsessed with controlling his wife that "if he couldn't have her, no one else would," they were offering jurors a story frame already familiar from television miniseries and popular romance novels. This is not to say, of course, that literary formulations of spousal abuse are merely "stories" unconnected to very real and horrifying violence. Yet the *literary logic* of such authorially shaped narrative versions of real events inevitably structures the way we "read" each successive version. Literary logic constructs specific plot expectations, and these establish patterns of sign and referent, evidence and inference, that guide the audience's interpretation of the unfolding dramatic "facts." Viewers know, for instance, that when the drama's first hour focuses on a series of increasingly violent incidents in an obsessive relationship, there will *always* be a climactic scene of violence later on, whether that violence is a brutalizing murder by the husband (*Star 80*) or a defensive execution by the battered wife (*The Burning Bed*). When these plot expectations are transferred to the courtroom, the legitimacy of a particular *legal* inference (when an abused woman is murdered, we can infer that her abuser was the murderer) is reinforced by what are essentially *literary* principles of narrative construction: consistency, economy, predictable causation.[3] Jurors are implicitly invited to use what they've learned as literary readers to solve the causal and evidentiary problems that confront them as juridical readers. By suggesting that this story is much like other stories jurors know—particularly if the story frame features unambiguous victims and perpetrators and a clear moral calculus—lawyers provide jurors with an accessible framework they can use as a guide in making credibility determinations and evidentiary assessments. Mountains of bewildering evidence, conflicting testimony, and seemingly unconnected detail suddenly become not just coherent but morally inflected, logically connected, and thus judgeable.

Three points should be noted about this process of literary appropriation and deployment. First, the use of "literary" forms to shape litigative narratives does not represent the invasion of a foreign, subjective, emotional discourse into an objective, rational one.[4] Narratives are not extraneous to legal process; they are its constitutive elements. Like literary fiction, litigation is a thoroughly discursive enterprise powered at every point by the act of storytelling. From the filing of a legal complaint to the presentation of testimony and argument at trial to the rendering of an appeals court decision, litigation is conducted by constructing, performing, and interpreting stories about anterior events. To win their cases, parties, witnesses, and their attorneys must do more than recite random facts; they must transform the ambiguous data of subjective experience into coherent, moral, persuasive narratives. That authorial, shaping process inevitably produces culturally familiar forms with their attendant characters, genres, plots, and—perhaps most important—with the predictable, pre-established responses jury-readers will bring to them. Consequently, the notion that forensic storytelling is necessarily deceptive misperceives not just the essential narrativity of all case presentations, but their consequent intertextual continuity with the wealth of narratives available in literary, political, and other discourses within a culture at the time. Yet the idea that consciously shaped narratives are "untrue" lingers, creating a stubborn taint that master storytellers can manipulate to advantage. At a conference on law and narrative held during the second month of the Simpson trial, for instance, Alan M. Dershowitz criticized the prosecution team for deceptively using "the power of storytelling" to argue that O.J.'s history of battering his wife predictably foreshadowed his involvement in her murder. When the defense's turn came, Dershowitz promised, they would eschew the seductions of fiction in favor of "hard data."[5] Dershowitz's attempt to undermine the prosecution's credibility by associating it with "fictionalizing" while casting his side as the sole purveyors of un"constructed" truth may have been a shrewd public relations tactic but was, of course, doomed. When the defense team finally presented its case, emotionally powerful stories about the racist history of a white policeman were used as predictors of his involvement in a racist frame-up. If anything, forensic storytelling reached a new apotheosis. The point here is not simply the ubiquity of courtroom storytelling in high profile cases. Rather, my point is that it is simply not possible *not* to tell stories in court. Even the dullest civil negligence suits necessarily generate recognizable stories whose persuasive power derives more from "literary logic" than from "hard data."

Second, while litigation is a storytelling process, it does not, like literary fiction, allocate to a single godlike author the power to create all the voices or to construct the entire universe of truth values that the plot's resolution will vindicate. Instead, our adversarial system is run as a storytelling contest in which each narrative must battle for acceptance against challenges and counternarratives. Each story is constrained, hemmed in and de-formed by its need to disprove or counteract what the other side is expected to say. Because at least two conflicting stories are always being made out of the same unrecoverably past events, a winning story frame must be not merely plausible or persuasive in itself, but *more* powerful and believable than the opposing story. It must simultaneously establish its own authenticity and efface the effectiveness of its narrative attacker. Thus, cases are won by whichever party can most successfully persuade the jury that this isn't a story about *that*, it's a story about *this*. As Susan Staves has demonstrated in her study of eighteenth-century civil adultery cases in England, the moral valences attached to different literary genres can become the fulcrum on which the case turns. In characterizing the husband's adultery, she notes, "there was often a very specific contest of interpretation, the plaintiff's counsel trying to assimilate the facts to a tragic narrative, and the defendant's trying to force them into a comic one."[6] If adultery is imaged through the optic of tragedy, it inflicts intense suffering, destroys lives, and ultimately erodes the stability of all marriages, all laws, and all stable civilization (and thus requires enormous compensatory damages). If, however, sexual misdeeds are presented as the stuff of comedy or farce, adultery becomes universal, laughable, pleasurable, a trivial sexual urge whose consequences are local and unthreatening (and therefore merit only minimal damages). While in each case "the facts" are the same, the genre used to characterize the adultery—*Anna Karenina* vs. *A Flea in Her Ear*—determines the weight, meaning, and financial assessment of the evidence.

Third, and perhaps most importantly, the relative power of a particular story frame—its ability to vanquish opponents, evoke guilty sympathy, or loosen purse strings—depends, ultimately, on its cultural currency. Story forms are not transcendental or essentialist; they change as authors and readers change. While culturally powerful stories may enjoy long reigns and frequent reruns (as for instance the perennial popularity of sentimental family narratives in the rhetoric of election campaigns), they are always fully historicized, always open to and limited by the values, fears, and assumptions of the culture that produces them. As those issues and attitudes change, stories lose their power, or, if they live, become reformulated to take new information into account. What worked in a courtroom in 1895 may be a good deal less effective one hundred years later. If juridical stories "win" by, in effect, annihilating their opponents' counterstories, the ammunition that permits one kind of story to execute another may be traced to the particular anxieties and evocable pockets of guilt animating potential jurors at a particular histo.ical moment.

Perhaps the most powerful contemporary example of such narrative annihilation is the much analyzed moment when Clarence Thomas, under examination by the Senate Judiciary Committee for allegations of sexually harassing Anita Hill, claimed to be the victim of a "high-tech lynching."[7] Lynching is not just a horrifying tag word from a now long-past moment. It suggests not so much a particular incident or incidents, but a compressed, almost allegorical master narrative of ultimate racial violence that shapes how all Americans "read" the ongoing story of racial interaction. It is a story with unambiguous villains and victims, with a central narrative episode, and, perhaps most importantly, with a well-established set of *responses* that white Americans have learned to make to each "character" and event in the story, responses that can be immediately triggered through the briefest invocation of the narrative lynching paradigm. By "reading" his confirmation hearings through this paradigmatic story frame of racial violence, Thomas both demanded uncritical sympathy for himself as the "murdered" victim and sought reflexive condemnation of his challengers as racial "murderers."

While the hearings, and Thomas's response to them, have already been analyzed in astonishing detail,[8] I want to spend a bit more analytical energy on this moment in terms of story-frame strategy. Thomas's brilliant rhetorical move worked so effectively, I would suggest, because it maximized the dynamics of litigative storytelling, which require shrewd deployment of historicity, audience casting, and what I call story-trumping. Let me take these one at a time. First, though the current guilt-inducing power of the racial lynching story is so intense that it may seem to transcend cultural specificity, we should remember that our contemporary horror at the idea of outlaw vigilantes taking the "law" into their own hands by lynching is a relatively recent phenomenon. In Owen Wister's 1902 Western classic, *The Virginian*, for instance, the schoolteacher girlfriend of the otherwise irreproachable hero is shocked to discover that he has participated in lynching a suspected cattle thief. Her horror is assuaged however, by none other than the town's judge, who persuades her that lynching, "so far from being a *defiance* of the law, is an *assertion* of it—the fundamental assertion of self-governing men, upon whom our whole social fabric is based."[9] The judge is careful to distinguish, and criticize, racial lynchings, on the ground that Southerners "take a negro from jail where he was waiting to be duly hung" and then burn him, while in Wyoming, cattle thieves are lynched without torture, "in the quietest way" by honorable men who are "determined to become civilized" but who have been frustrated by juries who, with "withered," "imitation" hands that have "no life in them, no grip," consistently let such accused thieves go instead of jailing and executing them.[10] To Judge Henry, "many an act that man does is right or wrong according to the time and place which form, so to speak, its context; strip it of its particular circumstances, and you tear away its meaning."[11] Lynching is barbarous where the law is strong enough to "duly hang" Negroes and the lynchers are weak enough to torture and burn their victims, but it is highly moral, civilized, courageous, and manly where law is weak and execution swift. Indeed, the judge infers, had the Virginian insisted on deference to the state's system of trial and punishment for cattle thieves, his strength of character and manly virtue would be open to question.

Clearly, to have likened an unpleasant juridical investigation to a lynching in 1902 would not have been a surefire strategy for defensive success. If some men deserve to be lynched, and some lynchers are honorable and courageous, then the lynching paradigm is morally ambiguous, context dependent, and insufficiently racial. Instead of solving the juror-audience's interpretive quandaries, it deepens them, inviting questions (is this a good lynching or a bad one?) instead of condemnations (this is like a lynching, so it must be an inhuman outrage). And, since lynching was not yet a crucial story about how "we" (all Americans) came to be the way we are, it did not automatically position every white reader inside a historical narrative of guilt.

This guilt-inducing effect was, of course, the primary goal of Thomas's invocation of the narrative lynching paradigm. At the same time that Thomas's characterization of the proceedings as a "high-tech lynching" cast himself as a blameless victim, it cast the members of the Senate Judiciary Committee as racist lynchers.[12] By locating his interlocutors *inside* the story's framework, Thomas constructed a story as much about them as about himself. And, because the accusation was made on national television, individual committee members could not decide for themselves that it did not apply; they had to respond, and behave, in ways that would negate their putative casting as racist lynchers in the eyes of millions of television-watching Americans. In short, once this powerful story was in place—and its power is so great that merely mentioning it is enough to put it ineradicably in place, regardless of its actual applicability to the facts at hand—certain forms of aggressive attack on Thomas simply became untenable.

While Thomas's rhetorical strategy may seem anomalous, even underhanded, its successful use of "juror casting" makes it in fact highly representative of the canon of successful forensic stories. The success of all litigative storytelling is measured by its ability to trigger the desired response from the juridical reader, that is, to elicit a favorable verdict from judge, jury, or, in the Thomas case, committee. The "best" stories therefore *always* draw juror-readers into their ambit, so that they see their verdict-vote as part of the story, and themselves as characters in it. Such stories connect jurors' private lives and values to the case at hand. Sometimes this takes the form of elaborate suggestions that only by vindicating the defendant's virtue and innocence can the jurors believe in the virtue and innocence of their own loved ones.[13] At other times, lawyers invite jurors to see themselves as the defendant's saviors, capable through their verdict-rendering power (and therefore the only ones who can accomplish the task) of righting the wrongs and healing the psychic wounds of the defendant.[14] In each case, as in the Thomas example, the suggestion is made that the critical moment when the juror shifts from passive reader to active author of the case's outcome, the moment of voting, signifies something important about the juror himself. By voting one way or the other, the juror can write himself into a narrative about his own life that either increases his security and self-esteem or destroys it.

Finally, the Thomas maneuver is noteworthy as a trumping mechanism. As discussed earlier, adversarial storytelling often produces not just competing interpretations of the same story, but quite different story frames through which the case's evidence is to be interpreted. One side's story "trumps" the other when it deploys a narrative framework that exerts so much response-evoking pressure that it effaces or nullifies the other side's story. Thomas's story was not uttered in a narrative vacuum. Over the preceeding days, the nation had been galvanized by Anita Hill's narrative of sexual harassment. Articles about the prevalence of harassment in the workplace poured into the media, and the *story* of gender, power, and abuse gained a sudden momentum. Like the lynching narrative as it appeared in Wister's novel, however, the American story of workplace harassment based on gender is not a single, powerful story, but a series of stories, with varying moral inflections (is it a story about a woman who "asked for it"? about men exerting power over women? about men unfairly accused by women they had sexually rejected?). Put simply, American culture has not decided that narratives of sexual harassment are factually credible or that they should evoke widespread moral outrage.[15] Thus, even if the alleged harassing behavior occurred as described, there was no universal agreement that such behavior was *truly* horrific rather than merely distasteful or annoying. And, because Professor Hill maintained a polite, nonaggressive posture, the harassment story was one that did not, at that point, cast committee members as successor-harassers to Thomas himself. In short, because the harassment paradigm was volatile, morally ambiguous and not well established, while the lynching paradigm was unparalled in its guilt-evoking power, Thomas's story easily vanquished Hill's.[16]

In every trial, whether watched by millions or by only the jurors and witnesses in the case, a battle to control the determining story frame can be discerned. Should we be troubled that story logic can so effectively shortcut detailed evidentiary assessment and inject seemingly extraneous stories into juridical deliberations? I don't think so. First, as I've argued here, even discursive presentations limited to the "facts of the case" will produce recognizably "literary" stories whose persuasive impact derives largely from their familiarity. Coherent and effective narratives of past events will always resonate intertextually with other narratives, factual and fictional, about similar events. The circulation of influence from literature to life and back again simply brings out the narrative logic that underlies litigative process; it does not violate it. Second, the larger scale trumping narratives of race and sex, the stories that appear to be about "something else," are not irrelevant. Like all storytelling, forensic storytelling occurs in a specific historical context and signifies differently to different audiences. Rhetorical strategies like the "race card" simply make visible the larger cultural context in which the trial is already occurring, and through which it will inevitably be judged. The battle between plaintiff and defendant is often a productive struggle to control the connection between text and context, between the forensic story used to frame the case's facts and the cultural story used to give those facts meaning and impact. The public courtroom is a central American arena for determining which stories, and therefore which conflicts and positions, we consider most true and important. As the Simpson case demonstrated, popular trials can catalyze fragmentation into race- or gender-identified groups that believe with equal absoluteness in the primacy of conflicting stories. But if powerful forensic rhetoric can thus prevent rather than produce a nationally unified "verdict" on issues of importance, it can also force us to recognize that such larger issues are always already in every case.

NOTES

1. The advent of Court TV, and of continuous CNN coverage of the O.J. Simpson trial, of course, brought real trials into viewers' living rooms. On one hand, this has led lawyers to intensify the theatricality of their courtroom behavior by, in effect, performing as law-drama actors for a national audience. Media access thus pressures "life" to imitate "art." On the other hand, the popularity of Court TV suggests that endless hours of *real* proceedings, in all their tedium, can exert a kind of hypnotic power precisely because they are authentic and unedited.

2. See, e.g., Philip Meyer, "'Desperate for Love': cinematic influences upon a

defendant's closing argument to a jury," *Vermont Law Review* 18 (1994): 721–749; and for a nineteenth-century version, Robert A. Ferguson, "Story and Transcription in the Trial of John Brown," *Yale Journal of Law and the Humanities* 6 (1994): 37–73.

3. The notion that readers bring to each new text the sum of their genre-based reading experiences, and that such experience governs their expectations and assumptions in moving through texts, is of course a cornerstone of reader-response theory. See, e.g., Stanley Fish, *Is There A Text in This Class? The Authority of Interpretive Communities* (Cambridge: Harvard University Press, 1980); Jane Tompkins, *Reader-Response Criticism: From Formalism to Post-Structuralism* (Baltimore and London: Johns Hopkins University Press, 1980). But if notions of interpretive communities and governing expectations are yesterday's news about literature, they constitute a relatively new field of inquiry with respect to trials, and the way that lawyers frame, and juries read, litigative narratives. Among the many scholars who have explored the connections between storytelling and trials are Anthony Amsterdam and Randy Hertz, "An Analysis of Closing Arguments to a Jury," *New York Law School Law Review* 37 (1992): 55–122; Kimberlé Crenshaw and Gary Peller, "Reel Time/Real Justice," *Reading Rodney King/Reading Urban Uprising*, ed. Robert Gooding-Williams (New York: Routledge, 1993); Lance Bennet and Martha Feldman, *Reconstructing Reality in the Courtroom: Justice and Judgment in American Culture* (New Brunswick: Rutgers University Press, 1981); Robert Hariman, ed. *Popular Trials: Rhetoric, Mass Media and the Law* (Tuscaloosa: University of Alabama Press, 1990); David Ray Papke, "Discharge as Denouement: Appreciating the Storytelling of Appellate Opinions," *Journal of Legal Education* 40 (1990): 145–159.

4. The seeming "objectivity" of legal discourse has been under attack from a variety of scholars and schools. The emerging field of "outsider" scholarship, for instance, "posits that law's traditional stories reflect neither neutrality nor consensus." William N. Eskridge Jr., "Gaylegal Narratives," *Stanford Law Review* 46 (1994): 607–646, 608. Such scholars emphasize the importance to the legal community of hearing and legitimating the voices of those (racial and ethnic minorities, women, gays and lesbians, etc.) whose "counterstories" challenge the complacent assumptions and exclusory discourse of traditional legal writing. Richard Delgado, "Storytelling for Oppositionists and Others: A Plea for Narrative," *Michigan Law Review* 87 (1989): 2411–2441. The Critical Legal Studies movement is often credited with popularizing the proposition that legal language, far from being "objective," is in fact a masking discourse that assumes a mantle of neutrality while carrying out the agenda of those who wield power—patriarchal, racist, classist, etc. See, e.g., "Symposium: Critical Legal Studies," *Stanford Law Review* 36 (1984): 1–674; Duncan Kennedy, "Form and

233

Substance in Private Law Adjudication," *Harvard Law Review* 89 (1976): 1685; Mark Tushnet, "Critical Legal Studies and Constitutional Law: An Essay in Deconstruction," *Stanford Law Review* 36 (1984): 623. Deconstructive work by both legal and literary scholars has effectively argued that legal discourse is, like every other linguistic enterprise, embedded in history, context, bias, and ideology. See, e.g., Stanley Fish, *Doing What Comes Naturally: Change, Rhetoric and the Practice of Theory in Literary and Legal Studies* (Durham and London: Duke University Press, 1989); Gerald Graff, "'Keep Off the Grass,' 'Drop Dead,' and Other Indeterminacies," *Texas Law Review* 60 (1982): 405–413; Clare Dalton, "An Essay in the Deconstruction of Contract Doctrine," *Yale Law Journal* 94 (1985): 997–1114. Recently, a number of legal scholars have adopted strikingly personal voices to present their arguments, vigorously, if implicitly, questioning the traditional "objectivity" of scholarly legal discourse. Such scholars may ground larger claims in their own personal experiences of racial discrimination (Patricia Williams, *The Alchemy of Race and Rights: Diary of a Law Professor* [Cambridge: Harvard University Press, 1991]), or childbirth (Marie Ashe, "Zig-Zag Stitching and the Seamless Web: Thoughts on 'Reproduction' and the Law," *Nova Law Review* 13 [1989]: 355–383), or may write their critiques in allegorical or story forms (Derrick Bell, "The Final Report: Harvard's Affirmative Action Allegory," *Michigan Law Review* 87 [1989]: 2382–2410; David Kennedy, "Autumn Weekends: An Essay on Law and Everyday Life," in *Law in Everyday Life*, ed. Austin Sarat and Thomas Kearns [Ann Arbor: University of Michigan Press, 1993]).

5. Quoted in Andrew L. Shapiro, "Reading O.J.," *The Nation*, March 6, 1995, p. 297. By treating the trial itself as an unfolding drama in which heroic defense counsel battle prosecutorial villains, Dershowitz participated in the construction of a story occurring in the present moment, one that competed with and often eclipsed the attention paid to the narrated story of the now long-past murders. Clever lawyers often work to bring the two stories together. Such a tactic might implicily suggest that jurors can transfer their feelings of sympathy, outrage, or pride in the ways that particular lawyers joust with each other in the courtroom to the underlying conflicts between the lawyers' clients.

6. Staves, Susan, "Money for Honor: Damages for Criminal Conversation," *Studies in Eighteenth Century Culture* 11 (1982): 279–297, 282.

7. The Thomas-Hill hearings were not technically a "trial," nor were they proceedings within a lawsuit. Nevertheless, they were conducted as adversarial hearings in which witnesses were examined (and cross-examined) and a "verdict" was produced. The narrative and counter-narrative process essential to trials was thus a powerful component in the nation's reading of the trial.

8. There is an extensive literature on the Thomas-Hill hearings. It includes two major studies: Jane Mayer and Jill Abramson's *Strange Justice* (Boston:

Houghton Mifflin, 1994), and David Brock's *The Real Anita Hill: The Untold Story* (New York: Free Press, 1993); as well as a collection of essays edited by Toni Morrison, *Race-ing Justice, En-gendering Power*, (New York, 1992); and a set of essays, "Gender, Race and the Politics of Supreme Court Appointments: The Import of the Anita Hill/Clarence Thomas Hearings," in *Southern California Law Review* 65 (1992): 1279–1582. Especially notable among those dealing eloquently with issues of rhetoric and stereotypes at the hearings are the essays by Nell Irvin Painter and Wahneema Lubiano in the Morrison collection, and by Amy Richlin, Hilary M. Schor, Tania Modleski and Charles R. Laurence III in the law review collection.

9. Owen Wister, *The Virginian* (New York: Penguin Classic, 1988) (1902), 341 (emphasis in original).

10. Id. at 339–340.

11. Id. at 336.

12. As Kendall Thomas and Kimberlé Crenshaw point out in the Morrison collection, the lynching paradigm cast Anita Hill in the role of false accuser, a role never played historically by black women because, as Garry Wills recently noted, "no white mob ever cared what black men did to black women." Garry Wills, "Thomas's Confirmation: The True Story" *New York Review of Books* 42 (Feb. 2, 1995): 36, 42. Thomas 370, Crenshaw 402–403. The reason Thomas's cross-racial casting of Hill worked, I believe, is that the lynching story made her both noncredible and essentially marginal. The story's real purpose was to shift the focus away from the Thomas-Hill relationship and onto the Thomas-committee interaction. The story controlled the behavior of committee members by forcing them to see a potential for racial violence in their hearings, and to see themselves as a group of white "perpetrators" with a black "victim." Both Hill and her charges of sexual harassment were extraneous to this story.

13. See Laura H. Korobkin, "The Maintenance of Mutual Confidence: Sentimental Strategies at the Adultery Trial of Henry Ward Beecher," *Yale Journal of Law and the Humanities* 7 (1995): 1–48, which argues that jurors at Beecher's trial were told that if they could not take Beecher's life of public virtue as persuasive evidence of his equally blameless private conduct, they would have to question the apparent virtue of their own wives and daughters.

14. In *United States v. Tindall* (D. Mass. 1981), for instance, attorney Joseph Oteri used a theory of "Vietnam syndrome," a form of post-traumatic stress disorder, to defend a Vietnam veteran who had become involved in drug smuggling. After suggesting that all Americans shared responsibility for the devastating psychological injuries the war inflicted on soldiers, Oteri told jurors that it was in their unique power to lift the burden of Vietnam from the defendant's damaged heart and mind. The defendant was acquitted.

15. I do not mean to suggest that "American culture" is a homogenous unit, or that

paradigmatic stories of race, gender, or sexuality will signify similarly to all Americans. The trumping power of a particular story often varies as much among different audiences as it does among different chronological eras. The extreme difference in reaction to the Simpson verdict among blacks and whites, men and women, vividly demonstrated, if any demonstration was needed, that the likelihood of certain narratives being accepted as "true" depends largely on who is reading that narrative.

16. As Kimberlé Crenshaw and others have noted, Hill was also attacked for her willingness to "compromise the upward mobility of a black man and embarrass the African-American community." Because race trumps sex every time, black women are often reluctant to report incidents of sexual and spousal abuse for fear of attracting negative attention to black men. Crenshaw calls this a "conspiracy of silence" that has "legitimated sexism within" the African-American community; it is also a powerful example of the difficulty gender stories have in achieving cultural authority. See Crenshaw, 420, 432.

26

Telling Stories, Telling Law

Martha Minow

Discussions among people interested in law and literature have taught me many things, such as the word "recursive." The *Dictionary of Philosophy* has an index entry for recursive that could also serve as a kind of definition; it says, "see recursive." There is always the temptation to become recursive in talking about stories. I will seize that temptation. Let me tell you two stories about stories and the law. Behind these stories is my own particular interest in asking what makes a good story, and how do stories relate to the practice of law.

The first story stems from my involvement with a program at Brandeis University titled "Doing Justice." It was originally designed through the extension school to respond to judicial burnout. The program invites judges to attend one-day sessions to discuss several assigned works of literature. This program has been under way for more than a decade. I have repeatedly participated as a facilitator of its discussion sessions.

The judges arrive somewhat nervously, clutching highlighted texts; some carry the corresponding *Cliff's Notes*. The texts themselves have included works of William Shakespeare, James Baldwin, Mary Gordon, Bertolt Brecht, Joseph Conrad, and Doris Lessing. A motley crew of academics—usually three for every group of fifteen to twenty judges—begin by telling the judges that we have as a group two sets of texts before us: the assigned literature and our own lives. These academic facilitators take turns asking questions to draw the judges into the literature and to connect the fiction to life experiences. Sometimes intense debates erupt about whether to admire a character in the text, or about how judges are or are not like ship's captains. Some revelatory moments occur.

In one session, I ask the judges to explain the tone of voice they imagine accompanied the first sentence of Mary Gordon's short story "Violation."[1] The sentence reads: "I suppose that in a forty-five-year life, I should feel grateful to have experienced only two instances of sexual violation."[2] One of the judges suggests "flat affect." Another said he is baffled by the sentence. Another bursts out with irritation: the sentence reminds him of the women who come to court seeking temporary restraining orders to halt physical abuse by their husbands or boyfriends and then do not return for the follow-up hearing required to make the order final. Those women, to this judge, seem passive or out of touch—like the voice of the story's narrator.

We turn back to the story, which explores two incidents. During a post-college trip to Europe, our narrator meets a sailor at a bar who takes her on a walk and rapes her. "She should have known better," says one judge. "She wouldn't have talked with a sailor in a bar at home; it's only that she felt free and adventuresome during her travels." One of the two women judges in the group of twenty says quietly, "Why should she have to watch what she does? Why should she be to blame for what happened?"

An intense discussion follows. The judges talk of daughters, of themselves, of cities they know, of dangers outside.

I turn to the other incident described in the story. An uncle visiting the family comes to the narrator's bed. He is drunk. He makes a sexual advance. After sudden inner paralysis, the narrator resists him successfully through a joking banter. She then lies awake knowing that telling anyone what happened would be a betrayal of the whole family. One judge comments, "She handled it perfectly." Another observes, "I don't understand what is the big deal here." Another responds sharply, "So it's okay if it happens in the family."

I return to the first sentence of the story. What do we know now about this person? Why would she describe herself as lucky? One judge says he feels sad for her because she seems repressed. Another disagrees, but says, "I still don't understand why she never told anyone."

We revisit the first incident. After the rape, the narrator has missed her travel connection and checks into a hotel. She describes how she gladly paid extra for a private bath because she could not bear the idea of sharing a bath-tub with others at the hotel. "It wasn't for myself I minded; I cared for the other people. I knew myself to be defiled, and I didn't want the other inno-cent, now sleeping guests, exposed to my contamination."[3] We talk about the way she felt and why she could not tell anyone. The judge who spoke earlier of the restraining orders jumps back to thoughts of the courtroom world and remarks: "I guess it's hard for anyone to come to court after something like this happens."

I tell here a narrative about using narratives. Of course I could tell others or reshape this one. Something often happens in talking about a story, some-thing I like to think of as a moment of insight. Other similar moments hap-pen; some wrenching, some comical. In discussing the confusion over public and private roles in *King Lear*, one judge volunteers that his son at home refused his directive to take out the garbage "because you're not the judge here." Even such a little moment, I hope, affords new perspective. But the risk that these sessions simply reassure the judges, patch them up, and send them back to the front lines with no new understanding is very real. Concerns like these have led me to wonder how judges, and other profes-sionals, actually make sense of their day-to-day experience.

Consider a similar narrative by another professional, a social worker who wrote:

The stuffed clown flies across my office and hits me in the head. "Use *words*" I say to my six-year-old patient, a little girl. "Use words to tell me if you're mad; don't throw the clown."[4]

The social worker continues:

Using words to teach and comfort, listening, I am witness and midwife to the slow painful rebirth of people whom language failed. For them, words had been used by others only to wound and destroy. A week later the six-year-old was carefully cutting paper. "This," she announced, pointing to a hole she had made in a piece of paper, "is a Door to the Land of Change."[5]

Like my story with the judges, this story offers a glimpse of insight and a sense of hope. I know from talking with the social worker that subsequent sessions with that little girl were not so hopeful, just as I know from the deci-sions and actions taken in the local courts that a less hopeful narrative could be told about my judges.

Nonetheless, stories invite the judges to make sense of the world. My sec-ond narrative similarly attends to the ways that legal professionals make sense of what they do. A colleague named Gary Bellow and I convinced eight peo-ple, lawyers and law students, to write narratives about their encounters with law.[6] We asked only that each essay pursue one case or problem and afford reflections about the experience from the author's point of view.

Gary and I looked around and found a surprising scarcity of narratives—whether hopeful, despairing, or something else altogether—by players inside the legal system about their experiences. We hoped that new narratives could do three things: (1) explore the subjective experiences of people who wield power and sense constraints within the legal system: what meanings, rationalizations, and dissonances would emerge? (2) expose the patterns of institutional and cultural practices, dense and thick patterns that vary by field of law and locale and yet almost invariably are invisible in law school teaching and scholarship; and (3) offer insights about points of leverage or opportunities for movement or change within legal worlds. It turns out these are hard tasks to fulfill.

I will narrate the narratives we have received. Individually, the stories have many points of interest, and some moments of tension and suspense. In one story, a hearing-impaired student advocates on behalf of a deaf man who lost his job—and not only does she prevail, she also learns about accommodations for disability that would help herself as well. She gains access during the hearing to a monitor that displays a reporter's transcript of the statements as they are uttered in the session. She realizes how this technology could have transformed her experiences in law school, where she had tried to "pass" as a hearing person.

In another story, a public defender confronts a dilemma after successfully defending a juvenile who did commit the offense. The defender now has to consider whether his client is better or worse off unpunished. A third essay recounts how the philanthropic gift creating the Armand Hammer Museum arose from resources not of Armand Hammer but of his corporation; the shareholders, without their knowledge, paid for Armand Hammer's philanthropy. The story then traces a lawyer's drawn-out fight to gain some restitution for the shareholders.

Another story explores how retired union members confronted both their union and former employer when they found themselves denied health-care benefits; their grievance reaches the unusual setting of a bankruptcy hearing. An essay by a legal services attorney-turned-professor looks at the opportunities for self-governance found by poor parents through the federal regulations governing Head Start. Still another considers how the attorney for an impoverished client neglected the client's own understandings of her experiences in the name of advocating for her entitlement to receive food stamps. The next essay recounts the advocate's efforts to get the state to return a child to her mother, efforts that include forty court appearances in an eighteen-month period. The last story is written by a criminal defense lawyer, who agrees for the first time to help the prosecution; she agrees to assist the victim who was assaulted at the same time that her lover was killed by the accused. That the victim and her lover were lesbians figures importantly for the author, herself a lesbian, who struggles with the experience of switching sides in the polarized world of criminal law.

There are striking differences among the stories in terms of contexts, institutions, and bodies of law. There seems little in common in the worlds of the Head Start mothers, the Armand Hammer shareholders, the criminal courts, and bankruptcy hearing. Patterns of activity familiar in one setting would baffle participants in another. The narratives convey, in effect, different cultures of law.

Nevertheless, all the stories can be read to some degree as challenges to the conventional media-shaped images of American law. The conventional picture depicts individuals who seek to right the wrongs specified in law, and construct oral and written arguments in order to persuade neutral decision makers. In contrast, these stories evoke the personal stakes of judges and hearing officers in what they do, and the palpable presence of delay as a medium or even an interest protected by public institutions. The stories shine light on the shifting shades of the familiar and the unfamiliar, the fixed and the mutable, that are not just the background but also the focus for legal actors.

Thus, the troubling account of one advocate's efforts to help a client regain custody of her child reveals an adversary on the other side who is not a contentious partisan. Instead, the adversary is the very caution and lethargy of public agency bureaucrats who treat delay as an inevitable and costless fact rather than ticking minutes of distance between parent and child. Similarly, the hearing-impaired law student who seeks unemployment benefits for her deaf client discovers no specific misinterpretation of governing laws, but instead widely shared attitudes that prevent accommodation of a particular individual's hearing difficulties.

These institutional cultures and dynamics shape not only the course, but also the focus and presentation of each story. None of the stories imagines a place to begin that is outside of or unframed by law. They offer, then, little clue to the process of translation and reconception as experiences cross and recross the boundaries of laws and legal institutions.

Some of the stories explore the lawyers' confusions about identity when one person claims to speak for another. Yet the stories do not much convey— how could they?—the way that clients shape what they want and who they are in relation to their audience. The authors are themselves audiences for their clients, but also actors trying to shape the wants and identities of others.

The stories indicate how much law work is word work. Lawyers' tools are words. Within public and private bureaucracies, in courtrooms and legislatures, on telephones and in one-on-one meetings with clients and opponents, legal workers use words to help clients get what they want or avoid what they do not want. Lawyers use words to press at the cracks of shut doors, to persuade the doorkeepers to open them, or to persuade the client that the door is not locked, or that one can learn to live with a locked door. Lawyers hope to use words to make doors to the land of change.

The lawyers sometimes use words to invent or reinvent the identity of a client; sometimes clients do that themselves. To get a daughter back from the state, a lawyer tries to convince the social workers and judges that the client is a "good mother." To get the unemployment benefits for the deaf client, the advocate has to fit him in the category of "effective" rather than "incompetent" worker. To pursue a sense of their own self-respect, the parents of Head Start children use legal procedures to claim the identity of "participant" rather than "at-risk family." To woo the sympathies of the reader, the lawyer for shareholders tries to convey a picture of them as powerless pensioners rather than well-off corporate types.

In each instance, a reader could ask, what do the authors leave out or invent? What words or images shift sympathies, identities? Does understanding better how words can do this help strengthen or help undermine a good story?

I myself still wonder and hope you can help me explore:

1) What makes a "good story"?
2) How can narratives convey not only what is unique but also what is repetitive and familiar?
3) When does the personal voice in a narrative persuade, and when not? When should its persuasive force be suspect, and when should the reader submit to it? I am reminded here of the medical school professor who asked an actor to appear in his class as a person with a terminal disease and convey to students a sense of that experience; the professor had found that the students were too uncomfortable with a "real" dying person in class. Does fiction, known to be fiction, lend a safe distance for exploring what we find dangerous?

And finally,

4) Is it possible that telling law stories may prompt insights, on occasion, for nonlawyers the way that literature may do so for lawyers and judges? What stories have I told here, with what effects for you?

NOTES

1. Mary Gordon, "Violation," in *Temporary Shelter* (New York: Random House, 1987), pp. 184–196.
2. Ibid., 186.
3. Ibid., 190.
4. Cornelia Spelman, "Introduction," *TriQuarterly* 75: 5 (1989).
5. Ibid.
6. Gary Bellow and Martha Minow, eds., *Law Stories* (Ann Arbor: University of Michigan Press, forthcoming).

PART EIGHT

The Literary and the Autobiographical

27

A Literary Approach
to Cultural Studies

Sacvan Bercovitch

It used to be an axiom of interdisciplinary studies that the relation of the literary to the cultural is one of text to context: literature understood in the context of philosophy, theology, psychology, national history, etc. The motive was to loosen, perhaps broaden disciplinary boundaries; but by and large the result has been colonization by context: literature psychologized, philosophized, theologized, nationalized. Cultural studies takes a radically different approach. It claims to make interdisciplinarity an enterprise in its own right—according to one of its leading exponents, a "bricolage of methodologies" ("semiotics, deconstruction…psychoanalysis, and so on"[1]) that challenges the very foundations of disciplinarity.

The force and scope of that enterprise are amply demonstrated in this volume; but the emphasis on methodologies leaves the problem of context unresolved. Is there a vantage point beyond disciplines? Insofar as cultural critics adopt the bricolage approach, they are also being used by disciplinarity: a certain controversial method in philosophy, deconstruction; a certain embattled method in psychology, psychoanalysis. And insofar as they are using such methods eclectically they are also claiming to have made informed choices within methodologies as well as between disciplines (Benjamin's Marxism, Lacan's Freudianism). This dream of metadisciplinarity seems to me a form of nostalgia born out of the frustrations of modern specialization. To paraphrase Emerson, it is lamentable but too late to be helped, the fact that we are culture bound and college trained. That fact is called disciplinarity.

The question for cultural studies is not to be or not to be, but *how* to be, disciplinary. The answer, I think, is to use disciplinarity against itself, and my proposal to that end is to see cultural "texts" in literary "context." The advantage lies in literature's peculiar mixture of rationality and artifice. On the one hand, literary study is the aesthetic field that's most closely connected with cultural disciplines. Language is their common denominator. We can read Gibbon's *Decline and Fall* as a literary narrative, but not as a work of music. We can argue technically as well as metaphorically, both formally and substantively, about whether Kafka's parables are philosophy or art, as we could not about the art of Rodin or Rembrandt. On the other hand, literature consists in works of the imagination. The evidence it yields is invented, make-believe.

Literary study is therefore more transparently *constructed* than any other textually based body of knowledge. Perhaps I should say *transparently* constructed, since my point is that it highlights the constructedness of all disciplines. Professionally, literary study is barely a century old; grounded, like other branches of aesthetics, in the vagaries of genteel appreciation (taste, tact, and sensibility); and in its brief career it has gone through several startling metamorphoses, from philology to poststructuralism. Is there a *literary* body of knowledge? Does it constitute *an* area of specialization? A discipline, after all, is a system of understanding. It demands a certain kind of rigor, certain modes of persuasion, certain standards of validation and invalidation. And, while "certain" here usually means processual, open to new developments, nonetheless, systematically, *as a discipline*, it re-presents process as cognitive certainty. It closes off earlier hypotheses. We *know* x because it corresponds to a *certain* Q.E.D., like the last house on the block. Another house might spring up, but when it does, that will invalidate the claim that x is the last house.

In the case of history, that pragmatic standard of certainty is empirical truth, and empirical truth is systemic. However provisionally or controversially, it offers true-or-false answers that claim to render earlier answers inadequate. That's why narrative theory has met so much resistance within the profession. Even when they acknowledge the importance of the "linguistic turn," historians want to know what verifiably happened, and they want to claim in this respect that *their* histories mark a certain progress. So do social scientists, for all their sensitivity to the intricacies of storytelling. And they should. It would be scandalous to revise the past without believing in some form of historical truth or to describe a society without strict regard to fact. So, too, it would be scandalous to call for legal reform without believing in some set of truths about justice (however provisional), or to advocate a philosophy that did not believe on some level in the logic of its own propositions. Disciplinary language necessarily tends towards closure and abstractions, even when closure is a proof of doubt; even when the abstraction is solipsism; and even when the Q.E.D. is that we have to go on talking forever. Different though they are in every other respect, disciplines are bound to the principles of propositional logic and hard fact.

Literary study is also bound to those principles; but insofar as it remains faithful to *its* hard facts, the "logic" of make-believe, it's also bound in principle to resist any propositional set of rules, or (what amounts to the same thing) to remain open to other rational systems of closure. "Whereof one cannot speak," Wittgenstein famously remarked, "thereof one must be silent." Philosophy, like all disciplines, tells us what we can articulate knowingly. Literature is the voice of cognitive silence. It keeps recalling us to areas where explanation fails.[2] It speaks to the multiple ironies (implicit in Wittgenstein's apparent tautology) distinguishing speech from knowledge. Speaking is not the same thing as knowing, and yet language and knowledge are coextensive. We often talk about what we *don't* know. It can make for very animated conversation. But disciplinarily, the point of conversation is to find answers. Literature often sets out to illustrate answers, but it does so in such a way as to leave us with the same old questions. For here answers are means, not ends. Disciplinarily, the literary text gets us nowhere—or worse, since in the course of leaving us where we began it also calls into question the answers we set out with. Philosophy disciplines language to the rules of reason. Literature opens language to its own nonreasonable, noncoherent *historicity*. Hence Plato's Republic, where philosophers, who *know*, and so tell everyone else what to do, tell poets to do something else. Wittgenstein's equivalent is a logical imperative: "one *must* not speak."

But granted the disciplinary claim—speaking is not the same thing as knowing—should the voice of not-knowing be silenced? Imagine a state that for enlightened purposes—because, say, fictions have been mistaken for morality—outlaws all verbal expressions of not-knowing. Literature is an antidote to that bleak utopia. It directs us, *as literature*—which as such may also include works classified as philosophy, social science, etc.—toward unanswered (and, for all we know, unanswerable) questions in the various explanatory systems we've inherited. Here the question of the last house on the block is the conclusion you arrive at.

I'm aware that this itself is an answer of sorts, a sweeping abstraction about the nature of literature. It's not offered as the last word on the subject. What I mean by literature is current professional common sense. It's the substance of what we expect when we scan the contents of a course in literary studies. Contents change, of course, but change may be a sign of professional vitality. In any case, we have no choice *but* to understand our subject disciplinarily. Literature meant something different in the Middle Ages from what it does now, but the only way for us to *know* that difference—indeed, the only way to understand the concept of the Middle Ages—is historiographically; which is to say, by means of a certain modern methodology. This is not to advocate relativism; it's to insist on limitation. One method can be superior to another (more persuasive, more comprehensive, more rigorous, etc.); but we can transcend disciplinarity itself *only by negation*—and to start with, the negation of transcendence.

That's the advantage I spoke of in literary study: on the one hand, its textual, linguistic aspect, which aligns it with cognitive disciplines; and on the other hand its explicitly made-up aspect, based upon the aesthetic rights of the imagination. The result may be termed a literary context by negation. By any name, it seems to me the approach most conducive to inter-, cross-, and at best counter-disciplinary studies. For example, the principles of resistance and multivalence apply to the language and narrative contents of both Freud's *Interpretation of Dreams* and Morrison's *Beloved*. But *The Interpretation of Dreams* seeks to provide a general explanation—if not once and for all, then at least for the time being: the last, best explanation on the block. On some level, no doubt, Freud meant to evoke the plethora of meanings that have been read into his work, but first and last he wanted to make a totalizing statement—or at least to take a giant step toward a totalizing statement—about the way dreams work, then and always. For Freudians, it's a guide to the perplexed that makes earlier theories of dreams as antiquated as the Ptolemaic system. Morrison may well have learned from Freud, but *Beloved* is a guide into a set of perplexities that challenge us partly because they do *not* supersede those of Ptolemy's world.

The difference is not that Morrison's work is timeless. It's that Freud's work as psychologist is different from Morrison's as novelist—differently deep—and that what makes for depth in Morrison's case is the opposite of timeless. It depends on the power of her text to keep recalling us away from the answers we're given, including those in which we believe, toward the sorts of questionable specifics out of which all answers are constructed. Freud returns to Oedipus in order to transcend: he tries to see the situation from outside, in its totality. Accordingly, he provides an interpretive framework that's adaptable to an infinite variety of persons and occasions across time and place. The play *Oedipus Rex* draws on an abstract design, an exemplum of fate, to tell a particular story about a man who married the wrong woman. No doubt Sophocles' story has served its exemplary purpose: it enacts the fateful answer to a riddle called Man. But insofar as the answer is the means to a particular story—insofar as the narrative details succeed as *a* story, in their own right—the relation between riddle and answer is reversed: the story provides the context for the exemplum; and this particular context opens the general exemplum to interpretation. In proving the power of Fate, it questions our norms of causality, agency, and self-knowledge. That's the literary context that connects *Oedipus Rex* to *Beloved*. The relation between the two works consists in the particulars of inside narratives that call different sets of absolutes ("ancient" and "modern") into question.

"Inside narrative" is Melville's term for stories that resist totalization. It's what Keats meant by negative capability: the readiness to assume limits. The ideal of disciplinary thinking is to say it all, as in Hegel's dictum that philosophy tells us the thoughts of God *before* creation. Wittgenstein compares undisciplined thought to a fly trapped in a bottle. The philosopher shows it the way out. So do the economist and the psychologist. Literary texts tell us what it's like to be the trapped fly. They challenge the solutions we inherit not because the authors are essentially rebels—the archetype of the Subversive Artist is a Romantic invention, one more (time-bound) absolute—but because their project, considered as literature, returns us to our bottled-in condition. Philosophy says: "I think, therefore I am." Literature says: "That's what *you* think." (And then again, with another universal limitation in mind: "That's what you *think*.")

The issue is not authorial intention; it's disciplinary intentionality. Philosophers who are contextual in principle (J. L. Austin, John Rawls) are nonetheless ahistorical in their reasoning—coherent, abstract, systemic. Writers who deal in ahistorical absolutes (God, the Eternal Feminine, Everyman) nonetheless represent these historically, in time and place, and therefore in terms of our universal human limitations of mind, imagination, knowledge, and endurance. Again, it's an issue of ends and means. Disciplinarily, particulars are the means toward abstractions. A good story in ethnography is a specific incident that's "true" (empirical, falsifiable) and representative: its cognitive value is that it represents a "larger" *conceptual* truth. Literature too offers itself as evidence for a larger truth; but the process of representation works the other way around. Here, the evidence is *historically* (not metaphysically) probable. Truth value is a function of communal norms and beliefs, the culture-specific absolutes by which we explain experience. Probability means that *this* general story—say, the fall of a great man (displaying the qualities that make him great, and the reasons for his fall)—is true to the moral or

251

rational expectations of a certain society. That's the sort of truth that literary study sets itself to explicate. But explication takes the story itself as context, and the cognitive terms of analysis may shift accordingly, toward a critique of the absolutes represented in the text. To learn from *Oedipus Rex* in this sense is to challenge the *particular, time-bound* norms and beliefs that the play embodies.

That's what I mean by counter-disciplinarity. Its principle is: absolutes are never universal and universals are never absolute. *Absolutes are never universal* because they're made up by limited human beings in certain times and places: *a* concept of God, *a* theory of justice, *a* view of history. *And universals are never absolute* because they're the limitations that define our common humanity: the narrative particulars, such as bleeding, laughing, and hating, which humanize the archetypal Jew; the historical and personal traits that make medieval Everyman *a* person, not unlike me *in his particularity*. In disciplinary terms, *absolutes* are answers that transcend time and place. They come attended by transhistorical dichotomies—objective, not partisan; scientific, not ideological, political, or fashionable—and at best they provide our means of progress: economically, psychologically, historiographically.

By contrast, what I've called *universals* are the "literary" representations that question the absolutes within which they operate. In appreciative literary study, the question usually leads to affirmation, as in Eliot's reading of the Metaphysicals. Their poetic achievement is his occasion for celebrating *an* undissociated sensibility, *a* holistic faith. In adversarial criticism, the same question usually leads to inversion, as in Blake's reading of *Paradise Lost*. The particularized God and Devil of *Paradise Lost* provide the context that questions the transcendence, reverses the "higher truth," that Milton began with. Blake goes on of course to substitute his own abstractions for Milton's; but we can carry his act of detranscendentalization one crucial step further. Literary study can serve counter-disciplinarily to question the process of cognitive abstraction.

I will return to this prospect in a moment. First let me note that in every instance I cited, literature is nonprogressivist. The literary text prevails because it does *not* transcend. We know a great deal more than the Renaissance writers did about death, medically and sociologically, but we can't claim that contemporary literature teaches us more about the problem of death—or about the problems of life, for that matter. What some aestheticians call progress in literature—free verse, the novel, stream-of-consciousness—is a locus of dispute, not a ground of consensus; and either way, progress means development only in the photographic sense of the word: as an enlargement, variation, or refinement in techniques of representing particulars. Literature teaches us about cultural "truths" past and present, but it contributes in its own right to knowledge only by negation—that is, by suggesting how the answers we've received are as suspect as those which our culture has (with good reason) long discarded.

Coleridge's doctrine of the suspension of disbelief is a paradigm for appreciative criticism: it's a leap into the religion of art, an unconditional ascent to the ideals that literature embodies. Far from being an unwilling act on our part, it's the sort of leap into absolutism that comes all too easily. We take it by cultural reflex every hour of the day in one form or another (moral, political, theological, intellectual). Aesthetic *understanding* requires something we're far less willing to entertain: a rational suspension of belief. Philosophically, for example, God *may* be dead; theologically, the answer *may* be Christ; historically, we *may* be advancing toward some end-time utopia; but it requires enormous arrogance or ignorance on our part to draw those conclusions from what science, religion, and history have taught us.[3] The counter-disciplinary truth is, *we don't know*. At most, we're midway between knowing and not knowing. That's also where disciplines stand, but with this difference: they tell where we are to the best of our knowledge. Literature speaks to us from the other side of the divide. "Imagination," said Einstein, "is more important than knowledge"—meaning important as a means to more knowledge; important as a context of discovery that precedes the *disciplinary* context of validation. Cognitively, the study of the literary imagination offers something like the opposite: it can show how our cultural knowledge consists in particular answers and absolutes—answers distinctive to particular sets of questions, absolutes made up by particular persons and accepted by particular groups. The literary text, so understood, is a context of validation that precedes the *interpretive* context of discovery.

This context is not superior to others; it's different. I believe absolutely in specialized knowledge. We *need* systems of understanding. We *should* want to find *the* answers. Not to try would make us less human, less than human. But it's the job of literary study to keep the search open. The problem is how to transform the disciplinary instruments of closure (coherence, causal relation, rational design) into a vehicle of open-endedness: e.g., how to make use of Freudian insights while challenging Freudia*nism*. To that end I venture six provisional principles for literary-cultural reciprocity:

One: The relation between the literary and the cultural is the reverse of what tradition since Aristotle has told us it is. In general, aesthetics has privileged the "higher" absolute over the "lower" particular. The closer the particular gets us to the general, the better. Literary texts, on the contrary, entail a *descent* from abstract to particular, hence from solutions to problems, hence from closure to open-endedness. The closer we get to specifics and predicaments, the better.

Two: This focus on specifics and predicaments by no means excludes the question of ends. On the contrary: it engages us profoundly, fundamentally, in problems of morality, politics, etc. In fact, seems to me just as profound, morally and politically, to focus on the particularist and problematic aspects of the solutions we consent to as it is to explore the depths of the solutions themselves. In any case, that's the cognitive work of literature: the literary detail, properly explicated, represents the ends we believe in as functions in context. So understood, the ends remain subject to question by the sorts of particulars from which they're abstracted. The terms of closure they provide change with changing abstractions; the questionable particulars remain constant. It amounts to an inversion of the New Criticism as cultural critique.

Three: Disciplines are closed systems by definition. They allow for open-endedness on the condition that the next solution will incorporate or invalidate the last "definitive" framework. Literary study allows for "definitive" status on the condition that we accept a variety of such frameworks, much as we accept a social and intellectual division of labor. Difference in both cases confirms the universality of human limitations, as against the totalizing claims of disciplinarity.

Four: The *common* subject of literature in all its forms is the networks of meaning that link text and context. Historians tend to emphasize materialist determinants (laws of history, patterns of culture). Aestheticians tend to emphasize creative agency, the free play of the imagination. Literary context, as I envision it, centers on the semantic meeting ground between. The literary is neither an abstraction drawn from another discipline nor a kaleidoscope of Great Books. Rather, it's a social symbology, the ordinary expressive forms that make for public discourse and shared meaning.

Five: Literature is not a criticism of life. It is life's criticism of absolutes; language's skepticism about the dogma of answers or the consolation of explanations. Often enough, literary texts aspire to archetypes, origins, and revelations, but in the process of doing so, they testify, on the contrary, to the powers of mutability and the commonplace. The so-called verbal alchemy through which ordinary language is refined into the extraordinary is a function in context, like a chemical combination of common elements that yields an extraordinary result. What's extraordinary about a literary text is not that it leaves the ordinary behind, but that it resonates with multiple ordinary meanings. Aesthetically and substantively, that resonance reaches *under* culture-specific absolutes. *Under* as in subject to those absolutes, but also within and through them, at once undergirding the rules they embody and undermining them; *under* as in underlie, involving possibilities that *these* absolutes *really* transcend—possibilities, too, of an unsettling kind, prospects that have been declared out of bounds or that have not yet been explored—

variations or innovations that may affect the status of the absolute, and so alter our current frameworks of transcendence. *Under* as in depth.

Six: Literary depth is a mediation between absolutes and universals (in my counter-disciplinary sense of these terms). I've just pictured this as a mediation *downwards*, an inversion of Aristotle's concept of aesthetic mediation as leading upward from historical possibilities toward (but not quite *to*) philosophical truth. We could picture it, too, as an inversion of Plato's concept of mimesis: what's universal about literary texts are the particulars that critique the reason's thrice-removed absolutes. That critique entails resistance to all totalizing systems, from Platonism to relativism. Its positive meaning derives from the negations of literary context: we are always more than our culture tells us we are, just as a language is more than a discipline, and just as a work of literature is more than the sum of the ideologies it accrues as it travels across time and place. What *more* means in this literary context is the proper subject of cultural studies.

NOTES

1. Quoted from a letter to me (March 22, 1995) from Marjorie Garber. I take the opportunity to thank Professor Garber for her generous commentary on this paper.
2. For this phrase, and the far-reaching ethnographic theory behind it, I am indebted to Eytan Bercovitch, "When Explanation Fails: Nalumin Discontinuity and Anthropological Understanding," delivered in 1988 as a paper at the American Ethnological Society. The paper itself advances a distinctive approach to culture that is elaborated in "Mortal Insights: Victim and Witch in the Nalumin Imagination," in *The Religious Imagination in New Guinea*, ed. Gilbert Herdt and Michele Stephen (New Brunswick, N.J.: Rutgers University Press, 1989), pp. 121–159, and "The Agent in the Gift: Hidden Exchange in Inner New Guinea," *Cultural Anthropology*, IX (1994), pp. 498–536. See also Stephen Greenblatt, "The Eating of the Soul," *Representations*, XLVII (1994), pp. 97–116.
3. See Hilary Putnam, "Beyond the Fact/Value Dichotomy," *Virtue and Taste: Essays on Politics, Ethics, Aesthetics*, ed. Dudley Knowles and John Skorupski (Oxford: Blackwell, 1993), pp. 130–136.

28

Criticism and the Autobiographical Voice

Susan Rubin Suleiman

Over the past decade, an increasing number of academic critics have sought to reach a larger audience, beyond the confines of specialized disciplines and vocabularies. Without sacrificing complexity of thought, they have tried to write in a language accessible to more people. Part of that process has been abandoning what used to be the first rule of academic writing—*Never say "I"*—in favor of a more personal way of discussing literature and culture. Some literary scholars have abandoned (at least temporarily) criticism altogether, opting for straightforward autobiography—what I call writing without footnotes. For academics, this is equivalent to a tightrope walker working without a net. Such work claims attention not based on scholarly authority but on literary skill.[1]

Is there always a clear line between criticism and literature, criticism and autobiography? Should there be one? What about the blurry line, wavering or zigzagging between the two genres? The operative term here is *between*. What interests me is not the "pure" form but the hybrid one: neither straight autobiography, aspiring to the status of literature, nor standard criticism, which keeps the critic's life strictly out of the commentary and claims the full authority of scholarly discourse. (Using "I" in a critical essay, instead of the editorial "we" or an impersonal construction, does not by itself constitute an autobiographical voice.) Critics who allow the autobiographical voice to enter their scholarly writing have to negotiate the transition from one kind of claim to another.

THE NECESSARY AND THE CONTINGENT

Some links between the autobiographical and the critical are more necessary than others. It's often said that "all criticism is autobiographical"; even the choice of subject can indicate something important about the one who writes. I am concerned here, however, with a more specific, more explicit connection. By "autobiographical," I mean a piece of life story, a bit of narrative related by the author-critic about her or his own life; by link (a more fancy word would be "articulation"), I mean the way that piece of life story is related to the critical or theoretical argument. On a continuum, one would move from the "necessary" link, where the personal narrative not only enhances but positively illuminates or even founds the critical argument, to the "contingent" link where the personal narrative may provide pleasure or a moment of relaxation, but is not intimately linked to a critical insight or to the development of a thought. To remove the first type from an essay would radically alter its meaning and structure; to remove the second would merely deprive the reader of a pleasurable diversion. Of course, since we are dealing with a continuum, it is not always possible to decide where on the continuum a particular autobiographical fragment belongs; furthermore, individual responses vary: one reader's "necessary" link may be another's "contingent" one.

Note that these terms don't correspond to "good" versus "bad," for the contingent is not in its essence less "good" than the necessary: "Reason not the need," as King Lear says. Still, I notice in myself a bias toward the necessary, or call it the "strong" link. To put it axiomatically, the necessary link is strong and moving, a successful piece of critical risk-taking; the contingent, on the other hand, threatens to fall into facility, self-indulgence, perhaps even an embarrassing self-exhibition on the critic's part. That's the risk of this kind of writing: there is a safety net (you still have your footnotes, your erudition), but you can fall off the rope from time to time and look silly—at least in some readers' eyes.

Let me risk illustrating these points by referring to a recent work of my own (autobiographical voice *oblige*), *Risking Who One Is: Encounters with Contemporary Art and Literature*.[2] A founding idea in that book is that if you write about the work of contemporaries (people who have shared at least some bit of your space/time), you are also necessarily writing about yourself, your own material world, your preoccupations, your history. This makes it more "natural" to put yourself, your own story, into the critical commentary—though it doesn't mean that you will do so, or should, or that if you do, you will do it equally well each time.

In *Risking Who One Is*, the "necessary"—and from my point of view, the most successful—links between the autobiographical and the critical occur in those essays where the personal story illuminates the theoretical or critical discussion in a unique, one might say overdetermined way. By the same token, the "contingent" (less successful?) links are those where the personal story is almost incidental, even if it is amusing—a little bit like the ice-breaking anecdote in a formal speech. (Granted, ice-breaking anecdotes may serve an important function leading to serious points, as writers of sermons know. Nothing is ever simple.)

Two examples:

A necessary link occurs at the beginning of the chapter titled "War Memories: On Autobiograhical Reading:"

> A few years ago, I realized with a jolt that I belong to a diminishing segment of the world's population: men and women who have personal memories of the Second World War in Europe. I don't have many, since I was only five years old when the war ended. But I have some, particularly from the last year of the war. Whereas for friends who are ony a few years younger than I, the war is at best a transmitted memory, for me it is a lived one. (p. 199)

The essay goes on to discuss memoirs of wartime experiences written by people who were children during those years, and to elaborate my notion of autobiographical reading—reading a narrative as if it were one's own, and possibly as a prelude to one's own writing. Later in the essay, I draw a parallel between some of the works I discuss and my own life; later still, I recount a recent event in my life, linked to this theme. The personal voice and the subject of the essay are so closely intertwined that any attempt to cut out the former would radically alter the latter.

At the other end of the continuum is the opening gambit of the chapter "The Fate of the Surrealist Imagination in the Society of the Spectacle," devoted to a novel by the British novelist Angela Carter. As an epigraph to the chapter, I quote from an essay by Carter: "In Japan, I learnt what it is to be a woman and became radicalized."[3] My own opening (slightly abridged here) takes off from that quote:

> What does Japan have to do with it? That requires a little story. In 1991, I decided to write an essay on an early novel by Angela Carter, *The Infernal Desire Machines of Dr. Hoffman* (1972), for a panel at the International Comparative

Literature conference to be held in Tokyo that summer. The general theme of the conference was "Imagination"—perfect, I thought, for this novel, which I had long wanted to write about because it was so obviously inspired by Surrealism, a subject in which I have a deep interest. [...]

Here the plot thickens. It turned out that Carter wrote *The Infernal Desire Machines of Dr. Hoffman*, a novel whose title points insistently to European art and literature (from the *Tales of Hoffmann* to the "bachelor machines" of Duchamp and the Surrealists), in Japan. It was in Tokyo, moreover, around 1970, that she first came upon two books about Surrealism and cinema that had a tremendous effect on her.

I then go on to recount some of the circumstances in the writing of the novel, and to say that Angela Carter herself informed me of these facts only a few months before her untimely death from cancer in February 1992.

This opening anecdote is not totally irrelevant (my reading of the novel emphasizes, among other things, the representation of women in faraway places), and I like to think it's not boring; it may even be moving, because of the personal reminiscence about Carter; but it does not illuminate my argument, or my reading of the novel, in a unique way. I could have communicated the same information differently, or even omitted it altogether without significantly altering my argument about "the fate of the Surrealist imagination in the society of the spectacle." In the "Autobiographical Reading" chapter, by contrast, my own status as a reader (and occasional memoir writer) with firsthand memories of World War II is absolutely necessary to the argument.

Between these two extremes of necessity and contingency, a wide range of possibilities exists. As I said, this is a continuum, not a set of strictly defined categories. (Close to the "strong" side: the account of my visit with Leonora Carrington in chapter 6, or my living in Budapest in the Epilogue about the politics of postmodernism. Closer to the "weak" side: the opening anecdote in chapter 8, about "alternatives to beauty in contemporary art.")

THE TYPICAL AND THE BANAL

Obviously, some stories are more dramatic than others. You might argue that the personal anecdotes in the "War Memories" chapter are not only more "necessary," but also intrinsically more compelling than the other one. Extreme experiences like war, torture, or mental illness exert a fascination by their very extreme quality. I would argue, however, that it is not so much their exceptionality but their typicality that makes them compelling. A reader responds to accounts of such experiences because she can imaginatively project herself into them—despite their extreme quality, she recognizes them.

To recognize another's experience as if it were (or could be, or could have been) one's own is to recognize its typicality. It is because the experience corresponds to a "type" that I can recognize it, even though its specific setting and circumstances may be totally unfamiliar to me.

But you might return to the charge: are some "types" (of stories) intrinsically more compelling, more interesting than others? Conversely, are some stories not typical but merely banal?

Stories of embarrassment or shame, like the one told by Svetlana Boym about her communal apartment in Leningrad (see her essay in this volume); stories of victimization or unfair treatment, like one told by Philip Harper at the "Literary and Cultural Studies Today" conference (Harper, an African-American, was stopped by police as if he were a criminal); stories of self-mockery or ironic self-correction (I attend a meeting of child survivors of the war, and feel I have nothing in common with these people, older than I—then I discover that three of them are professors of French literature, just like me[4]). These are typical patterns, or paradigms, which may take on specifically dramatic or even melodramatic form; but they may also occur in the "everyday." One quality they all have, I think, is a certain self-exposure (which is not the same thing as self-indulgence or self-exhibition, though sometimes it comes close) on the part of the one who tells the tale. If you're not willing to expose personal weaknesses or embarrassments in autobiographical writing, then it's probably not very good autobiographical writing. And ultimately, it's not the kind of story you tell that matters, but the way you tell it. Even the most banal experience can become, by virtue of the quality of its telling, moving and significant. If you will, typical.

ONCE YOU START, CAN YOU STOP?

Are all critical occasions appropriate for the autobiographical voice? Appropriateness in the sense of propriety or etiquette is not what is at issue; but the question remains: Is the entry of the autobiographical voice into critical discourse permanent, like a conversion? Or is it a mode, a mood, an inspiration depending on the moment? I would say the latter, certainly in my case. It would be boring and predictable to make the same moves each time, in critical writing as in any other kind. To the extent that criticism is creative, it remains open to the unforeseen.

NOTES

1. Among the most successful recent examples are Alice Yaeger Kaplan's *French Lessons* (Chicago: University of Chicago Press, 1993), which was nominated for a National Book Award; Henry Louis Gates, Jr.'s *Colored People* (New York: Random House, 1994), which won a National Book Award; and André

Aciman's *Out of Egypt* (New York: Farrar, Straus and Giroux, 1995), which received rave reviews in the *New York Times*.

2. Cambridge, MA: Harvard University Press, 1994.
3. Angela Carter, "Tokyo Pastoral," in *Nothing Sacred: Selected Writings* (London: Virago, 1982), p. 33; quoted in Suleiman, *Risking Who One Is*, p. 125.
4. Suleiman, *Risking Who One Is*, p. 213.

29

Unsettling Homecoming

Svetlana Boym

It might be tempting for an aspiring journalist to present the odyssey of contemporary criticism and the return of many academic theorists to auto-biographical writing as a parable of prodigal sons and daughters. After wandering and erring in theoretical wilderness they finally return home, to the "real world" of "authentic" personal voice. So why do they look back now and become enticed again by critical reflection? It seems that the greater taboo is not to cross over from critical to personal writing but to criss-cross between scholarship and autobiography, to mix genres and change voices, especially in the space of a single work. For how can one be at home in more than one place?

The pressure not to mix genres comes from both academia and the marketplace. The much-admired "writing for broader audiences" has to follow the commercial code; intellectual references are often censored like obscenities. From the point of view of professional scholarship, the intrusion of the personal voice into the supposedly impersonal space of scholarship, and the "confusion" between object of study and the critic's subjectivity, is perceived as bad professional manners.

Mixing genres could lead to professional and personal embarrassment. Yet these embarrassments are doubly revealing. On the one hand, the shift from impersonal to personal reflection sheds light on the unspoken assumptions behind professional conventions and on conceptions of objectivity and supposed consensus. On the other hand, the habit of distance and discipline could help to defamiliarize some of the personal obsessions and myths of pop psychology, to offer a necessary perspective on the potential self-righteousness and partiality of the personal. The word "personal," after all, comes from the *persona* mask. Any act of public speaking in the "personal" or "critical" voice is a performance; the difference is a matter of genre. The current division of American labor makes me nostalgic for the vanishing figure of the public intellectual (who dared to remain intellectual even when going public) and for that "heretic form," the modernist essay, described by Theodor Adorno.[1] The essay wandered between various commonplaces and across generic and disciplinary boundaries, undermining cultural myths and professional attachments. It presented an argument in the process, and was filled with lively contradictions. (Of course, some of the most successful practitioners of this risky essayistic writing, such as Benjamin and Barthes, never completed their dissertations.)

I believe that one has to write about what matters most—or at least to write about why it is so difficult to write about what matters most. Matters of passionate personal engagement are sometimes the most demanding of critical understanding. Now I must "get personal": I have just finished writing a book on Russian cultural mythologies, focusing on conceptions of everyday and aesthetics, of utopia and kitsch. My methodology required me to reveal my relation to the culture I've been studying. This proved difficult and ambiguous. Russia is not only my native country but also a country that I voluntarily left fourteen years ago for political reasons and where I did not belong to the ethnic majority. My return to Russian studies and to personal writing was hardly a simple homecoming. I found myself in an uncomfortable, yet exhilirating, position of an émigré-ethnographer, ex-native informant, cross-cultural mythologist, or displaced aesthetic critic. When it was necessary to record and bear witness to what is no longer there, I had to turn to autobiographical storytelling. In those instances, personal writing helped me to recover memories, not to recover and affirm a single identity. (After all, one does not always identify with one's "identity group"; one often partakes in many imagined communities.) The coexistence of various styles of writing, personal and theoretical, is akin to bilingualism. The moments of switching from one to the other reveal something crucial about an exilic conscience. Perhaps these practices of estrangement could tell us more than many direct confessions do about our common identity as intellectuals.

My "archeology" of the Soviet home embraces both the utopian conceptions of collective house-communes and actual everyday practices in non-utopian Soviet apartments. The central archeological site is the communal apartment—a specifically Soviet form of urban living, a memory of never implemented utopian communist design, an institution of social control and the breeding ground of grass-roots informants between the 1920s and the 1980s. In the communal apartments, corridor, kitchen, and toilets are shared with the neighbors, who are complete strangers thrown together on the whim of the local Housing Committee. I lived in a communal apartment for the first twenty years of my life; my observations, as a cultural ethnographer, are occasionally disrupted by the indelible memories of a communal apartment survivor, frequently scolded by the neighbors for unfulfilled communal duties.

Here is a primal scene of the Soviet family romance. The story is partly remembered by me, partly recollected by my mother, as one of our greatest embarrassments. My parents were having foreign guests for the first time in their life in our room in the communal apartment. Our neighbors "Aunt Vera" and "Uncle Fedia" were home. (Russian children call their neighbors "aunt" and "uncle" as if they were members of one very extended family.) Uncle Fedia usually came home drunk, and, if Aunt Vera refused to let him in, he would crash right in the middle of the long corridor—the central "thoroughfare" of the communal apartment—obstructing the entrance to our room. As a child, I often played with peacefully reclining and heavily intoxicated Uncle Fedia, with his fingers and buttons, or told him a story or two, to which he didn't have much to add.

This time we were all in the room listening to music, to tone down the communal noises, and my mother was telling our foreign guests about the beauties of Leningrad: "You absolutely must go to the Hermitage, and then to Pushkin's apartment-museum and of course, to the Russian Museum...." As the conversation rolled along, and the foreign guest was commenting on the riches of the Russian Museum, a little yellow stream slowly made its way through the door of the room. Smelly, embarrassing, intrusive, it formed a little puddle right in front of the dinner table.

This scene, with the precarious coziness of a family gathering, both intimate and public, with a mixture of ease and fear in the presence of foreigners and neighbors, remained in my mind as a memory of home. And the family picture is framed by the inescapable stream of Uncle Fedia's urine that so easily crosses the minimal boundaries of our communal privacy, embarrassing the fragile etiquette of communal propriety. (And it smells too much to turn it into a mere metaphor. It is something hard to domesticate....)²

If a Soviet cultural unconscious ever existed, it must have been structured as a communal apartment—with flimsy partitions between public and private, control and intoxication. The Soviet "family romance" that is now in its melancholic twilight was adulterated by the fluttering sound of a curious neighbor's slippers in the communal apartment, or by an inquisitive representative of the local Housing Committee. It was a romance with the collective, unfaithful to both communitarian mythologies and traditional family values.

The communal apartment was the cornerstone of the now disappearing Soviet civilization. It was not merely an outcome of the postrevolutionary housing crisis but also a result of a revolutionary experiment in living, an attempt to practice utopian ideologies. The archeology of the communal apartment reveals what happens when utopian designs are put into practice, inhabited, placed into history—individually and collectively. In my book, I present a kind of "thick description" of the communal apartment that helps to uncover the ruins of Russian and Soviet communality and illegitimate Russian "private life," and pays attention to the particular strategies of survival and minor everyday resistance that often become invisible in the panoramic historical or theoretical representations. Interestingly, the most common Soviet institution of everyday life has received little attention from historians, who tend to privilege public sites over the domestic spaces. Except for fiction and memoirs, these spaces have gone virtually unrepresented in the accounts of Soviet life. Few first-person accounts of everyday life in communal apartments have been recorded, and this kind of "grass-roots" social history has hardly been practiced.[3]

The work on my book coincided with my return to Russia after a ten-year absence. For a long time I thought that I would never go back. At the end of my chapter on communal homes comes a description of my own homecoming, which in some ways ironically mirrors my coming to personal writing.

I went to visit my house in Leningrad after a ten-year absence. The entrance was blocked, and on the broken glass door was an outdated poster advertising a newly open "video-salon" featuring Rambo II, The Slave Isaura Part IV, *and the Mexican serial* The Rich Also Cry. *Otherwise the facade looked exactly like the facade of my old house. But it seemed more like an impostor, a look-alike that imitated the "original" too literally.*

"What is happening here?" I asked an elderly woman, pointing at the blocked entrance. "Repairs," she answered. ("Remont"—that word that Walter Benjamin learned first during his travels in Russia. Then and now, the "repairs" seem to be ubiquitous.)

I sneaked into the interior yard through the cracks in the wooden fence.

Climbing through trash, I made my way upstairs. Our former communal apartment looked uncanny. Some of the partitions had been taken off, and the whole narrative of our interpersonal and communal interactions was broken. All the wrong doors, which once were locked and hidden behind the wallpaper to keep separate entrances for the neighbors, were open. It was not the space itself, not the house, but the way of inhabiting it that had made it home. That was forever lost.

I looked into the yard: black, bottomless balconies were still precariously attached to the building, and a few rootless plants continue to inhabit them. A local drunk urinated near the skeleton of the old staircase. In the center of the yard was an old truck that looked as though it was from the 1940s, with graffito of a single word—"DEATH." I thought it would make a good picture, but decided never to show it to my parents. They had come to Boston only a few years before and after spending most of their adult lives in this apartment. However, when I told them that our old house was in ruins, they seemed remarkably indifferent, as if far removed from my somewhat artificial search for memories.

—We heard they were making a movie in our yard...Leningrad film studio, I think...

—No, no, it was a film about a poet, Daniil Kharms, who wrote nonsense rhymes about a man who left his house one day and never, ever came back. And then Daniil Kharms left his house one day in 1937, to buy a pack of cigarettes and never came back....[4]

So much for the dramatic homecoming. Homesickness is a tricky ailment; one becomes homesick when one is too far away, and one gets sick of being home when one is too close. The word nostalgia has two roots—*nostos* (home) and *algia* (longing). One kind of nostalgia strives to reconstruct the ideal utopian home or a greater patria, while the other kind is about longing itself; it is ironic, self-reflexive, and individual. Perhaps it is the second type of nostalgia that would characterize my project. An unproblematic return to the personal voice is a kind of impossible homecoming. I would not rush to celebrate it as a definitive *Return of the Prodigal Theorist*. This is only another crossroads.

"There is no place like home," says the heroine of one of the most famous escapist fairy tales in the world cinema. But not all of our round trips are so magically seamless. I hope we have not yet entered the postcritical age: for now, the personal voice is not the *only* "true voice" by which, to paraphrase a long-distance telephone advertisement, we are able to "reach out and touch someone." There is always a place for critique, irony, and embarrassment.

NOTES

1. Theodor Adorno, "Essay as a Genre," in *Notes to Literature*, translated by Shierry Weber Nicholson (New York: Columbia University Press, 1991).

2. Svetlana Boym, *Common Places: Mythologies of Everyday Life in Russia* (Cambridge: Harvard University Press, 1994), pp. 121–122. The text is slightly abridged and modified.

3. In fact, there is a Russian proverb that does not translate well into American English: "*I* is the last letter of the alphabet." It is used as a caution against assertive uses and abuses of *I* (the letter "Я" indeed comes last in the Russian alphabet), a reflection of stylistic convention as well as a deep-seated cultural suspicion of truth spoken in the first-person singular. So the use of exilic *I* in a discussion of Russian commonplaces acquires an additional cultural meaning and a certain provocative resonance.

4. Svetlana Boym, *Common Places*, pp. 165–167. The text is slightly abridged and modified. This was a popular legend about disappearance of the Leningrad poet Daniil Kharms (pseudonym of Daniil Yuvachev, 1902–1942), a member of one of the last avant-garde groups, OBERIU, and the author of popular childrens poems. The poet was arrested in 1937 and died in one of Stalin's camps in 1942.

Contributors

KWAME ANTHONY APPIAH is Professor of Afro-American Studies and Philosophy at Harvard and the author of *In My Father's House: Africa in the Philosophy of Culture*; *Necessary Questions*; *For Truth in Semantics*; and three novels, of which the latest is *Another Death in Venice*. His interests are in the philosophy of language and mind, African philosophy, philosophical problems of race and racism, and Afro-American and African literature and literary criticism.

SEYLA BENHABIB is Professor of Political Theory in the Government Department at Harvard University and Senior Research Fellow at the Center for European Studies. She is the author of *Critique, Norm and Utopia: A Study of the Foundations of Critical Theory* (1986); *Situating the Self: Gender, Community, and Postmodernism in Contemporary Ethics* (1992); with Judith Butler, Drucilla Cornell, and Nancy Fraser, *Feminist Contentions: A Philosophical Exchange* (1994); and *The Reluctant Modernism of Hannah Arendt* (1996). She has edited with Drucilla Cornell *Feminism as Critique* (1987), and with John McCole *On Max Horkheimer: New Perspectives* (1993).

SACVAN BERCOVITCH is Charles H. Carswell Professor of English Literature and member of the Comparative Literature Department at Harvard. His books include *The Puritan Origins of the American Self*, *The American Jeremiad*, *The Office of the Scarlet Letter*, and *Rites of Assent: Transformations in the Cultural Construction of America*.

SVETLANA BOYM is Professor of Slavic and Comparative Literature at Harvard University. She is the author of two books, *Death in Quotation Marks: Cultural Myths of the Modern Poet* (Harvard University Press, 1991) and *Common Places: Mythologies of Everyday Life in Russia* (Harvard University Press, 1994), and of the play and film *The Woman Who Shot Lenin*.

NORMAN BRYSON is Professor of Art History at Harvard University. His books include *Word and Image: French Painting of the Ancien Régime*, *Vision and Painting: The Logic of the Gaze*, and *Looking at the Overlooked: Four Essays on Still Life Painting*. He is an editor (with Michael Ann Holly and Keith Moxey) of *Visual Theory: Painting and*

Interpretation (Harper and Row, 1991) and *Visual Culture: Images and Interpretations* (Wesleyan University Press, 1993).

LAWRENCE BUELL is Professor of English and a member of the Committee on Degrees in the History of American Civilization at Harvard University. His books include *Literary Transcendentalism, New England Literary Culture*, and *The Environmental Imagination*.

PATRICK K. FORD is the Margaret Brooks Robinson Professor of Celtic Languages and Literatures at Harvard University. He has edited and translated medieval Irish and Welsh texts, most recently the Welsh *Ystoria Taliesin* (from a single manuscript). He is coauthor, with J. E. Caerwyn Williams, of *The Irish Literary Tradition* (University of Wales Press, 1992).

PAUL B. FRANKLIN is a doctoral candidate in Fine Arts at Harvard University.

MARJORIE GARBER is William R. Kenan, Jr., Professor of English and Director of the Center for Literary and Cultural Studies at Harvard University. She is the author of three books on Shakespeare and of *Vested Interests* (Routledge, 1992), as well as an editor of *Media Spectacles* (Routledge, 1993) and *Secret Agents* (Routledge, 1995). Her most recent book is *Vice Versa: Bisexuality and the Erotics of Everyday Life* (Simon & Schuster, 1995).

HENRY LOUIS GATES, JR., is the W.E.B. DuBois Professor of the Humanities, the Director of the W.E.B. DuBois Institute, and the Chair of the Department of Afro-American Studies at Harvard University. He is the author of *Figures in Black; The Signifying Monkey; Loose Canons: Notes on the Culture Wars;* and *The Future of the Race* (with Cornel West). He is the General Editor of the *Schomburg Library of Nineteenth Century Black Women's Literature* and the *Norton Anthology of African American Literature*, and the editor, with K. Anthony Appiah, of *Transition: An International Review*.

MARY MALCOLM GAYLORD is Professor and Chair of Romance Languages and Literatures at Harvard University. She has written widely on early modern poetry, poetics, drama, prose fiction, and historiography in Spanish. At present she is completing *Tropics of Conquest*, a book which looks at how imaginative literature and other discourses reflect Spain's New World experience.

BEATRICE HANSSEN received her Ph.D. from the Humanities Center at The Johns Hopkins University. An assistant professor of German at Harvard

University, she is currently preparing a study on national and postnational identities in unified Germany.

MICHAEL HERZFELD is Professor of Anthropology at Harvard University. He has published numerous articles and books on themes of Greek enthnography, anthropological theory, and the history of ideas, nationalism, and bureaucracy. His most recent books are *A Place in History* (Princeton University Press, 1991) and *The Social Production of Indifference* (Oxford University Press, 1992). He is currently working on studies of apprenticeship and artisanship in Greece and Italy, and on an "ethnographic biography" of the Greek novelist Andreas Nenedakis.

BARBARA JOHNSON is Professor of English and Comparative Literature at Harvard University. She is the author of *The Critical Difference* (Johns Hopkins University Press, 1980) and *A World of Difference* (Johns Hopkins University Press, 1987), and an editor of *Consequences of Theory* (with Jonathan Arac, Johns Hopkins University Press, 1990) and *Freedom and Interpretation: Oxford Amnesty Lectures 1992* (Basic Books, 1993). Her most recent book is *The Wake of Deconstruction* (Basil Blackwell, 1994).

DAVID KENNEDY joined the Harvard Law School in 1981. He is currently the Henry Shattuck Professor of Law and Faculty Director of Graduate and International Legal Studies. He has worked for a variety of public and private international organizations, including the European Communities and the United Nations, and has practiced law with Cleary, Gottlieb, Steen and Hamilton in Brussels. In 1991, he founded and now directs Harvard's European Law Research Center. He teaches and writes about international law, international trade, the law of the European Union, and legal theory.

LAURA HANFT KOROBKIN is Visiting Assistant Professor of English at Williams College. She received her J.D. from Harvard Law School and her Ph.D. in English from Harvard University. She is the author of *Criminal Conversations: Stories of Gender, Adultery and the Law in Nineteenth-Century America* (forthcoming), and of articles in *The Yale Journal of Law and the Humanities* and *The New Nineteenth Century: Feminist Readings of Underread Victorian Texts* (forthcoming).

JEFFREY MASTEN teaches in the Harvard English Department. He is the author of *Textual Intercourse: Collaboration, Authorship, and Sexualities in Renaissance Drama* (forthcoming from Cambridge University Press), and articles in *ELH*, *Queering the Renaissance*, *Reading Mary Wroth*, and *Textual Practice*. He has edited the Middleton-Rowley-Massinger collaboration *The Old Law* for the forthcoming Oxford *Collected Works of Thomas Middleton* and is unediting Shakespeare's *Pericles*.

JANN MATLOCK is Associate Professor of Romance Languages and Literatures at Harvard University. She is the author of *Scenes of Seduction: Prostitution, Hysteria, and Reading Difference in Nineteenth-Century France* (Columbia University Press, 1994), and an editor of *Media Spectacles* (Routledge, 1993). She is currently completing a book on vision and aesthetics in nineteenth-century France entitled *Desires to Censor*.

MEREDITH L. MCGILL teaches in the English Department and in the History and Literature concentration at Harvard University. She has published on Edgar Allan Poe, the history of American copyright, and Wallace Stevens. She is currently completing a book on antebellum American literature and reprint culture.

MARTHA MINOW is a professor at Harvard Law School. She wrote *Making All the Difference: Inclusion, Exclusion and American Law* (1990), edited *Family Matters: Readings on Family Lives and the Law* (1993), and coedited (with Gary Bellow) *Law Stories* (1996). She coedits (with Austin Savat) a series for the University of Michigan Press on narrative, violence, and the law.

GREGORY NAGY is the Francis Jones Professor of Classical Greek Literature and Professor of Comparative Literature at Harvard University. He served as the elected president of the American Philological Association in the academic year 1990–91. He is the author of *The Best of the Achaeans: Concepts of the Hero in Archaic Greek Poetry* (John Hopkins University Press, 1979), which won the American Philological Association's Goodwin Award of Merit in 1982. Nagy's special research interests are archaic Greek literature and oral poetics, and he finds it rewarding to integrate these interests with teaching. As of July 1994, he has been Chair of the Classics Department at Harvard.

STEPHEN OWEN is Irving Babbitt Professor of Comparative Literature and Professor of Chinese at Harvard University. He is author on nine books on Chinese literature and comparative literature, the most recent being *An Anthology of Chinese Literature: Earliest Times to 1911* (Norton, 1996) and *The End of the Chinese "Middle Ages": Essays in Mid-Tang Literary Culture* (Stanford, 1996).

JUDITH RYAN is the Robert K. and Dale J. Weary Professor of German and Comparative Literature. She has published widely on twentieth-century literature and is the author of *Umschlag und Verwandlung* (1972), *The Uncompleted Past* (1983), and *The Vanishing Subject* (1991). She is at present working on a book on R. M. Rilke, provisionally entitled *Borrowed Plumes*.

ELAINE SCARRY is Professor of English at Harvard University and a Senior Fellow at the Society of Fellows. Author of *The Body in Pain* and *Resisting Representation*, she has also written a series of essays on war and the social contract.

DORIS SOMMER is Professor of Latin American Literature at Harvard University. She has written widely on literatures of the Americas in essays and in *One Master for Another: Populism as Patriarchal Rhetoric in Dominican Novels* (1984) and *Foundational Fictions: The National Romances of Latin America* (1991). Thanks to grants from the Guggenheim Foundation and from ACLS, she is now completing *Proceed With Caution: A Rhetoric of Particularism*.

MARY MARGARET STEEDLY is the John and Ruth Hazel Associate Professor of Anthropology at Harvard University. Her book, *Hanging Without a Rope: Narrative Experience in Colonial and Postcolonial Karoland*, was cowinner of the 1994 Victor Turner Prize for ethnographic writing. She is currently working on a book of Karo women's memories of the Indonesian Revolution of 1945–50.

SUSAN RUBIN SULEIMAN is Professor of Romance and Comparative Literatures at Harvard University. Her books include *Authoritarian Fictions: The Ideological Novel as a Literary Genre*; *Subversive Intent: Gender, Politics, and the Avant-Garde*; and *Risking Who One Is: Encounters with Contemporary Art and Literature*. She recently completed a memoir, *Budapest Diary: Excerpts from the Motherbook*—without footnotes—to appear in October 1996.

WILLIAM MILLS TODD III is Professor of Slavic Languages and Literatures and of Comparative Literature at Harvard University. His books include *The Familiar Letter as a Literary Genre in the Age of Pushkin* (1976) and *Fiction and Society in the Age of Pushkin: Ideology, Institutions, and Narrative* (1986). He has edited *Literature and Society in Imperial Russia: 1800–1914* (1978) and *Soviet Sociology of Literature: Conceptions of a Changing World*

(1990). He has also edited a collection of North American articles on Pushkin, which will be published in Russian in St. Petersburg.

HELEN VENDLER is Porter University Professor at Harvard University. She is the author of books on Yeats, Stevens, Herbert, and Keats; her essays have been collected in *Part of Nature, Part of Us, The Music of What Happens,* and *Soul Says.* She is completing a Commentary of Shakespeare's *Sonnets.* She writes frequently on contemporary poetry.

REBECCA L. WALKOWITZ is a graduate student in English and American literature at Harvard University. She is an editor of *Media Spectacles* (Routledge, 1993) and *Secret Agents* (Routledge, 1995).

IRENE J. WINTER is William Dorr Boardman Professor of Fine Arts at Harvard University, where she teaches ancient Mesopotamian art and archaeology. She has a B.A. in Anthropology, an M.A. in Near Eastern Studies, and a Ph.D. in Art History—which in concert permit multiple perspectives on her archaeological materials. She has excavated at sites in Iran, Cyprus, and Israel, and is currently working on aesthetics in cross-cultural context and on sculpture as a representational vehicle for the politics of the early state.